Astrotheology & Shamanism

Unveiling the Law of Duality in Christianity and Other Religions

Jan Irvin

Andrew Rutajit

Published 2005
The Book Tree
San Diego, CA

Astrotheology & Shamanism:

Unveiling the Law of Duality in Christianity and Other Religions

© 2005/2006 – Irvin/Rutajit

ISBN: 1-58509-107-3

For Hannah Rose and the future generations

Published by
The Book Tree
P O Box 16476
San Diego, CA 92176

We provide fascinating and educational products to help awaken the public to new ideas and information that would not be available otherwise.
Call 1 (800) 700-8733 for our *FREE BOOK TREE CATALOG*.

Table of Contents

If the truth can be told so as to be understood, it will be believed.
~ Terence McKenna

Genesis 3:22
And the LORD God said, Behold, the man is become as one of us, to know good
and evil: and now, lest he put forth his hand, and take also of the tree of life,
and eat, and live for ever:

We dedicate this book to the memory of:

John Marco Allegro (1923-1988)
For your integrity of research against all odds.
Few have risked as much in pursuit of truth as you.

~ Acknowledgements ~

We would like to extend a warm thank you to those whose artistic, intellectual, financial, material, and moral support made this book possible:

Especially to: Claudia Muñoz-Calderon and Andrew's wife, Diane, for giving the moral support, love and personal sacrifices required to make sure we survive many months of writing. Jack Herer for your intellectual, material and financial support; Scott Carr for coming through with extra funds when we needed help; also Eddy Lepp of Eddy's Medicinal Gardens, for providing us with much needed funds to make this book happen. We also thank Dr. Rick Strassman for answering our numerous questions in such a timely fashion; Paul Tice for quelling our publishing concerns; and Ray Hensley for your assistance in editing. Dan Hillman and Dr. Dennis McKenna for answering our chemistry related questions; George Clayton Johnson for your input and teaching how to observe; Jay Lynn for donating your entire life's research; Victor Wolf for your alchemical advice; John Major Jenkins for answering our Mesoamerican related questions; Nicholas Zervos for donating your artistic talent; Michael Hoffman (Egodeath.com) and John W. Allen for your photographs; Anna Partington for answering our numerous philological questions with cunning wit. In addition, we thank Monica Cavatiao, Todd Hoffarth, Marcel Battle, Jordan Maxwell, David Spess, Dr. Philip Davies, and any whose names we've forgotten. We also offer our warm appreciation to the Allegro Estate: Joan Allegro, Mark Allegro, and especially Judith Anne Brown (John Allegro's daughter), whose assistance in writing sections of this book was invaluable.

~ Special Note ~

This is a mind-expanding book. It helps us share the perspective of a shaman (a seer or wise man) on the world and on the interplay of sun and stars. In this world view, heaven and earth are the dual parts of a whole. Duality means correspondence rather than conflict: the confluence of stars governing our destiny; the roots and leaves of the world tree feeding each other; 'as above, so below'. The world is a web of interconnections, and to discover their oneness is to discover the God within each living thing.

As part of this world view, symbolism and mythology convey the truth and help us attain it. We need to understand the power that symbols used to hold – not merely decorative or reflective but as the doors to deeper meaning. Myths that nowadays seem fanciful conveyed themes such as redemption or rebirth – themes that underlie age-old religions.

By comparing the symbols and iconography of Christianity with those of different religions, we can see common ideas stemming from much older and deeper sources. For example, the similarities between the stories and images of Jesus, Horus and Krishna suggest a common ancestry in sun-worship. Since the Emperor Constantine's Council of Nicaea in AD 325, the story of Christ has been presented as a solid historical fact. Now we see how various aspects of the Christian religion have grown out of earlier beliefs based on the power of the sun and the seasons.

The book focuses on the central role of entheogenic plants, especially mushrooms, and the symbolism associated with them, in enabling the shaman or priest to attain divine knowledge. Ideas put forward by John Marco Allegro about the origin of religion in *The Sacred Mushroom and the Cross* in 1970 – which met universal condemnation – are here largely vindicated. In the development of language from Sumerian times, Allegro found evidence of a world-view based on the beliefs and practices of an ancient fertility religion; ideas that were handed down in the guise of many different stories through classical and biblical times. The dry philological approach of *The Sacred Mushroom and the Cross* is here supported by a wider study of symbols, iconography and mythology and further work on word derivation.

To read this book one should put aside the conventional outlook that hinges morality, ethics and history on the life of one religious teacher two thousand years ago. In its place one can open the mind to a sense of oneness with the world and all on it. Through rediscovering our heritage of symbols, myths and evolving languages, we can try to attain a deeper understanding and compassion for the world we share.

~ Judith Anne Brown
Daughter of John Marco Allegro
Author of *John Marco Allegro: The Maverick of the Dead Sea Scrolls*

~ Foreword ~

Our world is changing at a faster rate than any other time in recorded history. Managing these changes and handling the fast pace of life is difficult enough without worrying about a pending Apocalypse as described in the biblical book of Revelation. As we cross the threshold of a new Age, change is inevitable. Some see these changes as a descent into a sinful Babylon and are not only concerned for their own souls, but for future generations as well. While fewer in number, those who are informed about what the changes may actually be and what the future may have to offer, seem to be ready and eager for these changes to take place.

> Those who cannot remember the past are condemned to repeat it.
> ~ George Santayana

Entering into a "New Age" might sound like a nondescript way of saying that times are changing. However, these *Ages* actually exist; unfortunately, the understanding of just what these Ages are, is not well recognized. This knowledge has remained exceptionally cryptic and obscure. Consequently, those who recognize these changes for what they are and welcome this *turning of the Ages* are in the minority. Though, as we near the closing of an Age, the cryptic and secret teachings of this Age will be *revealed* to the public. This *revelation* serves as a public initiation into the coming Age of Aquarius, to which the authors of this book refer to as the "Aquarius Initiation." Among these secret teachings are the two pillars of *Astrotheology and Shamanism*. To my knowledge, the authors of this book are the first to combine these two fields of research.

These coming changes may reflect something archaic rather than futuristic. It is apparent that humankind once had understandings, which in the present day seem to remain beyond arms reach. Acquiring this perspective and gaining these understandings will leave no room for a literal belief in a mythological god-man. Additionally, one must consider the things our ancestors had at their disposal in order to create these myths, things that would withstand the test of time – things such as plants and celestial objects. Both have worked their way into the symbolism, rituals, and traditions of modern-day religion.

Religion is the source of much of man's inhumanity to man. Religious laws have been the foundation of most of the problems that have plagued humankind, and ironically, it has happened under the auspices of humans trying to convert other humans into becoming socially and morally better people. Astronomy was once just as taboo as the practice of Shamanism is today. In point of fact, the Church has launched inquisitions against both the astronomer and shaman alike.

These inquisitions were the result of religious enthusiasm, not unlike the majority of wars and other violence in our past. Those seeking personal liberty and self-transformation do not, by nature, build armies in attempt to spread their authority across the globe. Nevertheless, a *Pharmacratic Inquisition* has spread around the globe like a horrifying epidemic and most people don't even realize or acknowledge its existence. Like the hidden meanings in occult symbolism, the Pharmacratic Inquisition is buried beneath the organizations that employ it, like a wolf in sheep's clothing.

As Strong's Concordance points out (#5331 of the Greek dictionary), the Greek word *pharmakeia* (where we get our words pharmacy and pharmacist) is translated in the Bible as *sorcery* and *witchcraft*. Plant usage, consequently, was labeled as the worship of false gods; according to the Bible, your local *pharmacist* is a witch (if female) or a warlock. Few people keep in mind and in proper perspective that aside from demonizing the plants on the earth and the stars in the sky, it was also illegal for common people to read or write for hundreds of years. This period of history is known as the Dark Ages. Yet, at the same time the Church was burning and banning books, they were also amassing one of the greatest collections of rare manuscripts ever assembled. The collecting, sequestering and destruction of books was common practice in these inquisitions, and this mayhem did not end in the Dark Ages.

A good argument lies in claims that most, if not all, diseases are actually curable. However, those who are in charge of finding these cures are not concerned with *curing* disease; they would rather dedicate their time and research to *disease maintenance* (creating a drug that must be taken daily to stave off symptoms of disease). The HMO's many of us use are Health Maintenance Organizations. They are not health restoring organizations. They just *maintain* your illness and are not interested in curing it. You are maintained just enough to keep coming back and paying them for the "privilege" of having an illness. The facts are that all diseases may be cured if natural products were developed, rather than synthetic chemicals. This is a road not traveled by the pharmaceutical industries, because naturally occurring substances cannot be patented. A patent gives the inventor of these synthetic chemicals the sole right to make, use, and sell the new drug *exclusively*. Plants offer no monetary value to these industries; consequently, they are overlooked completely while people get sicker and sicker, and the pharmaceutical sales climb higher and higher. Don't forget that Adolph Hitler and the Nazis were financed and promoted by I. G. Farben, the largest chemical and synthetic drug company on earth at the time. Farben also owned the property where Auschwitz, the concentration camp, was located.

The Church's inquisitions have suppressed the knowledge of the plants, astronomy, mathematics, sexuality and brain function (among other things). Aside from women, their most blatant persecutions were waged against the astrotheologists and the shaman, yet as this book will confirm, the framework of Christianity rests upon the foundation of Astrotheology and Shamanism. While much truth is being released to the public in regards to astrotheology, shamanism is still receiving crushing blows and it all happens today under the guise of a "War on Drugs." This is accomplished by including the naturally occurring, shamanic plants with the highly refined, man-made *drugs* like crack and heroin.

The Spanish Inquisition, the burning of the witches; the holy crusades; the extermination of the pagan heathens; and the eradication, subversion and demonization of women (and the goddess-worshiping cultures) – these atrocities were all carried out in the name of the Christian God and the perpetrators behind these various movements continue to obscure (yet strengthen) their oppression of humanity to this very day. These religious leaders know all too well that people are quite prone to becoming manipulated into righteous anger, accusation, and pre-judgment. When these emotions are manipulated, people (especially in large groups) become easily persuaded to torture, mutilate, imprison and murder their fellow man. People need information, not manipulation; but instead, we are fed propaganda and kept in the dark about the facts. In this case, the *facts* are the history, the spirituality, and the benefits of entheogenic plants and natural medicines; as well as the significance of the turning of the Ages. Recognizing the link between these two to biblical themes is equally important.

The *propaganda* is that these plants are bad, evil, or witchcraft. The "war on drugs" keeps people in the dark and distorts the facts by continual media propaganda, thus creating the fear and detestation towards *drugs*; lumping all drugs that are not prescribed by a doctor or available at a *drug store* into a single (illegal) category. They associate all of the known dangerously addictive drugs with the sacred plants and mushrooms that have been used by nearly all of our ancestors throughout antiquity. This alone is a crime against human history and a literal tragedy for all humankind.

It is the desire of the writers of this outstanding work to shed light into a dark place by illuminating humankind to the spiritual connection and history of Astrotheology and Shamanism, dispelling once and for all the darkness created through ignorance and intentional obfuscation of the truth. Humanity is debilitated without this knowledge… ignorance is not bliss. The most important tool used by the Church and State to perpetuate their authority over humanity is the ignorance of the people. Our greatest defense against their dominance is truth, and sharing the knowledge it provides.

Humankind has enslaved itself with false beliefs and religious prohibitions. Only humankind can set itself free and this book is a sincere attempt to do exactly that. Let us rejoice and usher in the Age of Aquarius and leave the judgmental attitudes and desires to dominate one another to the past, where it belongs.

With this I am honored to present and I invite you, perhaps for the first time, to enlighten your mind with the history of astrotheology and shamanism.
Jordan Maxwell

~ Preface ~

The purpose of this book is to satisfy a desperate need: to fill a void in the basic understanding of humanity in regards to the founding principles behind the origins of religion. Most religious people do not recognize this void because mysticism, spiritism, and supernatural substances have replaced the physical elements long-ago extracted from the common teachings. Our intention is to offer some alternative explanations for dogmatic surrogates and reintroduce knowledge that has been sequestered completely. In brief, we shall attempt to enlighten the enquiring readership to how and why the major religions of the world are primarily based on star, sun, and moon worship known as astrotheology, and on psychedelic/entheogenic plant[1] knowledge known as shamanism.

Throughout history, humans have held a profound knowledge of the pattern of the stars in the sky and the pharmacopia of plants of the earth. Our ancestors' teachings consisted of both the above and below. Their celestial-timed holidays were celebrated with the ingestion of sacred plants in a group communion-like setting.[2] The usage of sacred plants was both a way of celebration via inebriation, and, in larger doses, these plants (and fungi) were used to induce out-of-body and near death-like experiences. The biggest obstacle faced was the language barrier, putting into words astral projections and ecstatic visionary states of consciousness from these experiences. In fact, it has been suggested that the ingestion of these sacred substances is what catalyzed higher consciousness and language, from which we've created our extremely complex systems of communication.[3] Language (including mathematics) has always been a barrier, this is why symbols hold such strong meaning, they have a language of their own. As symbols began to take their shape and written language evolved, words themselves became symbols.

The meanings of words are hidden within the words themselves. The following examples, both from antiquity and from modern day, are examples of the alchemical "Green Language" or "Language of the Birds" (or language of the *bards*, as in *poets*).

A word that we use quite often throughout this book is **anthropomorphism** or **anthropomorphized**, which is sort of a personification. **Anthropo,** meaning man, is where words like anthropology come from. Morphism is the transformation or correlation of a certain kind. To draw a smiling face on the sun or the moon is to anthropomorphize the sun or the moon. The Man in the Moon *is* an anthropomorphism of the moon. Simply giving an inanimate object (e.g. stars, plants, or natural phenomena) human features or qualities is to anthropomorphize it.

Archaeoastronomy is the study of the knowledge, interpretations, and practices of the ancient cultures regarding celestial objects or phenomena of this nature and consequently, tracking time (Kronos) and creating calendars.

Astrotheology is within the field of theology but *Astro*theology is theology founded on observation or knowledge of celestial bodies. Astrotheology is broken down into three parts. First, there is **Aster** (Astro), which is a star. Secondly, **Theo,** Theo is God (see below). Third, **logy** from logos (see below); is the word or study of the theology of the stars. This is the study of how our ancestors revered the stars, the sun and the heavens as gods or deities.

Entheobotany is the study and use of plants for spiritual purposes. This is the botany (plants) of entheos, which, in Greek, means enthusiasm. Enthusiasm means "GOD within" or "a connection with the Divine."

Entheogen is a compound word of **En** meaning within or into, (to **en**capsulate). Next is the word **Theo** again meaning God (see below). Lastly is **Gen**, "to generate or engender, to bring into existence." An entheogen is literally something (usually a plant substance) that generates God within you.[4]

> No one who respects the ancient Mystery of Eleusis, the Soma of the Aryans, and the fungal and other potions of the American natives, no one who respects the English language, would consent to apply 'hallucinogen' to these plant substances...[5]

---

[1] This includes plant combinations, fungus, and animal "poisons."
[2] *Plants of the Gods*, by Richard Shultes.
[3] *Food of the Gods*, by Terence McKenna.
[4] Ruck (1979); Ruck, Wasson, Ott and Bigwood, as an alternative term to use for "*psychedelics used religiously,*" coined the word *Entheogen*.

~ R. Gordon Wasson

Entheomycology is the study and use of mushrooms for spiritual purposes.

Ethnic is a word that refers to a particular cultural group, especially one who maintains the language or customs of the group. For an example of an ethnic group, one might consider the Huichol or Chumash tribes of North America, or the Yanomamö, Shipibo-Conibo, and Huitoto tribes of South America, or the Fulani and Hausa tribes of Africa.

Ethnobotany is the study of the plant lore and agricultural customs of a particular people. This is the study of the plants that these people use and the outcome or the impact that these plants have on the customs of their culture.

Logos is the *Word*, the creative word of God, which is itself God and an incarnate in "*Jesus*". Logos is also called "Word." This is a Latin definition. The Greeks considered logos to mean "*reason.*"[6] In Hindu theology logos (called "*vac*") and the sacred drink called Soma are synonymous.[7] This is also said to be true of the manna—the sacred food of the Bible.[8]

> John 1:1
> In the beginning was the Word, and the Word was with God, and the Word was God.

Macrocosm is a large representative system having analogies to smaller systems. Therefore, the macrocosm would represent *that which is above*.

Mazzaroth is not a very common word anymore, but was quite common at one point. Mazzaroth, by orthodox interpretation, simply means the twelve signs of the zodiac and their associated constellations. One can find the word Mazzaroth in Job 38:32 and in the *Catholic Encyclopedia*. A similar spelling, *Mazzaloth*, also appears in II Kings 23:5, though here it is typically transliterated as "planets," "constellations," *or* "zodiac."[9] Contrary to orthodox opinion, in 1905, Italian professor, G. Schiaparelli, published *Astronomy in the Old Testament*, which gives his evidence showing that the word Mazzaroth could be a plurality of the planet Venus:

> ...two stars of exceptional brightness, which keep guard in turn over the sun, the one preceding him in the morning at his rising, the other following him in the evening at his setting: Lucifer and Hesperus, the star of morning and the star of evening. [...] the planet Venus, apparently uniting two different manifestations as Hesperus and Lucifer, may have received a plural name from the first, i.e. the name Mazzaroth. When the identity of its two appearances at morning and evening was discovered, it naturally came to be thought of as one star, and hence the author of the Book of Job used it as a singular in a plural garb.[10]
> ~ G. Schiaparelli

Microcosm (*that which is below*) is a small representative system having analogies to a larger system. You can think of a hurricane, which is the microcosm as compared to a swirling galaxy. At the same time, the hurricane can be a macrocosm to a yet smaller tornado that would be a microcosm. However, this tornado can also be seen as a macrocosm to a smaller natural spiral, such as swirling water going down a drain. Often, many different levels of this duality are present. It is very important to understand the macrocosm/microcosm rule or law of duality of ancient philosophy because much, if not most of ancient philosophy is based on this ancient, dualistic principal.

Philosophy, alchemy, and many other ancient teachings talk of a *macrocosm* and a *microcosm*—that which is above is also below.[11,12] This macrocosm/microcosm relationship is one of the most *essential* (and most overlooked) elements in understanding ancient philosophy and religion. We call this relationship the "law of duality."

---

[5] *Persephone's Quest,* by Gordon Wasson, pg. 30.
[6] *Jesus Christ, Sun of God,* by David Fideler; also Oxford English Dictionary, 2nd edition.
[7] *Soma, The Divine Hallucinogen,* by David Spess, pg. 110.
[8] *The Mystery of Manna,* by Dan Merkur, PhD.
[9] See *Strong's,* #H4208.
[10] *Astronomy in the Old Testament,* by G. Schiaparelli, 1905. See ch. V, Mazzaroth, pg. 82.
[11] *The Secret Teachings of All Ages,* by Manly P. Hall .
[12] *Alchemy & Mysticism,* by Alexander Roob.

The Lords Prayer:

Our Father, who art in heaven,
hallowed be thy name.
Thy Kingdom come,
thy will be done,
<u>on earth as it is in heaven</u>[13]

Give us this day our daily bread.
And forgive us our trespasses,
as we forgive those who trespass against us.
And lead us not into temptation,
but deliver us from evil.
For thine is the kingdom, the power and the glory.
For ever and ever.[14]

Mycology is the study of fungi or mushrooms; **Ethnomycology** is the study of fungi and their use and customs within a particular culture, and the outcome or the impact that these fungi have on the customs of that culture.

Pagan, from Latin *paganus* means *rural*, the *country people*, but was a word coined by the Catholic Church in order to excommunicate any persons who used plants for spirituality or medicine. These people later became known as witches, another generic term for the shaman. Today, many people who call themselves "pagan" or "witch" have no clue as to the background of their so-called philosophy that has, most often, become nothing but a bunch of misunderstood symbology from shamanism and astrotheology.

> With the passing years, the Wasson[15] Theory [of Shamanism] has become so widely accepted by specialists as to be considered beyond serious dispute. Shamanism is the earliest manifestation of culture; the shaman the first professional and the precursor of the priest, physician, musician, and every artist alike. Visionary ecstasy is the primal heart and soul of shamanism and religious revelation. [La Barre 1979; Ott, The Age of Entheogens 1995] Shamanism is at least 50,000 years old. [Furst 1976; La Barre 1970, 1979, 1980; Ott 1995]

Psychedelic means to make the mind clear or visible. From Greek we take "**psyche**" (mind) and "**dēlos**" (clear or visible) and can loosely be translated as "mind manifesting" or "mind revealing" or to make the mind clear or visible.[16]

Shamanism: It is better to consider shamanism as more of a practice than a belief or a religion. People who claim to be shamans, but do not put into practice the consumption of psychedelic (entheogenic) plant sacraments, are not shamans. There is a misunderstanding of what shamanism is by the "neo-shamanism" crowd; these people just enjoy the title, though they don't practice true shamanism. The word "shaman" originates from Siberia, and the Siberian shaman consumed psychedelic mushrooms. Today, the generic definition of shamanism covers all societies who use psychedelic plant sacraments, but people who believe that the word "shaman" encompasses everything that is mystic and holistic often misuse the word. The word shaman comes from the Norse, Ostiak, Samoyedes, Finish and Siberian tribal people who use the *Amanita muscaria* mushroom. It does not necessarily pertain to the spiritual leader or healer of others.

The Christian/Catholic-controlled world in 1853 defined shamanism as, "The Idolatrous worship or religion of the Ostiaks, Samoyedes, and other Finnish Tribes."[17] This is clearly a misrepresentation or misunderstanding of shamanism as a whole, but that was the Christian world's view at that time, and for the most part, it still is.

The term today has been adopted to mean those people in any entheogen-based culture, whether they be curanderos, peyoteros, or ayahuasceros, etc. The modern definition of the word *shaman* by Jonathan Ott, reads:

> Shaman - A medicine-man or priest-doctor of preliterate societies in northern Asia and, by extension, of other areas, particularly the Americas; a specialist in 'archaic techniques of ecstasy,' originally in ecstatic states *naturally* catalyzed by entheogenic plants, later

---

[13] As with all quotations in this book, the bold, italics, and/or underlining has been added by us.

[14] Notice that *above* the words "on earth as it is in heaven," the prayer is speaking about that which is above; *below* the words "on earth as it is in heaven," the prayer speaks about that which is below.

[15] See Chapter 4.

[16] "However, not only is 'psychedelic' an incorrect verbal formation, but it has become so invested with connotations of the pop-culture of the 1960s that it is incongruous to speak of a shaman's taking a 'psychedelic' drug." *Psychedelic Drugs*, by Ruck, J., 1979 11: 145. Quote from Ott, 1995.

[17] *Webster's Encyclopedic Dictionary*, 1853, pg 1017.

artificially induced by secondary techniques like drumming, chanting, fasting, breath control, etc.[18]

So, shamanism is a set of techniques and tools used to generate the god within, with the primary technique being the use of entheogenic plants.

Theo comes from the Greek word *Theos*, which literally means God. It is used in words like theomorphic, theology, and atheist. **Theology** is the study of the nature of God and religious truth; it is a rational inquiry into religious questions.

Philologist, Jay Lynn, spent 33 years researching the origins of words and the alphabet. He suggested that many words, especially discontinued words, reveal a hidden sexual past of the origins of the alphabet and the Church's censorship of language. For instance, "oon" is the liquid egg of the *male*. Woman was spelled "ooman," showing that she *receives* the liquid egg from the man.[19] Women were unknown to have eggs in those times because it was believed that the men had the seed (egg). "OO" is the root of words like ooze and oops. The letter "P" was of late arrival and derived from the Greek letter "rho" (ρ), and is where words like rain, river and run originate. Rho means "to flow," as in the flow of God's seed, often seen as rain. Rho is also the root of words like diarrhea and gonorrhea.[20] The development of p from ρ brings us things like penis and pen from the Greek "peos" (pee + os = bone, or "pee bone" (of God)). The letter "S" (also Z and N) meant God. Referencing the words "sblood," "sfoot," "sflesh," etc., in the Oxford English Dictionary reveals that these words mean "God's blood," "God's foot," and "God's flesh" respectively.[21] The words sea, see, seed, semen, spittle, son, sun, sacred, snake, etc., are all holy "S" words. Bodily fluids were especially sacred.[22] Each letter of the alphabet dating back to hieroglyphic times had specific meaning, usually related to physiology. By understanding those meanings, a deeper level of understanding is obtained.[23] The word "oops," using Lynn's theory, would be broken down as "God's flow from the testis"— "Oops, she's pregnant." Thus, if Lynn's theory is correct (see Appendix B), our very own vocabulary was larger in ancient history because of the knowledge of "letter words." This is the reality of the censoring and dumbing down of humanity that George Orwell called "Newspeak" in his prophetic novel, *1984*. Language needs to evolve and expand, not deteriorate through selective reductionism.

> Don't you see that the whole aim of Newspeak is to narrow the range of thought?... Every concept that can ever be needed, will be expressed by exactly one word, with its meaning rigidly defined and all its subsidiary meanings rubbed out and forgotten...Every year, fewer and fewer words, and the range of consciousness always a little smaller...by the year 2050, at the very latest, not a single human being will be alive who could understand such a conversation as we are having now. How could you have a slogan like "freedom is slavery" when the concept of freedom has been abolished? The whole climate of thought will be different. In fact there will be no thought, as we understand it now. Orthodoxy means not thinking – not needing to think. Orthodoxy is unconsciousness.[24]
> ~ George Orwell

The ancient Babylonians, who invented the 60-minute hour, the 24-hour day, and the 360-degree circle, wholly understood mathematics. Splitting day from night while showing reverence for the 12 helpers of the sun god (the zodiac), the 24-hour day was split into two 12-hour sections, with minutes being 60-seconds, and hours being 60-minutes. Sixty is the smallest number with **twelve** different divisors = 1, 2, 3, 4, 5, 6, 10, 12, 15, 20, 30, 60. Normally, we would expect an *advanced* civilization to have such a thorough comprehension of mathematics and time rather than our ancestors. It is important to recognize that these people were constantly seeking to increase consciousness. This is but one example showing that these ancient cultures were copiously more advanced than most of us assume. It may likewise seem implausible for some readers to consider psychedelics to have been the

---

[18] *The Age of Entheogens & the Angel's Dictionary*, pg. 134-135.
[19] O, OON Gr. Egg, more specifically, OON, the liquid egg of the male. OO egg and N, a suffix denoting Liquid. OO upright is 8, and OO is a sign of infinity. See Appendix B for more examples.
[20] *Oxford English Dictionary*: Rhea or Rea - Rhea: Jocular aphetic form of diarrhœa, gonorrhœa, etc.; See also spermatorrhea, blennorrhoia, gonorrhoia.
[21] *Oxford English Dictionary* - See also Sfire, Sbodikins, Sbobs, Sbody, Sbores, Sbuds, etc.
[22] Spittle and Spitting – *The Encyclopedia of Religion*, ed. M. Eliade, Vol. 14, pg. 37.
[23] *The Alpha and Omega, the Greek Alphabet and Other Root Words*, by Jay Lynn.
[24] *Nineteen Eighty-Four*, by George Orwell, 1949, excerpts from Chapter 5.

cause of (or catalyst for) this advancement. However, we contend that that theory is not only plausible, but it is actually most probable.

Today, the consciousness-expanding plants have been stolen from us as we sit in awe of what our ancestors achieved. This isn't really a case of the blind leading the blind, but rather the blindfolded leading the blindfolded in a society where it is illegal and taboo to remove your blindfold. Over the last 2000 years, we have been trapped in the Age of Pisces, the "Dark Age," while the Church and State have turned truth into blasphemy.

With rumors abounding of things like Big Foot, the Loch Ness Monster, haunted houses, UFOs, X-Files, Reptilian Agendas, conspiracy theories, bleeding or crying statues and paintings, and other anomalies[25], it appears that people today are anticipating a paradigm-shattering event. It has become obvious that society *wants* this...we want something earth-shattering and paradigm-shifting. The psychedelic experience is this and nothing less. To describe the psychedelic experience, Terence McKenna often referred to a slightly modified John Haldane quote:

> It isn't just stranger than you suppose, it's stranger than you *can* suppose.
> ~ Terence McKenna

Although it seems that we want this paradigm-shattering event, it also seems as though most people do not want any change to actually take place. They just want something novel to happen, then, they can return back to work or go watch an equally exciting football game. The buildup to the "Y2K" was a big letdown for the multitudes of people who were ready for something novel to occur (even those who feared the changes seemed to be disappointed when the world's computer-based infrastructure failed to collapse). At the same time, it has become routine for us to expect this paradigm shift to be like everything else in our lives. We want it to fall right into our laps or have it shipped to our doorstep overnight so we can glance at it as we go on about our busy day.

The truth of the matter is that the real mystery is in the *Self*. It seems as if the biggest obstacle facing humanity in this new millennium is that we are afraid of exploring our own minds. In fact, this is one of our society's paramount taboos. The techniques for true spiritual illumination that the religious authorities have put in place today are guaranteed to miss the mark because the holy plant sacraments have been removed and replaced with placebos and the false doctrines of transubstantiation.

> Shamanic ecstasy is the real 'Old Time Religion,' of which modern churches are but pallid evocations.
> ~ Jonathan Ott

Most people do not expect this paradigm shift to be a matter of individual courage. Nevertheless, that's what it is. It's a matter of courage, and the experience is personal to each individual. It cannot be held up to the light or examined on a chalkboard. Like Carl Sagan's book *Contact* suggested, we cannot simply send out a representative to report back to the community. If the experience could be put into words, the experience itself would not be that important. Otherwise, we could just hire a musician, or a poet, or an artist to interpret the experience for us. However, this is quite literally walking into another dimension wherein one of the most important aspects of the experience is that we are profoundly able to fully experience ourselves as our *Selves*. No one can do that for you or sell it to you. We are not only here on earth at the most opportune time to witness this paradigm shift, but we are actually in a prime position to become an integral part of it. These thoughts are reflections of philosopher Terence McKenna, who in a concert-lecture titled, *Alien Dreamtime* once said:

> And now with the engines of technology in our hands, we ought to be able to reach out and actually exteriorize the human soul at the end of time. Invoke it into existence like a UFO and open the violet doorway into hyperspace and walk through it, out of profane history and into the world beyond the grave, beyond shamanism, beyond the end of history, into the galactic millennium that has beckoned to us for millions of years across space and time. *This is the moment*. A planet brings forth an opportunity like this only once in its lifetime, and we are ready, and we are poised. And as a community, we are ready to move into it, to claim it, to make it our own. It's there... go for it....

Having this shamanic experience is more than just experiencing something astonishing and unbelievable. In fact, it is insulting to the shaman and the experience itself to suggest that the psychedelic experience is merely a "trip" for

---

[25] See the Art Bell and/or the Jeff Rense audio archives online.

recreation. The shamanic death and rebirth experience is believed by many to be an integral part of the reincarnation process. After all, one cannot conquer death without practicing for such an event. .

> Religion is a defense against a religious experience.
> ~ Carl G. Jung

The shamanic death and rebirth experience (being "born again") should be held in very high regard. Those who attempt to practice these techniques in a loud, party-like atmosphere should not expect the same results as the shaman who carries out these techniques in silent darkness. This is a very personal experience whereby the person literally feels like he (or she) is going to die. After consuming the plant medicine, the shaman is flat on his or her back while having an out of body experience. The shaman is leaving the body, just as people report having experienced on an operating table or after a severe car wreck. The difference is, the following day, the shaman will be safe and sound, feeling well and knowing fully that the shamanic death experience was just practice for the real thing. When one dies, one must let go, one cannot hang on to worldly possessions or worry about the past or future. Many theologies suggest that this is why we reincarnate. Fearing death is the result of misunderstanding it.[26, 27] Anxiety about death is a major obstacle.

> The Los Angeles Biomedical Research Institute at Harbor-UCLA Medical Center is conducting a study designed to measure the effectiveness of the novel psychoactive medication *psilocybin* on the reduction of anxiety, depression, and physical pain.
> ~ CancerAnxietyStudy.org

All participants in this study have stage IV cancer and anxiety, they are between the ages of 18 and 65, and do not have a history of major psychiatric disorders. Participants spend two nights at the hospital, undergo an MRI scan of the brain, and receive psilocybin.[28] This is a double-blind study, meaning the participants are given a placebo *and* the active medication, but they are not told which drug is administered when. Participants are encouraged to bring along personal photos and some of their favorite music. If *this* experience could be put into words, these cancer patients could either simply be *told* about this mystery or undergo counseling. Only through the *ingestion* of a true sacrament (in this case, psilocybin) can these terminally ill cancer patients have such a profound experience that they no longer fear death. This is a personal paradigm shift for each participant.

When it comes to religion, most are set in their ways and do not like to discuss the opinions, theories, or ideas of other faiths. It is just not politically correct. Some businesses even have strict policies regarding the discussion of religion in the workplace. Talking to co-workers and clients about things that you do not entirely understand, yet believe in wholeheartedly, is a recipe for disaster. If people completely understood what it was they believed in, there would not be such a problem. However, it seems as though most people do not even want to ask *themselves* questions about their religion, even within the privacy of their own minds, on the chance that God might hear them thinking and pass judgment on their soul. Through personal experiences, we have found that seeking out the answers to the questions that many people will not even ask themselves has quickly turned into what is known to many as heresy and blasphemy. We call it *necessary*! To some, this kind of blasphemy is a sin. To others it is just a part of the learning process.

Today, we are lucky to have information at our fingertips as knowledge that previously eluded us, since it is now only a mouse-click away. As a result, people can research for themselves without having to ask a priest or rely on someone's prefabricated opinion. If you are a member of an organized religion, please ask yourself the following questions as you read this book:

- Is there anything that can be said that, if proven factual, would make me reconsider my spiritual options?

- Do my beliefs rely on faith rather than experience?

---

[26] *Creative Meditation and Multi-Dimensional Consciousness*, by Lama Anagarika Govinda, 1976.
[27] *Transformations of Myth Through Time*, by Joseph Campbell.
[28] A hallucinogenic compound, often obtained from the mushroom *Psilocybe cubensis*.

- What do the rituals that I perform, and symbols that I see at my church/temple represent? [29]

Christianity teaches that the only way to find God is through the Church, or through *Jesus*. This literalist teaching denies any attempt to find God by looking within your Self, yet simultaneously you are told that your body is the Temple of God. Religion is the main thing in this world that separates humanity. How many people have killed and/or died in the name of their god? Modern Gnostics on the other hand, have no template to follow. A gnostic[30] is a spiritual "do-it-yourselfer." A gnostic does not need another person or group of people to set dogma or creeds before them or dictate morality to facilitate enlightenment. If someone else's *morals and dogma* are laid before the gnostic, they are recognized as nothing more than beliefs and doctrine that are open to interpretation and scrutiny.

A gnostic, by definition, is "one who knows" and many central themes of this knowledge are contained within these pages. This means that by definition, you too will "know" many of the secrets when you finish reading this book. Gnosticism primarily focuses on personal experience, and therefore we highly encourage you to seek out the answers to your own mysteries and start asking questions. It has been stated in the mythology of the Aquarian Age that over the next few years, the greatest secrets of humankind will begin to be revealed unto the masses. We have termed this as "the Aquarius Initiation" Our hope is that this book will act as a catalyst to help effect this change.

The facts presented here will confront religious and political "authorities" on many topics and some people may be offended. One must remember how the character of Jesus is *depicted* in the Bible. The religious authorities persecuted Jesus. The Bible says that he confronted the religious authorities and called them fools. In history, people like Socrates and Galileo upset the religious authorities.[31] This is what it means to be a gnostic. One stands up for what is believed to be true based on experience, despite what is politically correct or accepted as conditioned thought and action. So if you hear us say that ingesting mushrooms that cause "visions" is enlightening, stop and think for a moment. The Bible is full of people having visions, and sacred plants (and fungi) have been used in nearly every culture and religion as far back as we can trace human history.[32,33,34,35,36] Only through religious and governmental prohibitions and inquisitions have these plants been made out to be "illegal and immoral." The "authorities" are telling us that if we eat of this *forbidden fruit*, they will kick us out of *this* so-called paradise, and put us in a jail cell. The forbidden fruit will not kill you or any person. To the contrary, it will open one's eyes – you will become as the gods, knowing yourself and knowing *for* yourself what is good, and what is evil as opposed to having some "authority", whom you have never met, to decide this for you.

---

[29] Baptism, communion, for rituals; for the many symbols that cannot be aptly covered in a footnote we recommend the work of Jordan Maxwell and Acharya S; and the book *Symbols, Sex and the Stars*, by Busenbark, among others.

[30] Gnosis is where the English word 'knowledge' is derived.

[31] Timothy Freke and Peter Gandy expound upon this in a radio interview with Laura Lee in 2001

[32] *The Sacred Mushroom and the Cross*, by John Allegro.

[33] *Soma*, by Gordon Wasson

[34] *Mushrooms and Mankind*, by James Arthur

[35] *Plants of the Gods*, by Richard Schultes

[36] *Pharmacotheon*, by Jonathon Ott

Figure 1 - Cathedral "Portal"

The Gospels quote Jesus as saying, "I am the door." It is obvious that one does not walk up to a door and just stand there. You walk *through* it. Once you have walked through the door, the door is behind you. As we are entering a new Age, we must leave the Age of Christianity and move on. We have stood at the doorstep of spiritual evolution long enough. The time has come for humankind to enter the *temple*, to walk through the door.

Part I
The Aquarius Initiation

The Aquarius Initiation is a "people's" worldwide initiation into the ancient occult mysteries. No longer are the mysteries to be reserved for the ancient secret societies or contemporary groups of men practicing authoritarian elitism.[37] *Astrotheology and Shamanism* is about disseminating the knowledge of the heavens *and* the earth, by providing a fundamental understanding in the fields of astrotheology and shamanism. Both are equally important in finding our place in history and understanding religious history itself. Failing to understand the mystic nature of both astrotheology and shamanism has been a tragic oversight by many researchers and truth seekers.

Searching for the truth is a lifelong devotion. It is not something that can be handed to someone in a word or a sentence, or even in a single book. Truth is an understanding that only the observer can comprehend. Living a life in the quest for truth and influencing truth upon others can be quite difficult when popular belief and truth are on opposite sides of the same coin. Manly Palmer Hall spoke of truth not as a word, doctrine, system, philosophy, or religion. Hall often said that truth is *alive*, it is a conscious creature in and of itself. It has its own beginnings and it has its own ends. These beginnings and endings, whether they are conscious or not, are what we call "paradigm shifts" and as truth goes through these great cycles, so shall humankind. The Age of Aquarius is the age when today's mysteries become tomorrow's common understanding.

This book is part of the dispensation of the new Age, and this new Age is the Age of Information - the Age of Enlightenment. In the first part of this book, we will provide evidence that the earth enters a physical "new Age" every 2150 years based on proven astronomy and the planetary Precession of the Equinoxes, and show how this has shaped religious symbolism and philosophy throughout history. Of utmost importance to humanity is the fact that we are physically leaving the old Age of Pisces and beginning the new Age of Aquarius. There is a lot of debate as to when this new Age of Aquarius begins and when the old Age of Pisces ends.

Most religions are (and were) based on this ancient knowledge of (and reverence for) the heavens. This knowledge has been suppressed from the general public. On May 5, 2000, there was a grand planetary alignment.[38] This came directly on the heels of the Grand Cross of August 18, 1999 and the Solar Eclipse of August 11, 1999. These events marked the end of the Aztec calendar and many people have accepted this rare occurrence as the beginning of this 'New Age.' Others will debate that the end of the Mayan calendar on December 21, 2012 marks the start of the new Age.

> Precessional motion, as we know, moves backward through the zodiac, and a problem arises when we consider that the end of the Age of Pisces occurs when the vernal point is actually at 0° Pisces, preparing to enter 29° Aquarius, rather than at the "last" degree of Pisces. However, perhaps we should acknowledge a hidden intention within Western astrological tradition and take the notion of Pisces as the last zodiacal age at face value. Doing so, Western astrology proclaims that the Zero Time of precession is when the Age of Pisces—the "last" zodiacal sign—ends, which would be sometime in the next two centuries. From this perspective the Zero Time of Western astrology appears to be in general accord with the Maya end-times.[39]
> ~ John Major Jenkins

---

[37] *The Secret Teachings of All Ages,* by Manly P. Hall.
[38] Earth, Moon, Mercury, Venus, Sun, Mars, Jupiter, and Saturn were the "seven known planets" to the ancients. While this list includes eight celestial bodies, one was not included in the count because of those who placed either the earth or the sun in the middle of the cosmos. Whichever was placed in the middle was not counted as it is today.
[39] *Maya Cosmogenesis 2012,* by John Major Jenkins, pg. 325.

Figure 2

Thomas 1
"...Whoever finds the interpretation of these sayings will not experience death."

Global knowledge and understanding of the ancient mysteries has not happened in recorded history. Previously, small and intimate mystery schools and secret societies were the only ways to be initiated into the *Secret Teachings of all Ages*. In the present day, bits and pieces of the mysteries are told in various ways. These pieces are hidden in religion, television shows, movies, music, and other media. However, the majority will still overlook or even demonize the core teachings of astrotheology and shamanism. The authors of this book recognize the twelve year period between the ending of the Aztec and Mayan calendars (roughly, the years 2000-2012). We are simply calling this 12-year period the Aquarius Initiation. The Christian Church, knowing their *hidden* knowledge would someday become *common* knowledge, refers to the time we live in as the "End of Days" or the "End Times."

Figure 3 - Yggdrasil Tree   Figure 4 - Yggdrasil Tree

4

AS ABOVE – SO BELOW

Figures 3, 4, and 5 are all representations of the Yggdrasil Tree[40], which portray the concept "that which is above is also below." As above, so below. Figure 3 depicts the leaves reaching up to the sky with the bird Aquila (sometimes called Sophia), in the tree displaying its wings. Notice the tree and its roots under the ground where the dirt has been stripped away showing the underworld, known as the *chthonic realm*. The chthonic realm is the dwelling place of the serpent, winding its way around the root system of the tree. The wings are above the serpent. This too is something that is applied all throughout religion, alchemy, and mysticism. In the middle of the image are deer. The significance of the deer will be discussed toward the end of this book.

Figure 4 is showing the branches that extend into the heavens, as well as the branches (roots) that anchor the tree to the earth. As in the heavens, so on earth. This dualistic philosophy is applied throughout religion, alchemy, and mysticism. The further out into the heavens we go (Figure 5), we see the World Tree. The axis of the earth (the *poles*) is now acting as a tree, branching out into the heavens above the earth *and* below the earth.

> One of the great motifs of myth is the wondrous tree so often described as reaching up to heaven. There are many of them—the Ash Yggdrasil in the *Edda*, the world-darkening oak of the *Kalevala*, Pherecydes' world-oak draped with the starry mantle, and the Tree of Life in Eden.[41]
> ~ Giorgio de Santillana & Hertha von Dechend

Figure 5 - Yggdrasil Tree as World Tree Axis

---

[40] Pronounced **Ig**-dra-sil.
[41] *Hamlet's Mill,* by de Santillana & von Dechend, pg. 223.

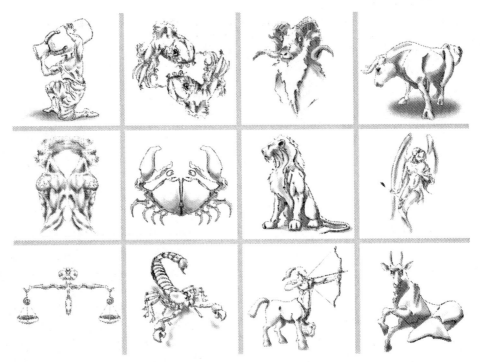

Figure 6 - The Mazzaroth

In this image, you will notice the representation of the zodiac constellations with their animal-like characters given to nearly all of them. In the heavens there are many different zodiac signs and constellations. The animalized gods and the human-like gods can all be found in the nights-sky. Consequently, as above – so below, both animals and humans share the heavens and the earth.

Figure 7 - Different zodiac signs apply to different parts of the microcosmic universe.

Within the sign of Taurus there is also a small group of stars **called the Stable (Aurega). This is the same Stable of Augeas** which Hercules mythically cleansed as his sixth Labor and Justin Martyr proudly boasted that Christ was born on the very day when the sun takes his birth in the **Stable of Augeas in the sign of the Goat (Capricorn).** [42] [bold—ours]
~ Ernest Busenbark

All of these are different degrees of this macrocosm/microcosm relationship. We must apply this macrocosm and microcosm theory again in our own bodies because the elders have always spoken of the *Grand Man* as the universe itself, and we humans as the tiny universe. Accordingly, we symbolically apply the zodiac signs to *our* universe, or our bodies, and this philosophy is found throughout antiquity.[43] In *The Sacred Mushroom and the Cross*, Allegro explains that early "Theraputae" healers used plants and astrology for diagnoses and treatment. This is also said to be true among shamanic cultures and the Essenes/Zadokites at Qumran.[44]

---

[42] *Symbols, Sex, and the Stars,* by Ernest Busenbark, pg. 126.
[43] As an example, see *The Doctrine of Signatures,* by Jacob Boehme in *Signatura Rerum: The Signature of all Things,* which was popularized by Paracelsus; and *Judgement of Diseases,* by Nicolas Culpeper; 1600's.
[44] *The Sacred Mushroom and the Cross,* by John Allegro, pg. 60.

The secret philosophy of the R.C. [Rosicrucian] is founded upon that knowledge which is the sum and head of all faculties, sciences, and arts. By our divinely revealed system—which partakes much of <u>theology and medicine</u> but little of jurisprudence [philosophy of human law]—<u>we analyze the heavens and the earth; but mostly we study man himself, within whose nature is concealed the supreme secret.</u> [underline—ours]
~ Confessio Fraternitatis of the Rosicrucian Order

Pictured left is a mystical image of the Great Prototypal Man or the "Grand Man of Zohar."[45] A similar adaptation of this image is depicted in Manly P. Hall's monumental work, *The Secret Teachings of All Ages*. Similar images are found all throughout religion and alchemy. The rings represent the celestial spheres, which all represent different stages of consciousness, human development, and initiation. The top ring is the "sphere of fixed stars," which are the constellations with their zodiac signs. The lower ring represents the "seven spheres of the planets." In ancient mythology, the seven spheres of the planets represent the seven known planets at the time (ancient times) including the sun and the moon, the seven stars of the Pleiades, the seven days of the week (divided by the four phases of the moon), and the seven chakras[46] in the human body, and other associations.

Figure 8 - The Grand Man of Zohar

The earth represents the lowest level of consciousness, and the sun was considered mediator between heaven and earth. In the center, the God figure himself is representing the sphere of divine intellect, the *Middle Pillar*. God (the Grand Man or Great Architect) is standing on both land and in water. Overall, the image suggests that God is testing the waters of the new Age to see if it is ready to begin. Notice how the sun is the head of the sky god's penis. This is not censorship, the reasons for placing the sun in this location of the anatomical figure will be discussed in chapter three.

> The name of the Great Architect—is "Jahbulon" or "Jahbelon," which breaks down into Jah, Bel and On, three ancient names of the God Sun.[47]
> ~ Acharya S.

---

[45] Original image titled *Grand Man of Zohar*—modern artist interpretation (Nicholas Zervos).
[46] Seven centers of spiritual energy in the human body and their associated endocrine system glands.
[47] *Suns of God*, by Acharya S, pg. 550.

~ Chapter Two ~
The Paradigm Shift

FINDING YOURSELF

The Christian church will tell you that in order to find God you need the foundation of church, priest, communion, confession, etc. In other words, it teaches that the only way to find God is through the Church, or through *Jesus*.

> John 14:6
> Jesus saith unto him, I am the way, the truth, and the life: no man cometh unto the Father, but by me.

The typical interpretation of this denies any attempt to find God by looking within your Self.

> 1 Corinthians 3:16
> Know ye not that ye are the temple of God, and that the Spirit of God dwelleth in you?

> Colossians 1:27
> To whom God would make known what is the riches of the glory of this [Shamanic] mystery among the Gentiles; which is **Christ in you**, the hope of glory...

When St. Paul talks about the Christ in You, he is saying that your essential identity, the fabric that makes you alive and awake, is divine. Your *essential identity* has nothing to do with how a person physically appears to others, but rather how one appears to oneself as a whole. The final judge and jury of your own soul will not be a man on a throne in heaven. It will be you. It seems that much greater time is spent dealing with outward appearance as opposed to inward appearance. Instead of looking at the world and seeing a tiny little body wandering around inside this vast universe, it should be understood that this tiny little body *is* this vast universe.

All great teachers have taught that there is only the One, or that there is only God and through finding yourself, you in turn find God. If Joe and Jane were looking at each other, a gnostic would suggest that whatever it is that's looking at Joe, and whatever it is that's looking at Jane, are the same entity... the entity that we have come to know as God or the Great Architect of the Universe. This is the essence of the "I Am" consciousness.[48] Individually, I am God and you are God. Together we are all God. Everything that we see, hear, smell, taste... everything that we experience, the good and the bad – is God. Take this theory to the Church and they will tell you that God is omnipresent. Take this theory to science and you will learn how everything is made from "general relativity" and "quantum mechanics" which combined give us "strings" ("The Theory of Everything"). This mathematical String (M) Theory reveals that we could all be literally connected multidimensionally on some sort of vibrating string level[49]--a sort of Gaian consciousness. Another unifying and interesting proposal is the *Holographic Universe* model first suggested by Alain Aspect, which we'll discuss more toward the end of this book.[50]

Christianity teaches separation and division of God and man. God is in heaven and man is here on earth. However, the Church also says that God is omnipresent, meaning that God is everywhere at once. How can God be everywhere at once and ***not*** be the only thing that exists? If you follow this theory, then, you will understand that by finding your *Self*, you will in turn find God. If everything is made of atoms, energy and strings, then the air we breath, our lungs that do the breathing, the hair on our heads, the car we drive, the food we eat, the fork with which we eat, all that we see, smell, touch, taste, etc., are all woven from the same material. Then all is truly connected. We are all literally (the) one. Comedian Bill Hicks said this best when he was complaining about all drug stories on the news being negative. He would explain that he had experienced epiphanies while on drugs and that he was upset that *those* stories never make the evening news:

---

[48] Timothy Freke and Peter Gandy expound upon this in a radio interview with Laura Lee in 2001.
[49] *The Elegant Universe*, by Brian Greene.
[50] *The Holographic Universe*, by Michael Talbot, see also David Bohm.

"Today a young man on acid realized that all matter is merely energy condensed to a slow vibration, that we are all one consciousness experiencing itself subjectively, there is no such thing as death, life is only a dream, and we are the imagination of ourselves. Here's Tom with the weather."
~ Bill Hicks

On one hand, there is religion which is a set of beliefs about God and, on the other hand, there is shamanism which is a set of techniques used to discover that you *are* God. The primary belief in religion is that of God, and the primary technique for a shaman is the usage of sacred plants to engender God within you. With shamanism *and* religion on the table now, we find ourselves at the cusp of a true-to-life paradigm shift. This will not be the end of the world, but the end of the Dark Age and the beginning of a new Age of Understanding.

The literal understanding of the Bible, from which many seem to be breaking away, is the fundamentalist viewpoint. This is the essence of the literalist's viewpoint (the opposite from Gnosticism) whereby the Bible was literally written by a heavenly deity. From this viewpoint, Jesus was literally the son of God, incarnated into a real person, who literally healed the sick by brushing up against them, who actually died and came back to life (reincarnated), etc. The literalist take on the Bible is that it is all 100% accurate and divine, historically as well as morally, which of course is absurd.[51,52] This is where the *"a woman's place is in the home"* mentality comes from. Their god is male, the priests have always been male, and only recently have women been permitted to become active in church and community. This paradigm is shifting, too.

This breaking away from the literalist point of view is natural when we realize that it has only been because of the selfishness of man that the truth is kept from fruition.

THE GALILEAN SHIFT

Ancient pagan religions in the Mediterranean area and throughout the Middle East taught that the universe was quite tiny. These included the religions of ancient Egypt, Babylonia, Canaan, etc. The earth was often thought of as flat, like a dinner plate. Mountains around the edges held up a rigid metallic dome, which formed the sky. The gods and angels pushed the sun, moon, planets and stars across the dome of the sky on a daily basis. God sits on his throne in Heaven, which lies above the great dome or canopy. Doors or windows in the dome could be opened through which water, fire (in the case of Sodom and Gomorrah), and brimstone could be poured. This is the view of the universe that the writers of the Bible appear to have adopted from these pagan religions, i.e., if one interprets their writing literally.[53] The problem came after Aristotle suggested that the earth is a sphere. Many members of the clergy could not accept that as truth. There are a number of implications in the Bible that suggest it is the sun that moves, not the earth. This suggestion was contradictory to the "Word of God," therefore, in the minds of many, it could not be true.

---

[51] *The Catholic Encyclopedia of the Bible* admits that nearly 40% of the Bible is fabricated interpolation. *The Christ Conspiracy*, by Acharya S.

[52] The fact that there are over 20 known English translations of the Bible also shows us that there is no "infallible word of God."

[53] www.religioustolerance.org.

Figure 9 – Astro-Theology

Joshua 10:3
And the sun stood still, and the moon stayed, until the people had avenged themselves upon their enemies. Is not this written in the book of Jasher? So the sun stood still in the midst of heaven, and hasted not to go down about a whole day.

Over two millennia ago, Aristotle taught that the earth was the center of the universe. Greek astronomer Claudius Ptolemy worked out this idea into great detail by expanding Aristotle's ideas into what has become known as the Ptolemaic system. Within this system, all the heavenly bodies that could be seen with the naked eye (the moon, the stars, the planets) were all in motion and circling our stationary earth. Many astronomers would account for the observed motion of heavenly bodies by assuming that they were attached to translucent crystal spheres, each sphere rotating within the other.

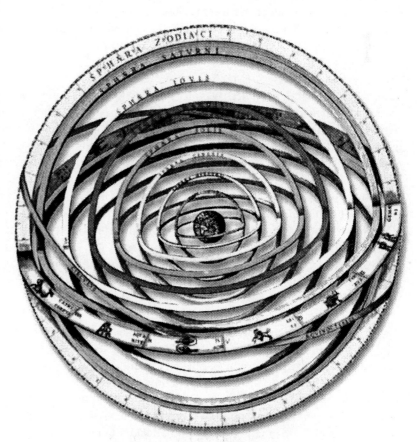

Figure 10 - The Ptolemaic system

11

In contrast, Copernicus thought that this could be simplified if one were to modify the model by replacing the *earth* as the central stationary object with the sun. However, his theory was rejected due to the lack of visual evidence to support it. Consequently, Copernicus became the laughingstock of Europe. But in retrospect, knowing that the sun was actually the *risen savior* that the Church was worshipping, it would make sense for the Church to reject the claims of a man who described the sun as a king sitting on a royal, heavenly throne, ruling over the celestial bodies that circled around it.

After working for quite some time making lenses and designing telescopes for the Navy, Galileo Galilei pointed his homemade telescopes to the heavens. In the early 1600s, after observing Jupiter for several days, Galileo noticed that the four "stars" near this planet were actually moons. He had already spent many sleepless nights observing *our* moon and its phases, taking particular notice to its similarities to the earth. Galileo knew that if our moon circled the earth, that the four moons of Jupiter are circling that planet as well. This discovery clashed with the belief that the heavens were solely restricted to revolving around the earth. Planetary bodies circling *other* planetary bodies did not fit into the model that was supported by the Church. Galileo learned this the hard way when he moved from Venice to Tuscany, where he was accepted into the Medici court as a philosopher and mathematician. Venice was much more liberal in its thinking and teaching than any community with close ties to the Vatican. The Medicis had close ties to the Vatican. The family had produced many Popes and Cardinals.

Although he believed it to be true, Galileo could not see a way of *proving* the Copernican system, even with the discovery of Jupiter's moons. It was one of Galileo's students who suggested to him that if the planet Venus does in fact revolve around the sun, rather than the earth, that it, too, would be seen in phases, similar to those of our moon. Galileo then observed Venus for months and noticed that it did indeed have phases, sometimes seen as a disk, and other times as a crescent. He then understood that if the sun was truly in the center, that Venus *would* be seen as a crescent as it circled in an orbit between the sun and the earth. With Galileo's telescopes, one could visually witness Venus circling the sun by watching its shadow, thus proving the Copernican system and shattering the notion of a stationary earth.

Almost immediately, Galileo was scrutinized by the Church and by the scholars who supported the Ptolemaic system. Galileo contradicted the Bible and he knew that others who have dared commit such a crime were dealt with in an extreme and public manner, e.g., burning someone alive for making such claims against the Bible was not unheard of (case in point, Giordano Bruno, just a few years earlier in 1600). The Church had already started a dossier on Galileo, and Rome was becoming aware of the implications that his claims could have.

Rather than retreat to a more liberal community, Galileo went to Rome in the winter of 1616 with the intentions of standing his ground and explaining his claims. One of the men to whom he would have to explain himself was Cardinal Bellarmine (a.k.a. "The Hammer of the Heretics"). Bellarmine was one of the inquisitors of former priest, Giordano Bruno, who also suggested accuracy in the Copernican doctrine. Bruno was subsequently burned alive. But Galileo was anxious to meet Cardinal Bellarmine because he was bringing to Bellarmine the *visual proof* that would be needed to convince such a man. Consequently, as soon as Cardinal Bellarmine realized that science was a threat to the Church, "scientific heresy" was added to the Inquisition.

Galileo never had the chance to prove his theories to Cardinal Bellarmine. Just three days prior to their meeting, the Holy Office of the Inquisition held a vote. The results were 11-0, concluding that the Copernican doctrine and the notion that the earth moves was not only irrational, but (scientific) heresy as well. Three days later, when Galileo met with Bellarmine, there was no conversation or discussion. Galileo was formally issued a warning from Bellarmine to discontinue his belief that the earth moved. Cardinal Bellarmine then cautioned him and other scientists to treat Copernican views as a hypothesis, not fact. Galileo was warned not to speak of Copernicanism as anything other than a method for hypothetical calculations.

> To assert that the earth revolves around the sun is as erroneous as to claim that Jesus was not born of a virgin.
> ~ Cardinal Bellarmine

Galileo was permitted to write about his ideas, as long as they were treated as hypothetical. He then wrote his theories as a dialog between two men, a simpleton who reflected the Church's dogma and spoke on the side of the stationary earth, and the other as a learned man and supporter of Copernicus. At the end of the *Dialogue*[54], Galileo put the words of Pope Urban the Eighth into the mouth of the simpleton, basically stating that if God wanted us to understand such complex matters, we would. Years earlier, the Pope had said this to Galileo and now Galileo was putting those words into the mouth of a simpleton, consequently making the Pope look foolish. The Pope then called together a commission to examine Galileo's book. Upon doing so, they recommended the case be turned over to the Inquisition.

At 70, Galileo was tried before the Inquisition Court, which limited itself to only two questions: 1) Did the late Cardinal Bellarmine forbid Galileo to advocate Copernicus? And 2) Had Galileo violated this order by writing his *Dialogue*? Galileo was found guilty and sentenced to life in prison. At this point in his life, he was old. Rather than spend the rest of his days in a dungeon, he did as he was asked, got upon his knees, renounced his sins against the Church, and verbally abandoned the Copernican doctrine. As Galileo rose from his knees after making this required humiliation to the Catholic judges, he is said to have muttered under his breath, "but still it moves." Galileo was later sentenced to home imprisonment and ordered to recite weekly prayers of penitence. His *Dialogue* was soon added to the growing index of forbidden books and remained banned for 200 years.

MORE SHIFTS

Our ancestors lacked the technology that we pride ourselves on today. For them, it made sense that the earth was the center of the universe. As high up on any mountain as one could climb, the earth appeared to be as flat as a chessboard. Additionally, the sun and moon *do* appear to move across the sky. These theories have been proven wrong over time, but this is what the masses were once taught, in part because this is what they could see with their own eyes. Still, to this day, we use words like sun<u>rise</u> and sun<u>set</u>. While these words obviously imply movement of the sun, they are common solecisms that almost everyone gladly overlooks.

What it took to change the minds of the masses, who believed what they were told, was a paradigm shift. A paradigm shift happens quite often in the grand scope of humankind's history. One example of a paradigm shift that many of us were a part of would have been the introduction of computers into the workplace. Today, that paradigm shift has been completed as computers have gone from being unheard of and unneeded in the workplace to becoming completely indispensable. This is but one example of a paradigm shift, as there are many others. By exposing the truth behind Christianity and other religions regarding shamanic plant/drug use and the reverence for celestial bodies, we hope to speed up the paradigm shift that will usher in the new Age of Aquarius.

Shifting the paradigm requires more than just thinking outside of the box. To shift the paradigm, the box must be rebuilt. In the past, those who had questioned their current paradigm or dared to suggest a new one were seen as unbalanced or crazy. These people were once vilified by their peers for following the truth beyond the realm of political correctness. However, they were soon seen in a new light as their theories were proven factual (oftentimes, long after their deaths). Today, with the power of the Internet, the Law of Duality can literally be known worldwide overnight.

Suppose you were living back in the era when the Christian church had declared mathematics to be the work of the devil. Imagine also that you had just seen the calculations of Galileo explaining the motion of the moons around a planet and the phases of Venus[55], something that propelled your understanding into the next paradigm. This would

---

[54] *Dialogue Concerning the Two Chief World Systems*, 1632 Galileo Galilei.

[55] Venus was also considered Lucifer (the "Devil"). Regarding Venus, the Day-star (Morning-star), Pliny the Elder stated: "Before the sun revolves a very large star named Venus, which varies in course alternatively, and whose alternative names in themselves indicate its rivalry with the sun and moon—when in advance and rising before dawn, it received the name Lucifer, as being another sun and bringing the dawn whereas when it shines after sunset it is named Vesper, as prolonging the day-light, or as being a deputy for the moon.... Further, it surpasses all the other stars in magnitude, and is so brilliant that alone among the stars it casts a shadow by its rays. Consequently, there is great competition to give it a name, some having called it Juno, others Isis, others Mother of the gods..." --*Natural History* II 36-37; see also *The Dead Sea Scrolls and the Christian Myth*, by John Allegro pg. 182, and *Oxford English Dictionary*: Lucifer - 1. The morning star; the planet Venus when she appears in the sky before sunrise. ...Misused for: A devil.

be fine if you were to keep these thoughts to yourself. But it would be impossible to explain what you know to those who mirror the Church's view of your new insight as being evil (mostly because "evil" mathematics would be necessary in your explanation). In other words, telling the wrong person the right information could get you burned at the stake.

However, times have changed and knowledge isn't evil anymore, but the truth isn't quite politically correct yet either. This current paradigm is shifting too and it's only a matter of time before the visionary shaman plays a major role in our society.

Perhaps, there is a reality out there that we cannot understand or recognize because we don't yet have the combined determination of the community to discover it. We have no way to build machines that will open *the doors of perception* to us because the keys that open those doors grow in nature. And because there is no way to put a patent on nature, these plants are pushed to the side in order to make way for highly-priced and highly-refined mood-altering chemicals that you see on television and can buy at any corner drug store. All you need is a note from a doctor (or "chemical shaman").

It is unfortunate that the drugs that society will acknowledge as politically approved or correct are the ones that promote thinking *inside* the box. The recreational drugs that are politically correct are the ones that make you sluggish, submissive, and stupid, while the politically incorrect plants that the shaman uses, promote thinking *outside* of the box. When using these shamanic techniques, you can no longer be told what is right and wrong. You can see and judge this clearly. In Christian mythology, Adam and Eve were kicked out of a garden of paradise for this very same thing.

> *The Papyrus of Ani* (The doctrine of eternal life)
>
> He thirsts not, nor hungers, nor is sad; he eats the bread of Ra and drinks what he drinks daily, and his bread also is that which is the word of Keb, and that which comes forth from the mouths of the gods. He eats what the gods eat, he drinks what they drink, he lives as they live, and dwells where they dwell; all the gods give him their food that he may not die. Not only does he eat and drink of their food, but he wears the apparel which they wear, the white linen [hemp] and sandals; he is clothed in white, and he goeth to the great lake in the midst of the Field of Offerings whereon the great gods sit; and these great and never failing gods give unto him [to eat] of the tree of life of which they themselves do eat.

Perhaps visionary plants do not warp reality or disfigure your perception as commonly thought. Shamanic techniques offer gateways into novel degrees of perception that truly exist at a level that our society does not yet appreciate. Perhaps today's shamanic voyagers using visionary plants are peering into the future, at the next paradigm, at the different ways of seeing things that *normal* people may not find for many years. In the future, when we look back to these times as history, perhaps those who helped to return the modern day exploration of human consciousness[56] will be remembered for their bravery for standing up as voyagers and surveyors of the final frontier, fighting for the collective consciousness.

For these reasons, it is sad that today's shamans or anyone using plants to expand their consciousness are being persecuted, mocked, pushed aside, and made out to be criminals for not being "normal." We can only reflect back into history on those who were persecuted for their outrageous beliefs, beliefs that later became common knowledge. We contend that the role of shamanic techniques in our future will become so profound that many will someday ask how we ever survived without visionary plants and altered states of consciousness.

---

[56] Terence McKenna (1946-2000), John Marco Allegro (1923-1988), Timothy Leary (1920-1996), Gordon Wasson (1898-1986), Aldous Huxley (1894-1963), et al.

~ Chapter Three ~
The Christian Myth and the New Age

DISCIPLES OF THE MACROCOSM

In attempting to dissect Christianity by only looking to the stars, many of the important and *secret* traditions are overlooked completely. The sacred meal is one of them. The following references are brilliant when attempting to understand astronomy as it applies to Christianity throughout antiquity. These authors mention very little (if anything at all) about the ingestion of the holy sacraments, and few dare to suggest what these sacraments could have been.[57]

Among other works, Manly P. Hall wrote *The Secret Teachings of All Ages*. The larger versions of this book contain plate after plate of amazing alchemical and religious art. It has in-depth explanations regarding the meanings behind ancient symbols, as well as (to a fair extent) the origins of those ancient symbols. One can find this book in most larger libraries, or for sale at PRS.org, the website for the Philosophical Research Society, founded by Manly P. Hall in 1934.

That Old-Time Religion by Jordan Maxwell, Paul Tice and Alan Snow is a very interesting book on the history of religions. This book includes a chapter written by Gerald Massey. Jordan Maxwell has conducted dozens of intensive seminars, hosted his own radio talk shows, guested on more than 600 radio shows, and written, produced and appeared in numerous television shows and documentaries (including three 2-hour specials for the CBS TV network), as well as the internationally acclaimed 5-part Ancient Mysteries series.[58] Maxwell is also the author of *Matrix of Power*.

Acharya S has also written books dissecting Christianity. *The Christ Conspiracy* is an excellent book on the forgery that depicts itself as Christianity and how astrotheology is applied to the origins of religion. She also wrote *Suns of God: Krishna, Buddha and Christ Unveiled*, which is one of the best-documented books on these subjects. Acharya is a member of one of the world's most exclusive institutes for the study of ancient Greek civilization, the American School of Classical Studies in Athens, Greece. She served as a trench master on archaeological excavations in Corinth, Greece, and Connecticut, USA, as well as a teacher's assistant on the island of Crete. Visit truthbeknown.com for more information about this author and her books.

Gerald Massey was a social reformer, a poet and an Egyptologist who wrote a number of informative books. Many of Massey's lectures have been transcribed and are available online and in bookstores. His books titled *The Natural Genesis* and *Ancient Egypt:Light of the World* are both recommended reading and are available in a two-part series.

The World's 16 Crucified Saviors: Christianity before Christ, by Kersey Graves, is another fascinating book. The title of this book alone speaks volumes. It discusses how many of the characteristics applied to Christianity are associated with many of the religions that came *long before* Christianity. Since the publication of this book in 1875, Graves has received numerous unfounded attacks against his scholarship. Regarding the matter, Acharya S, who has re-substantiated Graves ideas[59], had this to say:

> Contrary to popular opinion, Graves did not fabricate any of these correlations, which means that he has been unfairly judged over the past century, although more careful citation on his part would have avoided much of the problem.[60]
> ~ Acharya S

Timothy Freke and Peter Gandy have authored several books together: *The Jesus Mysteries: Was the 'Original Jesus' a Pagan God?*, and *Jesus and the Lost Goddess* are two of our favorites. Both of these books provide wonderful insights into Christian Gnosticism *and* Christian Literalism.

---

[57] In *The Book Your Church Doesn't Want you to Read*, Tim C. Leedom suggested the forbidden fruit was a banana! Pg. 210.
[58] From bio at www.JordanMaxwell.com.
[59] *Suns of God* –by Acharya S (2004), see chapters 5 thru 9.
[60] Ibid pg. 161.

Ernest Busenbark wrote *Symbols, Sex, and the Stars*, originally published in 1949. This book provides an excellent overview of the mysteries of archaeoastronomy, fertility worship, and symbolism. We highly recommend this book.

THE EARTH MOVES

Figure 11 - Flat Earth?

Psalm 93:1 – "thou hast fixed the earth a movable and firm..."

The Bible typically portrays the earth as flat, not spherical (e.g. "the four corners of the earth/land," "*one* end of the earth even unto the *other* end of the earth," etc.[61]). Numerous members of the Catholic Church, who controlled and disseminated the authorized beliefs for the people (believers), mirrored this philosophy in their teachings. One thing that is not often mentioned is that the female anthropomorphism of the earth in these ancient philosophies was often considered to open up like a flower (or vagina) and was believed to *derive from* the sun (shaft). The sun was anthropomorphized as the head of the sky god's penis, which plunged into the womb of mother earth nightly in the heavenly act of coitus. The semen was symbolized by rain, which originated from the sky god's penis and fell onto the womb of Mother Earth, impregnating her and thus bringing life into the world.

> Now they have to be told that their Lord was a mushroom, his mother a fungus vulva, and his heavenly Father a mighty penis in the sky.[62]
> ~ John Marco Allegro

However, not every ancient culture on earth believed that the earth was stationary and even fewer were under the impression that the earth was flat. These theories happened to be primarily an Indo-European belief. It was not necessarily a belief held in the priesthood and by those who were educated in any of the ancient mystery schools. Eratosthenes (276 - 195 BCE), and many others long before Galileo correctly calculated the circumference of the earth. The stationary and flat earth theories may have been primarily just hypotheses (or lies) promulgated to the masses, who, as a whole, were ignorant by force. Reading, writing, and mathematics were forbidden sciences throughout the Dark Ages.

---

[61] Isaiah 11:12; Ezekiel 7:2; Revelation 7:1; Deuteronomy 13:7.
[62] *The End of a Road* – by John Marco Allegro.

Once mathematical systems were developed, they looked at the stars in the heavens and documented what they saw. Our ancestors (the first astronomers and mathematicians) founded what we today call archaeoastronomy. Archaeoastronomy was created for the measurement of time.[63] By removing this knowledge from the common folk, these educated priests appeared to be able to perform magic when they could do simple things like predict lunar and solar eclipses. They could tell the masses how many days until planting season, or they could announce the beginning of spring. How easy it would be, by understanding the heavens, for a king or clergy to trick their people (who could not to read or write) into believing that they actually had something to do with a solar eclipse. The ancient cultures had great amounts of knowledge in mathematics, as evidenced by their architectural alignments to the stars.[64]

Ancient Olmec and Mayan archaeoastronomy shows that these natives (acknowledged as the greatest timekeepers in all history) created one of their *seventeen* calendars between 400 and 100 BCE[65], which aligned with the *Great Year* or *Precession of the Equinoxes*. Based on the Tzolkin and Haab calendars, this sacred calendar, referred to as the Long Count Calendar has more accuracy today than any other calendar known. This calendar has an end-date[66] and works backward through time. The calendar ends on December 21st of the year 2012, ending the Aquarius Initiation, and beginning the next Mayan cycle (13.0.0.0.0).

> The Maya estimate of precession, if we assume that 5 Great Cycles (65 baktuns) were intended to represent a full precessional cycle, is 25,626[67] years. Since the end-date of the 13-baktun cycle of the Long Count calendar identifies a rare alignment in the cycle of precession, and Long Count dating first started appearing in the archaeological record in the first century B.C., the ancient skywatchers apparently had already calculated precession at that time. Their forward projection, some 2,100 years into the future, was very accurate and reveals that the ancient skywatchers possessed an advanced cosmological knowledge.[68]
> ~ John Major Jenkins

To prove the knowledge of the Precession of the Equinoxes was/is established in western culture, we traced the word *precession* back to 1828 in *Webster's Dictionary*:[69]

> In astronomy, the precession of the equinox, is an annual motion of the equinox, or point when the ecliptic intersects the equator, to the westward, amounting to 50 1/2. This precession was discovered by Hipparchus, a century and a half before the Christian era, though it is alleged that the astronomers of India had discovered it long before. At that time, the point of the autumnal equinox was about six degrees to the eastward of the star called Spica Virginis. In 1750, that is, about nineteen hundred years after, this point was observed to be about 20 deg. 21' westward of that star. Hence it appears that the equinoctial points will make an entire revolution in about 25,745 years.

---

[63] From our research, there appears to be evidence to suggest that (in part) the progression/creation of various religions (outside of drug-based shamanism) could be in direct relation to the progression of man's ability to measure time. As man's ability to track time proceeded, old and inaccurate methods and mythologies were abandoned. For example: As the 13 month, 364-day lunar calendar was proven inaccurate, people moved to the age of sun worship, and the 365.24-day solar calendars based on the winter solstice. Moon worshipers then became known as "lunatics." As the sun worshiper's calendar was proven inaccurate, these people suppressed the new knowledge of the precession and later developments. This stage of evolution eventually went stagnant in the old world due to the suppression of learning by the Church. In Mesoamerica, people (the shaman-priests) created yet greater and more accurate measurements of time based on Galactic cycles, with ever-greater mythologies and religion.

[64] *The Wisdom of the Knowing Ones*, by Manly P. Hall.

[65] The Long Count Calendar was perfected between 400 and 100 BC, and put in use in the 1st century. See John Major Jenkins.

[66] "The Calendar Round and the Long Count calendars are precession-tracking tools, but each system uses a different methodology.... The important concept in the Long Count calendar for understanding how World Ages were tracked involves the position of the sun on the end-date and the "cosmic center" marked by the **Maya Sacred Tree** [Axis Mundi]... the crossing point of the Milky Way and the ecliptic near Sagittarius. They came to understand the Galactic Center as the true cosmic center, the Womb of All, which renews the world in A.D. 2012." *Maya Cosmogenesis 2012*, by John Major Jenkins, pg. 24, 38.

[67] Modern astronomers estimate a cycle of the Precession to take between 25,600 and 26,000 years.

[68] *Maya Cosmogenesis 2012* –by John Major Jenkins Pg. 41-42.

[69] Webster's: *An American Dictionary of the English Language*, 1828, in two volumes quarto.

Similarly, *The Oxford English Dictionary 2nd Edition* (1989) had this to say about the *Precession of the Equinoxes*:

> Astron. precession of the equinoxes, often ellipt. precession [æquinoctiorum præcessio (Copernicus): called by Hipparchus and Ptolemy μετάπτωσις| mutation]: the earlier occurrence of the equinoxes in each successive sidereal year, due to the retrograde motion of the equinoctial points along the ecliptic, produced by the slow change of direction in space of the earth's axis, which moves so that the pole of the equator describes a circle (approximately: see nutation) around the pole of the ecliptic once in about 25,800 years. Hence commonly used to denote this motion of the equinoctial points, of the earth's axis, or of the celestial pole or equator; also the motion of the earth itself which manifests itself as the precession of the equinoxes.
>
> As a result of the precession, the longitudes, right ascensions, and declinations of all the stars are continually changing, and the signs of the zodiac shift in a retrograde direction along the zodiac, so that they no longer coincide with the constellations from which they were named (cf. the statement s.v. cancer n. 2b).[70]

By tracing the very names of this phenomenon back into our history, it becomes quite clear that our ancestors not only knew of this phenomenon, but also had a deep understanding of it. The pioneering book, *Hamlet's Mill* by de Santillana and von Dechend, argues sufficiently that the precession was known some one-thousand years before Hipparchus' so-called discovery of it. Most ancient sun worship is based on this same Precession of the Equinoxes.

> Hipparchus in 127 B.C. called it the Precession of the Equinoxes. There is good reason to assume that he actually rediscovered this, that is, had been known some thousand years previously, and that on it the Archaic Age based its long-range computation of time. Modern archaeological scholars have been singularly obtuse about the idea because they have cultivated a pristine ignorance of astronomical thought, some of them actually ignorant of the Precession itself.[71]
> ~ Giorgio De Santillana & Hertha Von Dechend

In *The Invisible Landscape: Mind Hallucinogens and the I Ching*, Terence & Dennis McKenna lay out Terence's mathematical timewave theory called Habit and Novelty Theory, which is based on the I Ching. Aligning the peaks and troughs of the wave, matching them with novel events in history, produced this same end date, Dec. 21, 2012. Habit & Novelty theory states that as novelty increases, time is *speeding up*. Thirty thousand years ago, we learned agriculture. At least fifty-five hundred years ago, our ancestors invented the wheel. Three hundred fifty years ago, we learned how to mass-produce machinery. Roughly one hundred years ago, the assembly line was invented. Roughly fifty-five years ago, humans learned how to build the first computers. Thirty-five years ago microchips were invented. Today's microchips will soon become extinct, only to be replaced with "nanochips" that offer millions of times more computing power in a microscopic package. The *rate* of change is ever increasing as we build upon our previous achievements. This year, more inventions are likely to be registered than all inventions throughout history. Novelty is accelerating faster and faster as the spiral of time is tightening. With computers we now have the ability to build things that are *more* efficient, we can also educate more people in a shorter amount of time, etc. Each of the tools that we build furthers our development at a faster rate until, as Terence McKenna hypothesized, *"some protean force smacks right into us on (or around) Dec. 21st 2012."*[72]

IN THE BEGINING

Many believe that the Roman Emperor Constantine *converted* to (or simply tolerated) Christianity, but what is often spoken of regarding Emperor Constantine is that in 325 CE, he called together the ecumenical[73] council, also known as the Council of Nicaea. This consisted of 300 or more of the world's leading philosophers, mathematicians and some of the greatest minds of the time. The choice of Nicaea was favorable to the assembling of a large number of bishops. It was easily accessible to the bishops of nearly all the provinces, but especially to those of Asia (Asia Minor), Syria, Palestine, Egypt, Greece, and Thrace.[74] Most of the bishops present were Greeks. Among the Latins

---

[70] *Oxford English Dictionary 2nd edition*, 1989.
[71] *Hamlet's Mill*, by Giorgio De Santillana & Hertha Von Dechend, pg. 66.
[72] Terence McKenna, *She Who Remembers Audio Archives;* Note: There exists arguments both in favor and against McKenna's theory. See *Autopsy for a Mathematical Hallucination?*, by Matthew Watkins, and *Delineation, Specification, and Formalization of the TWZ Data Set Generation Process - Philosophical, Procedural, and Mathematical*, by John Sheliak.
[73] The Oxford dictionary defines *ecumenical* as: "Belonging to the whole world; universal, general, world-wide."
[74] Catholic Encyclopedia online.

we know only Hosius of Cordova, Cecilian of Carthage, Mark of Calabria, Nicasius of Dijon, Donnus of Stridon in Pannonia, and the two Roman priests, Victor and Vincentius, representing the Pope. The assembly numbered among its most famous members, St. Alexander of Alexandria, Eustathius of Antioch, Macarius of Jerusalem, Eusebius of Nicomedia, Eusebius of Caesarea, and St. Nicholas of Myra.[75] At this council, Emperor Constantine literally created Christianity. Constantine was in no way *converted* to Christianity, he created it. By the end of his life, it is reported that Constantine went back to his "old pagan ways."[76]

> Recent investigations have challenged the traditional outlook and the traditional conclusions and the traditional "facts." With some today, and with many tomorrow, the burning question is, or will be, not how did a particularly silly and licentious heresy rise within the church, but how did the church rise out of the great Gnostic movement, how did the dynamic ideas of the Gnosis become crystallized into dogma?
> ~ Rev. Lamplugh (1937)

What most people call the Christians in the first 300 years of "Christianity's existence" were actually Gnostics, and Mithra and Krishna (sun) worshipers—the Therapeuts—the Zadokites, Essenes, and others.[77,78] The Roman Empire's official religion became Christianity under Constantine as he created a *one-world religion* from the doctrines of all existing religions. Thus was born the "Roman Catholic Church" ("Catholic" means *universal*) and Constantine was the religious *and* secular leader of the new Christian state authoritarian patriarchy. In order to explain how this brand-new religion should be accepted, "Church authorities" *imagined* all sorts of scenarios, which they purported into fact.

> That which is known as the Christian religion existed among the ancients, and never did not exist; from the beginning of the human race until the time when Christ came in the flesh[79], at which time the true religion[80], which already existed, began to be called Christianity.
> ~ St. Augustine, 354 CE

The fact that Rome just happened to be in total control of this eternal religion must have been, of course, "divine will." The uneducated Romans eventually believed this and took up the sword to exterminate anything non-Christian at the behest of the Roman Catholic authority.[81] The Council of Nicaea is where Christians today get their common prayer known as the Nicaean Creed. This Nicaean Creed is nothing more than a list of what a Christian is to believe and this is, in part, what came out of the Council of Nicaea in 325:

> We believe in one God the Father Almighty, Maker of heaven and earth, and of all things visible and invisible; And in one Lord Jesus Christ, the only-begotten Son of God, begotten of the Father before all worlds, God of God, Light of Light, Very God of Very God, begotten, not made, being of one substance with the Father by whom all things were made; who for us men, and for our salvation, came down from heaven, and was incarnate by the Holy Spirit of the Virgin Mary, and was made man, and was crucified also for us under Pontius Pilate. He suffered and was buried, and the third day he rose again according to the Scriptures, and ascended into heaven, and sitteth on the right hand of the Father. And he shall come again with glory to judge both the quick and the dead, whose kingdom shall have no end. And we believe in the Holy Spirit, the Lord and Giver of Life, who proceedeth from the Father and the Son, who with the Father and the Son together is worshipped and glorified, who spoke by the prophets. And we believe one holy catholic and apostolic Church. We acknowledge one baptism for the remission of sins. And we look for the resurrection of the dead, and the life of the world to come.

---

[75] Ibid.
[76] Jay Lynn.
[77] *The Dead Sea Scrolls and the Christian Myth*, by John Allegro; *Suns of God*, by Acharya S.
[78] "Eusebios, in compiling his history of the Christian Church for the Emperor Constantine, with only Philo's essay as his source, mistook these Therapeutai for an early Christian community, even citing the Platonic metaphor of the mirror." – *Apples of Apollo*, pg 162; *Eusebios, Ecclesiastical History*, 2.17.
[79] Notice St. Augustine backpedaling here as he states that the True Religion already existed before Christianity, but still claims that Jesus existed as a historical figure.
[80] Meaning shamanism & astrotheology.
[81] *Social Record of Christianity*, by Joseph McCabe.

Emperor Constantine worshiped Sol Invictus. Sol Invictus is often referred to as Mithra because of their strong correlation. The Latin words, 'Sol Invictus' literally translate into "the unconquered sun." Emperor Constantine was a sun worshiper (astrotheologist). He directly incorporated his sun worship knowledge into Christianity. The similarities between Sol Invictus and Mithra are well published and is not the focus here.[82,83]

The Persian sun god Mithra, in the Mithraic Kronos (the Personification of Infinite Time), and in other artwork, is in the center of the zodiac. He is surrounded by his 12 helpers or the 12 helpers of the sun. Mithra has 12 helpers like the Jesus character does, making Mithra and Jesus the number 13. Consequently, the number 13 is unlucky for *you* because it is reserved for divinity.[84,85] One will often find a goddess, a sun, or some sort of divine entity inside the zodiac when depicted in art. There are even old paintings of Jesus sitting on a throne surrounded by his 12 helpers, sometimes 12 angels other times the 12 disciples.

Figure 12 - Personification of Infinite Time

In Figure 13, Christ, whose crown of thorns is an obvious sunburst, is depicted with the 12 signs of the zodiac surrounding him. As we mentioned in chapter one, an old Hebrew word for "zodiac" is "Mazzaroth," found in the Old Testament (Job 38:32). In the book of Genesis, God (the Elohiym, often spelled Elohim) explains that the stars in the heavens are for "signs." Each of the 12 *houses* of the Mazzaroth is a *sign*. Aquarius is one of these 12 signs.

> Genesis 1:14
> And God said, Let there be lights in the firmament of the heaven to divide the day from the night; and let them be for signs, and for seasons, and for days, and years...

Figure 13 -Christ in the Zodiac, Northern Italy, 11th century.[86]

[82] *Suns of God* –by Acharya S.

[83] *The Worlds 16 Crucified Saviors*, by Kersey Graves.

[84] Usually the unlucky number 13 is associated to the Freemasons with Knights Templar Grand Master Jacques De Molay, who was purportedly arrested by King Philip IV of France on Friday the 13 1307. For more information on 13, see *Matrix of Power*, by Jordan Maxwell, pg. 37.

[85] 13 is also the number of months in a 364-day Lunar year. It is probable to suggest that the sun worshiping Christians took this idea from the moon worshipers and applied it to their sun worship in relation to the precession of the equinoxes. Some precessional calendars also show 13 primary constellations instead of 12. The numbers 3+6+4 also equal 13.

[86] *Alchemy & Mysticism – The Hermetic Museum* –by Alexander Roob. Pg 63

There are thousands of examples of this knowledge that we are not normally familiar with because it is not found through "mainstream" sources. As a result, we often do not have the ability to recognize it and attempt to understand it. The Internet is a very handy tool to the modern-day truth seeker. Online libraries and image galleries abound on the Internet. We must use this resource as a stepping-stone to increase our knowledge and consciousness. This is true all throughout history. For example, we had to continue pushing the envelope until we dissolved the boundaries between us and things that are too tiny to see before the microscope could be invented, or was needed. In addition, if there were things that were once beyond the extremes of our senses, then there are still things out there that we still have not been able to observe. At the time of this writing, scientists do not know what makes up 96% of the universe.[87] That is an incredible statistic. Everything that we know (stars, planets, people, household items, everything) contributes to just 4% of the universe. The rest of the universe is comprised of an even more mysterious fabric called dark energy. Yet people cheerfully assume that 100% of everything that surrounds us is exactly how it appears to be. This is a tremendously naive perspective.

If there are things beyond the boundaries of our awareness, perhaps there are also *doors of perception* and degrees of consciousness that we have not yet discovered. Nevertheless, like some of the greatest wonders of the world—the great Pyramid of Giza, Stonehenge, and other mysterious monuments—humankind may have already achieved these higher degrees of consciousness in the past. Somewhere along the line, *we started to take our anthropomorphisms literally* and we all but lost the essence of the Greatest Story ever told.

THE ONLY STORY EVER TOLD

Some of the characteristics of Jesus are as follows[88]:

- He was born of the Virgin.
- His father was a carpenter.
- His birth was attended by angels, wise men and shepherds, and he was presented with gold, frankincense and myrrh.
- He was persecuted by a tyrant who ordered the slaughter of thousands of infants.
- He was of royal descent.
- He was baptized in a river.
- He worked miracles and wonders.
- He raised the dead and healed lepers, the deaf and the blind.
- He used parables to teach the people about charity and love.
- "He lived poor and he loved the poor."
- He was transfigured in front of his disciples.
- In some traditions, he died on a tree or was crucified between two thieves.
- He rose from the dead and ascended to heaven.
- He is the second person of the Trinity, and proclaimed himself the "Resurrection" and the "way to the Father."
- He was considered the "Beginning, the Middle and the End" ("Alpha and Omega"), as well as being omniscient, omnipresent and omnipotent.
- He is to return to do battle with the "Prince of Evil," who will desolate the earth.

For many Christians, these characteristics may sound very similar to the Nicaean Creed, but those who have studied other religions may find similarities with something or someone else. That's because all of the attributes listed above, while they do apply to the Jesus character, were originally characteristics of Krishna.[89] Krishna is a Hindu deity worshiped at least 500 years and possibly as much as 3000 years before Christianity. If you take away from Jesus all of these characteristics that indeed make him divine (because they did not belong to him in the first place), the Jesus character is not left with a leg to stand on. For more information about this topic, research Gerald Massey, Jordan Maxwell, Kersey Graves and Acharya S.

---

[87] NASA.gov: 4 percent ordinary matter, 23 percent dark matter, and 73 percent dark energy.
[88] *The Christ Conspiracy, The Greatest Story Ever Sold*, by Acharya S.
[89] Jordan Maxwell, Acharya S, Kersey Graves, Gerald Massey and others.

There is an image in *The Hindu Pantheon* by Edward Moor and in Higgins' *Anacalypsis*, with a drawing of what looks to be Jesus. Although the deity is pictured with long hair and a beard, standing with his arms out and his feet together, with holes in his hands and feet, wearing a crown of thorns and a sash around his waist, it is not Jesus, it was actually intended to represent Krishna.

One important thing to know about this character is that it represents some*thing*, not some*one*. It is the character's posture and life cycle that is important, the name of the character can be interchanged and applied to different cultures and Ages, but the characteristics will always remain the same. It is very important that the characters assume this posture. This will be discussed more in depth later.

Figure 14 -The Crucifixion in Space

Mithra of Persia was born from a rock. Standing inside the gateway (Figure 12), Mithra stands on top of the primordial mound, with wings on his back, and he is entwined with something that resembles a serpent climbing his body. These are very important symbols and understanding them is the key to understanding many of the ancient mysteries.

Mithra has the following in common with the Christ character[90],[91]:

- Mithra was born on December 25th.
- He was considered a great traveling teacher and master.
- He had 12 companions or disciples.
- He performed miracles.
- He was buried in a tomb.
- After three days he rose again.
- His resurrection was celebrated every year.
- Mithra was called "the Good Shepherd."
- He was considered "the Way, the Truth and the Light, the Redeemer, the Savior, the Messiah."
- He was identified with both the Lion and the Lamb.
- His sacred day was Sunday, "the Lord's Day," hundreds of years before the appearance of Christ.
- Mithra had his principal festival on what was later to become Easter, at which time he was resurrected.
- His religion had a Eucharist or "Lord's Supper."

The characteristics that are shared with Jesus do not end with Mithra. Horus from Egypt is thousands of years older than the Jesus story and also shares many characteristics with Jesus[92]:

- Horus was born of the virgin Isis-Meri on December 25th in a cave/manger, with his birth being announced by a star in the East and attended by three wise men.
- He was a child teacher in the Temple and was baptized when he was 30 years old.
- Horus was also baptized by "Anup the Baptizer," who becomes "John the Baptist."
- He had 12 disciples.

---

[90] More attributes that must be removed from the newer, "historical Jesus."
[91] *The Christ Conspiracy, The Greatest Story Ever Sold*, by Acharya S.
[92] Ibid.

- He performed miracles and raised one man, El-Azar-us, from the dead.
- He walked on water.
- Horus was transfigured on the Mount.
- He was crucified, buried in a tomb and resurrected.
- He was also "the Way, the Truth, the Light, the Messiah, God's Anointed Son, the Son of Man, the Good Shepherd, the Lamb of God, the Word," etc.
- He was "the Fisher," and was associated with the Lamb, Lion and Fish ("Ichthys").
- Horus' personal epithet was "Iusa," the "ever-becoming son" of "Ptah," the "Father."
- Horus was called "the KRST," or "Anointed One," long before the Christians duplicated the story.

Christians believe that all of these attributes and many more are only applicable to Jesus Christ and, as we can see, this is in no way true whatsoever. There are *at least* thirty ancient deities who are all thousands of years older than Jesus and share a great degree of commonality with him.[93,94]

HE IS RISEN INDEED

This great story can be found in nature. In the spring and summer, the sun in the sky is large and the days are hot and long. During the fall and winter, the sun is farther away on the horizon (smaller) and the days are shorter and colder. During the summertime, the northern hemisphere tips toward the sun as the earth rotates on its axis. Because of this tipping of the axis, the sun appears to be larger on the horizon and the days are longer and warmer. During the wintertime, the northern hemisphere tips away from the sun and we experience colder months as the sun appears smaller on the horizon and the daylight hours grow shorter and shorter.

Figure 15

The sun in the sky is truly our savior. It saves us from a sure death by giving its energy to us. Like all stars, someday our sun will also burn out. Consequently, the sun is quite literally giving its life so that we may live. When the sun in the sky is being anthropomorphized as a human deity (the baby Jesus for example), the birth is depicted to occur underneath a star. This is because the sun in the sky truly is born underneath a star, or at least that is how it appears from our earthly perspective. The baby Jesus is usually depicted in a stable with a star over his head. As the story goes, Jesus was born in a stable in between a goat and a horse (also known as Capricorn and Sagittarius[95]). It is common to put a Nativity scene underneath the Christmas tree with a star on top of the tree. Horus is also depicted with a star over his head in sculptures and other artwork. Wise men are said to have followed this star to the birth of Jesus. What role could these wise men and this star play in all of this?

The sun is the main star of all stars, the only star that is of real importance to us because it sustains our lives. Similarly, in this macrocosmic anthropomorphism, the sun and all other stars in the sky (the cousins or brothers of the sun) are *Kings* and Jesus, representing the sun, is the King of kings.

---

[93] Ibid, pg. 105-25.

[94] *The World's 16 Crucified Saviors*, by Kersey Graves; *Suns of God*, by Acharya S.

[95] *The Christ Conspiracy: The Greatest Story Ever Sold*, pg. 161, by Acharya S.

Imagine that you are sitting by the pond in this picture, facing the East, and watching the sun's cycle all year long. Imagine further that you are only going to document where the sun first appears on the Eastern horizon each morning. Beginning in the spring and early summer you would notice that the sun is at 7 a.m., already raised from its nightly sleep and above the eastern horizon. You will also notice that it is consistently rising on the northern side of due east.

As we approach autumn, at the same time of the morning, the sun will not be rising on the north side of due east, now it is crossing over and rising on the south side of due east. The sun appears to be moving to the south and shrinking as well. As we progress further towards winter, the days get shorter and shorter as the sun appears to get smaller and smaller. It is as though the sun is falling to its death. It would appear that if the sun were to continue on this course, our days would continue to get shorter and shorter until there were no daylight hours at all. Eventually, all life on earth would cease to exist.[97]

It is fortunate for us that this does not happen. The sun will soon be traveling back to the northern part of the sky. When doing so, the sun will appear to grow larger and stronger, bringing the warmer weather of spring and summer. However, the transition between this southerly movement and northerly movement of the sun does not happen overnight. (It appears as though) the sun has been moving toward the south and growing smaller every day, but on the evening of the winter solstice[98] (typically December 21st), this comes to an end. On December 22nd, 23rd, and 24th the sun does *not* rise one degree closer to the south as it has each day in the previous 6 months.

Figure 16 - Movement of the Sun[96]

---

[96] These images are for visualization purposes only and are not to scale.
[97] Jordan Maxwell: lectures, videos, and books.
[98] The word *solstice* literally means "sun stands still."

Instead, the sun will rise in the exact same location, it is without movement. The sun is *considered* dead for three days. There is a three-day period when our savior, the King of kings, the son of God (the sun god) is dead. The new sun is born on December 25th, rising on the horizon and advancing one degree toward the north as it begins its new life and the days begin to grow longer. In fact, above 66.5° to 67° latitude[99], the sun will actually disappear from the horizon during this three day period:

> According to my tables for this year [2004] at the 67 degrees latitude, the sun is not visible for three days from the Dec. 21, to Dec. 25... but at noon it is still bright outside... the sun must be 6 degrees below horizon for total darkness.[100]
> ~ Prond Robertson - Meteorologisk Institutt of Northern Norway

Though it is not the scope of this book to look into this in depth, it has interesting implications on the origins of so-called Mesopotamian and Vedic religions, and further research is required.[101]

New Year's and Christmas are essentially the same holiday, the celebration of the birth of the sun. But how can *you* tell when this happens, like our ancestors did? There is a simple technique to recognize when this time of year occurs. As the typical story goes, three kings follow a star in the east to the birth of the Christ child.

Figure 17 – The Kings

---

[99] Depending on specific annual calculations.

[100] A phone conversation with Prond Robertson of the Meteorologisk Institutt Forecasting division of Northern Norway, Tromsø. Sun. Nov. 28, 2004.

[101] The implications of this hypothesis on religion are important. This could place the origin of the death of the sun *tale* with people living above the 65.5° latitude. If this is true, it could mean the origins of Middle Eastern, Mediterranean and Vedic religions who celebrate this would actually be developments from Ural-Altaic shamanism of the Arctic Siberian north! Gordon Wasson suggested this in 1968! There is evidence to show that the Turkish and other peoples (possibly even Sumerian) are just that! Peter Wilson's ideas of Soma always being bought or stolen from the tribal people (see chapter 4 or Wilson, *Ploughing the Clouds*) would also reinforce this theory. Wilson derived this idea from Gordon Wasson in *Soma: The Divine Mushroom of Immortality* pg. 23-24.

Christmas Eve

Christmas Morning

Figure 18 - Christmas Eve and Christmas Morning, Split screen showing 3 Wise men following the star.

The three wise men, or the three kings, are anthropomorphisms of the three stars of Orion's Belt.[102] Like the sun, Orion's Belt also rises on the eastern horizon. In early December, Orion's Belt will rise above the horizon approximately an hour after sunset. In mid-January, Orion's Belt will rise above the horizon approximately an hour before sunset. However, on Christmas Eve, Orion's Belt will rise above the eastern horizon just after the sun sets. This occurs on the evening of December 24 to the morning of December 25. Symbolically, the three kings (Orion's Belt) are following the star of "Bethlehem," known as Sirius (also called Sithus by the Egyptians).

We three kings of Orient are
Bearing gifts we traverse afar[103]
Field and fountain, moor and mountain
Following yonder star

O Star of wonder, star of night
Star with royal beauty bright
Westward leading, still proceeding
Guide us to thy Perfect Light
~We Three Kings[104]

---

[102] The Bible only mentions kings or wisemen, not "three." However the number thee is found in more ancient mythology and folklore of the same tale.
[103] To travel a great distance.
[104] *We Three Kings of Orient Are*, written by Rev. John Henry Hopkins Jr., 1857.

The tale tells us that these *kings* traveled a great distance. This is because on this day, these three stars begin their journey across the night's sky immediately at twilight. When this alignment with Sirius occurs, it appears to point straight down at the earth as if it were pointing down to the place where the sun in the sky is about to rise. On this night, we know that God's son, the sun in the sky, is about to be born. When this occurs it is Christmas morning. It is the dawning of God's sun/son, the beginning of the New Year, and the first day of the sun's journey to the north.

During the summer months the belt of Orion and Sirius are turned up in the sky at a different angle and are often hidden by the daylight sun. Only one night of the year, do they swing fully down and point directly at the earth in alignment with the sunrise while appearing on the horizon just after twilight.

In this image (Figure 19), the star is aligning with the head of Jesus, the sun god. This is a microcosmic anthropomorphism of what is occurring in the sky in the early morning hours of December 25. It is a clever way to represent *that which is above*, and *that which is below* by depicting the actual star *and* the personified deity.

> Thomas 77
> Jesus said, "It is I who am the light which is above them all...

Days are actually degrees, there are 360 degrees in a full circle and yet there are 365 degrees or days in a full calendar year. When we understand that the sun actually appears *dead* for several days (or stands still), we realize where these days come from. The average length of a year in the Julian calendar is 365.25 days, differing from the value of the mean solar year by about .0078 days. This resulted in a slow shift of the Julian calendrical year with respect to the solar year (i.e. to the solstices and equinoxes). By the 16th Century the Julian calendar was seriously out of synch with the seasons. Pope Gregory XIII introduced the Gregorian calendar (our "modern" calendar), which is still in use. The Maya recognized this problem early on, and created a five-day month in their "Haab" calendar at the end of their 360-day cycle called the *Vayeb* which accurately depicts the 365-day year, and because they calculated this calendar in conjunction with the Tzolkin calendar for the Long Count, there was no future chance for inaccuracy.

Figure 19 - Born under a star

EAST STAR

People everywhere celebrate the sunrise every Sun-day by going to their churches and temples during the rising of the sun in the sky and facing an altar located in the eastern side of the church. This is blatant sun worship in itself. The churches themselves are temples built in honor of the sun. These temples will often face the east, or rather, the altar will be facing the east.

Some simply claim that this is done so the sun shines through the stained glass over the altar during the worship service. While this is true, there is a lot more to this than just visual effects. In the example before, we were documenting the sun's movement by facing the <u>east</u> and watching the sunrise as it dies and is reborn. The microcosmic image of Jesus on the cross (his halo in particular) is a depiction of the sun dying in the sky.

Figure 20 - Examples of Jesus at the Crucifixion looking to his right.[105]

In most of the older paintings and sculptures of the crucifixion, Jesus is always looking to his *right* or his head is hanging to the right side of his body.

It is common for Freemasons to hang banners on their walls. Often, these banners contain the four letters representing North, South, East and West on the outer border. What may go unnoticed is that East is usually placed at the top. Maps in general (whether they are street maps, weather maps, or other maps) usually have north at the top. However, when referring to the death and rebirth of the sun god, one must face the East because that is where the new sun is born. Therefore, East is at the top of the banners of the mystery schools.

Ancient cultures oriented[106] themselves with due east,[107] not the north. As a result, they built their temples facing the sunrise. They often put two pillars at the front of the temples (representing Boaz and Jachin, Isis and Osiris, Ishtar and Tammuz, Castor and Pollux, *Amanita* and *Psilocybe*, et al.), positioned in such a way that when the sun crossed the front of these temples, the shadows created by these pillars actually told them what time of year it was. They literally created a clock and a calendar out of these temples that only the priestly class could understand. The shadow would move across the floors of these temples that were tiled in a checkerboard pattern, telling them the time and the day of the year.

Figure 21 - Masonic Banner

---

[105] From left to right: Albrecht Altdorfer, *Christ on the Cross*, c. 1520; Andrea Da Firenze, *Crucifixion*, c. 1365; Jan van Eyck, *Crucifixion*, c. 1420; di Bondone Giotto, No. 35 Scenes from the *Life of Christ*: 19. *Crucifixion*, c. 1304; Francesco Francia, *Crucifixion with Sts John and Jerome*, c. 1485.
[106] The word "Orient" means east, or in the heavens, the sun. (Orient - <u>Archaic</u> - The place on the horizon where the sun rises; the east.)
[107] *Stellar Theology and Masonic Astronomy,* by Robert Hewitt Brown, 32nd degree, pg. 62.

Figure 22 Crucifixion of the Sun[108]

Various artists from different times and locations, all illustrating Jesus with his head hanging to his right or looking to his right (Figure 21) is not mere coincidence. When facing these paintings, the same concept applies as when you are facing a Freemasonic banner, you are still facing east, because the sun rises in the east.

If we superimpose the four directions over the image of the crucifixion, placing East at the top as the mystery schools do, we see Jesus is not just looking to his right, saving the soul of a thief hung next to him. Jesus is looking to the north. Or rather, the sun god is *moving* to the north. By stripping away the background – we see that the sun has been traveling south until it dies. The two thieves stayed on the cross for three days, while the sun will spend three days in the tomb. The sun cannot move any further to the south, just as Jesus cannot look in that direction.

When taking into consideration that Jesus is referred to as the *Door*, the two crosses on either side of Jesus could be seen as the two pillars of Boaz and Jachin standing on either side of the doorways of the cathedrals.

A quote from Bishop Youssef from the St. Mina Orthodox Church says, "In our church we face the east for several reasons. One reason is that the sun itself rises from the East. Similarly, Jesus is our light and we are always looking to him as our Lord. Also with the birth of Christ, the three wise men saw a star that was in the east that led them to the Christ Child."

I John 1:5 -
and declare unto you, that god is light, and in him there is no darkness at all.

Malachi 4:2 -
but unto you that fear my name shall the sun of righteousness arise with healing in his wings.

The fact that the "sun" is spelt s-u-n is no mistake in the verse from Malachi. The Hebrew word translated as sun is "shemesh."[109] The definition reads "to be brilliant, the sun, by implication the east...." Therefore, the sun is truly our savior and you can find these quotes in the Bible and in songs, poetry, and seemingly everywhere telling us this.

GOD'S SUN IN HEAVEN

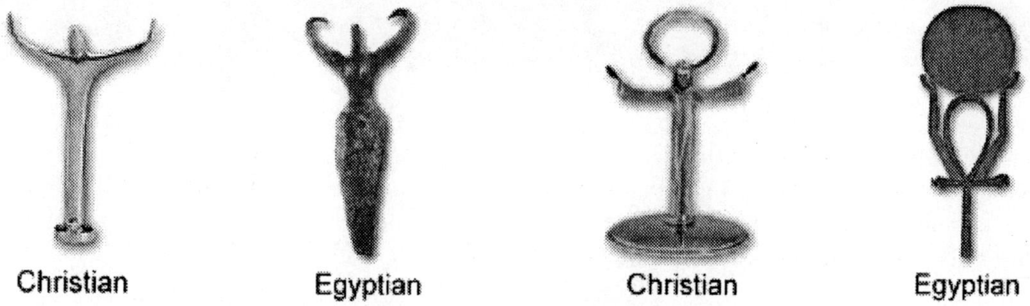

Christian   Egyptian   Christian   Egyptian

Figure 23 - Christian and Egyptian Icons

These are Christian and the Egyptian icons representing the worship of the sun god. Many Egyptian icons are very similar to Christian ones, one obviously appropriated from the other, and it only takes a simple history lesson to decipher which is which.

---

[108] Original artwork by Giovanni Bellini, *Crucifix*, c. 1455.
[109] *Strong's*: 8121– shemesh sheh'-mesh from an unused root meaning to be brilliant; the sun; by implication, the east; figuratively, a ray, i.e. (arch.) a notched battlement: + east side(-ward), sun ((rising)), etc.

One will often come across pyramids when researching sun worship. The pyramids point to the sun and the pyramids were built in honor of the sun. We even find a capped pyramid blatantly displayed on the back of the one dollar bill, with 13 steps leading to the All Seeing Eye… the eye of God, the eye of Horus, your third eye, the sun, etc. The word pyramid, or Pyra-Mid, means "fire in the middle"…*Pyro* and *mid*.[110] An Egyptian word for pyramid was "Khuti" meaning glorious light. According to Robert Hewitt Brown's book *Stellar Theology and Masonic Astronomy*, the word 'Freemason' is derived from Egyptian 'Phre' (the sun) and 'Mas' (a child) and actually means "Children of Light."

The word *masonry* in Greek is *Mesouraeneo* meaning "in the midst of heaven."[111] The sun is in the midst or middle of the heavens and here we see that the word masonry itself means *in the middle of heaven*, directly linking it to sun worship. As we previously pointed out, the sun is the King of kings, God of gods, light of light, very God of very God, and considered the mediator *between* heaven and earth. These terms strongly suggest that the symbolism behind the Freemasons, the pyramids, Solomon, Boaz and Jachin, Jesus (and many other *occult* symbols) is all in reference to sun and star (astrotheology) understanding and worship.

The sun was represented as the head of the sky god's penis, and as we mentioned earlier (Figure 8), the spheres of the constellations or the spheres of enlightenment surround him. The sun, depicted in this location of the Grand Man or Great Architect of the universe, was a common representation of the era.

Understanding the religious motifs of the past is important in order to understand the religions of today. Also important is how these religions have been functioning for the past 2000 years in a dualistic or macrocosmic/microcosmic way of thinking. There is the unconcealed (Macrocosmic) decree of dogmatic religions that can be heard day after day in church and by many Christians: the literalist biblical interpretations. Then there is the enigmatic (Microcosmic) level of these teachings that was kept only for the ecclesiastic and the secret societies.

Figure 24 - Leonardo da Vinci - Last Supper – 1498

Leonardo da Vinci was an initiated artist who understood the macrocosm of Jesus with his 12 celestial helpers and painted them accordingly. What da Vinci painted was four groups of three disciples, totaling 12, with Jesus in the center.[112] Jesus being the number thirteen. Here you can see the four seasons with Jesus, the sun, in the center. Each disciple represents one of the signs in the zodiac constellations.

There is a book in print and easily available from Harper Collins called, *The Other Bible*. In this book, there are many sacred texts and gospels, e.g. *The Gospel of Thomas*. The book contains Dead Sea Scrolls text, Nag Hammadi texts, Gnostic works and other "Gospels" similar to those found in the New Testament. Scholars familiar with this astrotheological content recognize that the creators of the Bible included only four Gospels to show the connection to the four seasons.[113]

---

[110] Jordan Maxwell - numerous radio interviews available online.

[111] *Stellar Theology and Masonic Astronomy*, by Robert Hewitt Brown 32nd degree, pg. 34.

[112] Jordan Maxwell.

[113] Jordan Maxwell, Acharya S.

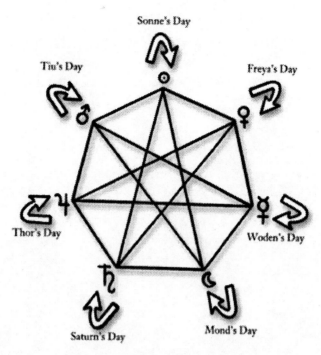

Figure 25

This image (Figure 25) was originally discovered by G. H. Frater D.D.C.F., and is found in Aleister Crowley's *The Book of Thoth*, and in David Fideler's book *Jesus Christ, Sun of God: Ancient Cosmology and Early Christian Symbolism*.[114] It is a representation from Gematria of the seven known planets and the seven days a week. All of these are represented on the microcosm by the actual days of the week and on the macrocosm by the planets, the sun, and the moon in the sky. A particular planet represented each day of the week and people worshipped these planet-gods by naming the days of the week after them. The language varies for each, so the Greeks had Kronos, in English we have Saturn, in Saxon Saturn, and today we call it Saturday, etc.

> ABOVE: The order of the planets around the outside of the heptagon follows their traditional order from the earth. By connecting the points inside to form a heptagram or seven-pointed star, the planetary cycle of the week is revealed.
>
> BELOW: The names of the planets and their relation to the names of the days of the week.[115]
> ~ David Fideler

Sonne's day (Sun-day) is Sunday; Mond's day (Moon-day) is Monday (Spanish: Lunes); Tiu's day (Mars) is Tuesday; Woden's Day (Mercury) is Wednesday; Thor's day (Jupiter) is Thursday; Freya's day (Venus) is Friday; and Saturn's day is Saturday, the Sabbath. This is where our names for the days of the week came from. Sunday is an important one to note, Acharya S suggests *Helios* is where we get the word "holy." As an example, "Holy Bible" would translate into "Sun Book" or *Helios Biblia*.[116]

> Helios - The sun god, son of Hyperion, depicted as driving his chariot across the sky from east to west daily.[117]

The Christian "savior" is actually the sun, which is the "Light of the world that every eye can see." The sun has been viewed consistently, from time immemorial, as the savior of humankind for reasons that are obvious. Without the sun, life on this planet would not last very long. So significant was the sun to the ancients, that they composed a *"Sun Book,"* or *"Helio Biblia,"* which became the *"Holy Bible."*[118]

---

[114] *Jesus Christ, Sun of God: Ancient Cosmology and Early Christian Symbolism*, by David Fideler, pg. 245; also *The Book of Thoth*, by Aleister Crowley, pg. 11.
[115] *Jesus Christ, Sun of God: Ancient Cosmology and Early Christian Symbolism*, by David Fideler, pg. 245.
[116] Jews worship the "Sabbath" on Saturday because of Saturn worship.
[117] *The Christ Conspiracy* –by Acharya S.
[118] Ibid.

Figure 26 - Axis Mundi

When we look at a ball or a sphere, we do not see an axis unless it is spinning. When we back up far enough away from the earth, we see that it too is a sphere and we do not notice that it is tilted on axis until we watch it spin. This *Axis Mundi* (Axis of the Earth), often represented as the *World Tree*, is the axis on which earth rotates.

Not only do we spin upon this axis, but due to the gravitational pull of the sun, moon, and other planets, we also wobble on this axis. One complete *wobble* has been called a 'Great Year,' 'Stellar Year,' and 'The Precession of the Equinoxes.' The word *precession* is defined as: A slow gyration of the earth's axis around the pole of the ecliptic, caused mainly by the gravitational pull of the sun, moon, and other planets on the earth's equatorial bulge.[119] As the earth, wobbles, the axis makes a circle through the heavens. Periodically we need to adjust for this wobble by adopting a new North Star. Consequently, in 12,000 years, the North Star will be Vega. One complete Great Year takes roughly 25,800 years. This 25,800-year period is divided into 12 houses of the zodiac or *Ages* (the macrocosm) just as a normal year is divided into 12 months (the microcosm). Each month, the Sun appears to be in front of one of the signs (houses) of the zodiac. We rotate through all the signs during one-year. The wobble of the *precession* moves through the 12 signs in the *reverse order* than our yearly zodiac sequence. As a result, we enter a new "Great Month" or new *Age* every 2150 years which is 30° of one complete wobble or Great Year, just as one month is approximately 30° of a calendar year. Furthermore, one Age is broken down into "Great Days," in which one Great day lasts 72 years.[120] In Numbers (11:24-26) the number 72 is significant in that there were 70 elders who received the impartation of Moses' spirit by the laying on of hands and two who received the same spirit spontaneously in the camp. As well, in Luke 10:1 after Jesus had commissioned the twelve apostles, he also sent out 72 evangelists (prophets) before him. Depending on which version of the story you read, there were 70 or 72[121] translators of the Old Testament from Hebrew to Greek, called the "Septuagint," which means *seventy*. Even the name of God is composed of 72 letters according to the cabalistic tradition.

---

[119] www.dictionary.com.
[120] The number 72 may relate to the "seventy-two virgins in heaven" in Islamic folklore and is also the lifespan of the average man. Muslims offer seventy-two virgins (a metaphor for one Great Day) to the life of a man. The virgin is a metaphor for the Holy mother Isis-Meri (Mary) or Virgo.
[121] The *Oxford English Dictionary* gives both 70 *and* 72 for the number of authors of the Septuagint.

The 72 actually represent the decans or dodecani, divisions of the zodiacal circle into 5° each, also considered constellations. In addition, it takes 72 years for the precession of the equinizes to move one degree.[122]
~ Acharya S

The early star gazers, after dividing the zodiac into its houses, appointed the three brightest stars in each constellation to be the joint rulers of that house. Then they divided the house into three sections of ten degrees each, which they called decans. These, in turn, were divided in half, resulting in the breaking up of the zodiac into seventy-two duodecans of five degrees each. Over each of these duodecans the Hebrews placed a celestial intelligence, or angel, and from this system has resulted the Cabbalistic arrangement of the seventy-two sacred names, which correspond to the seventy-two flowers, knops, and almonds upon the seven-branched Candlestick of the Tabernacle, and the seventy-two men who were chosen from the Twelve Tribes to represent Israel.[123]
~ Manly P. Hall

We have probably all heard of the song lyrics, "this is the dawning of the Age of Aquarius." The Ages really do exist.

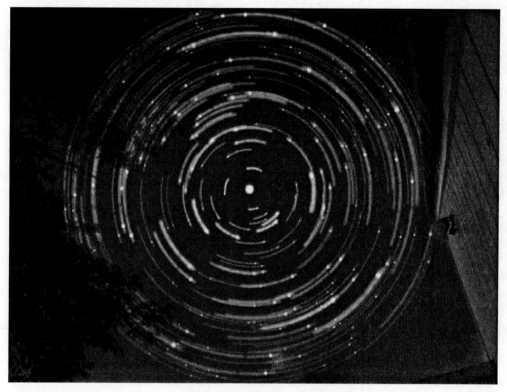

Figure 27 - The StarGate

When we go outside at night and look at the stars, we see the same things that our ancestors did. We notice that one particular star in the night's sky remains stationary while all of the other stars revolve around it. This is the North Star. With time-lapse photography, you can actually see the stars spinning around the axis by watching stars rotate around the North Star. This axis leading to the stars in heavens above the North Pole and below the South Pole is known as the 'Axis Mundi' or 'World Tree.' Many ancient cultures had mythologies wherein the Earth was actually within a tube, the body of a snake, as if a great serpent had eaten the Earth. It was common for the shaman to meditate towards this point in the night sky, primarily because they believed that if they went out of body and went out of the mouth of this serpent, not only would they travel toward the center of the galaxy, but they could also *enter* the mouth of the serpent to find their way home. This spinning of the stars in the night's sky, also symbolized in Christian artwork and even modern-day media, is often called the 'Stargate.'

---

[122] *The Christ Conspiracy*, by Acharya S. pg. 231-32.
[123] *The Secret Teachings of All Ages*, by Manly P. Hall, pg. 159 (reader's edition).

Figure 28 - Precession of the Equinoxes, moving backward through the zodiac.

Figure 29 - Mithra holding the cosmic sphere and turning the zodiac to the new Age.

Again, during the *precession* of the equinoxes, we go *backward* through the zodiac as we enter new Ages, unlike the *procession* of the equinoxes, which runs *forward* through the zodiac in the normal monthly progression, or *procession*. By working our way backwards through the zodiac, we may begin to understand how the signs of the zodiac have affected symbolism throughout history. This is documented quite well in the Holy Bible (the Sun Book).

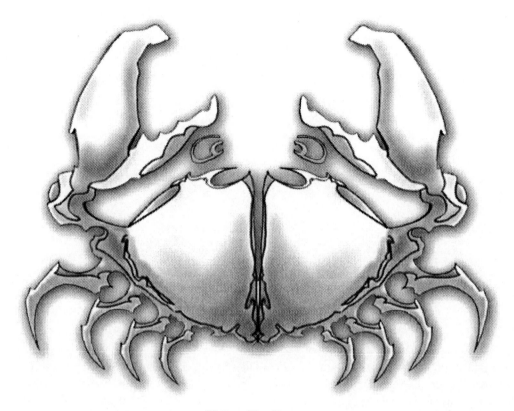

Figure 30 - Cancer

The Age of Cancer is as far back through the Ages necessary for us to explore in order to illustrate points relevant to this study. The summer solstice is known to happen when the sun is in the sign of Cancer. Appropriately, at this time of the year, the sun appears to reverse its course and descend the zodiacal arch resembling a crab, a crustacean walking backwards.[124] The Egyptians symbolized this sign with the scarab beetle and it was also associated with the phoenix. The beetle sank into the dung heap to be *reborn* from its own egg in a behavior paralleling the phoenix. The mythological phoenix will later be shown as the representative life cycle of the *Amanita muscaria* mushroom (ashes/spores, youth/serpent, maturity/bird, fire/red cap, ashes/spores—as the cycle continues).

Like the ox (represented by Taurus, the bull, which will be discussed in a moment), symbolically pulling the sun across the sky, the scarab beetle, rolling balls of dung across the ground, became associated with a celestial deity. The *celestial* crustacean is Cancer. Cancer is a water sign and the moon, passing through its phases, is well known to influence the tides. Many ancient cultures recognized Cancer as the origin of all life because it embodied the matriarchal principals in nature and was considered to be the nature domicile of the moon.[125] Cancer is primarily a feminine sign and this Age embodied matrilineal ideologies. Could there be a connection? During summer, Cancer represents the pinnacle of the sun's power (in its lifecycle). The feminine nature of Cancer's symbolism reveals to us that the masculine principle in nature (the sun) can only satisfy its full potential when the feminine is also exalted.

---

[124] *Secret Teachings of All Ages*, by Manly P. Hall.
[125] Ibid.

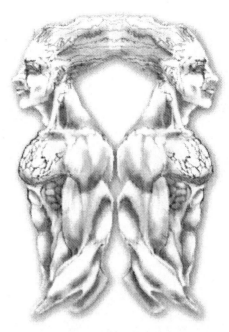

Figure 31 - Gemini

Between 6000 and 8000 years ago, humanity was considered *pre-civilized*.[126],[127] The Age of Gemini is visually considered to have been an Age of egalitarian societies[128], but these societies were often products of, and went directly hand in hand with, matriarchal social structures. Gemini is the Age that gave birth to the many variations of creations myths, most of which concern a pair of primordial parents of civilization. The twins are often depicted as one male and one female. When the twins are represented as male and female, they embody harmony between polar opposites. The sign represents the androgynous nature of God as well as the dualistic nature of the physical universe. It was the Middle East in this Age that produced the earliest known records of creation, epics, and Adam and Eve stories, roughly 6000 to 8000 years ago (4000 to 6000$_{BCE}$).

The Middle East also gave birth to the epic concept of the Great Polarities in conceiving a battle in the heavens between light and darkness. Ahura Mazda (light) and his angels fought against Angra Manyu (darkness) and his angels. The two opposite principals will later be shown as two serpents entwined in battle, often battling for control of the mundane egg—symbolizing the physical universe and everything within it[129], including the souls of humanity. The Greek twins, Castor and Pollux are associated with Gemini, it was common for patriarchal mythology to eliminate the female principals (and even androgynous aspects of the deity) and replace it with male characteristics.

The myths of twins, such as Castor and Pollux, Jachin and Boaz, Romulus and Remus, Jacob and Esau, and Adam and Eve, are likely the result of amplifying the merged yet dualistic nature of the mushrooms[130], along with the celestial motif of the Gemini twins. Temples and cathedrals often reflect these twins in their architecture with their twin pillars, which have also been described as "ancient-symbol limits of the course of the sun in the heavens."[131] The Age of Gemini, in our most recent passing, embodied the final Age that is generally thought of as pre-civilized. This Age saw the culmination of human physical evolution, the decline of the matrilineal social environment, and the commencement of religious development.

---

[126] *World History Encyclopedia*, Millennium Edition.

[127] "[I]t is necessary to focus some sharp criticism upon the central concept of civilization, which as popularly viewed is entirely self-serving. How do we define "Civilization"? Traditionally, this word was reserved for "High Cultures," which had devolved agriculture, animal domestication, writing, monumental architecture, transportation methods, and technology. [...] It should be apparent ... that something is radically wrong with the above-given definition of civilization, which is equated mainly with technology and the Central State. A more revealing definition can be formulated if we focus upon the word itself, which implies civil behavior and peaceful social conduct." *Saharasia*, by James DeMeo, pg. 14.

[128] Favoring social equality; see also *Saharasia* –by DeMeo.

[129] *The Symbolism of Freemasonry*, by Albert Mackey, 1882.

[130] See Part II: The Pharmacratic Inquisition.

[131] *Suns of God*, by Acharya S, pg. 109, quoting Robertson in *Christianity and Mythology*, pg. 368.

36

Figure 32 - Aries

The Bible stories tell us that Moses came down from the mountain with the tablets of the new law on two separate occasions. The first time that he came down the mountain with the new law, he notices that his people had fashioned a golden calf and were worshiping it. Moses gets angry with this and throws the tablets against the rocks, literally *breaking the law*. Moses was trying to usher in the new Age, the new dispensation, but his people were still caught in the old Age. One will sometimes find artwork of the Ten Commandments showing the bull in the background with a sun disk between its horns, similar to Apis of Egypt.

In the story, when Moses came down from the mountain and noticed that his people were worshiping the bull, he did more than just get angry with them, breaking the tablets of the law and returning to the mountain for a new set of commandments:

Exodus 32: 27-29(KJV)
And he said unto them, Thus saith the LORD God of Israel, Put every man his sword by his side, and go in and out from gate to gate throughout the camp, and slay every man his brother, and every man his companion, and every man his neighbour. And the children of Levi did according to the word of Moses: and there fell of the people that day about three thousand men. For Moses had said, Consecrate yourselves today to the LORD, even every man upon his son, and upon his brother; that he may bestow upon you a blessing this day.

The word "bless" actually means 'to make sacred or holy with blood'.[132] To be blessed is to have the blood of a sacrifice on you. We will further discus the Holy Blood as well as the Holy Grail in a later section.

Psalm 118:26
Blessed is he who comes in the name of the LORD. From the house of the LORD we bless you.

---

[132] *Stellar Theology and Masonic Astronomy*, by Robert Hewitt Brown 32nd degree; *Oxford English Dictionary*; bless.

Figure 33 - Taurus

Moses finds his people worshiping the bull and orders them to kill one another, and 3000 of them died because they resisted change and continued worshiping in the old Age of the Bull, Taurus. After fleeing Egypt (land of the bull/Apis/Taurus), Moses (the ram/Aries) begins a new Age with his followers. No longer were the Jews to worship Taurus the Bull, they were in the new Age of Aries and were to worship the ram with Moses. Still today, the Jews blow the ram's horn (shofar) in worship. They are still foundering in the Age of Aries and continue to resist the Age of Jesus (Pisces), inherently skipping over it completely.

Mithra, like Nike, also kills the bull. In many statues and paintings one will see Mithra stabbing the bull, taking humankind out of the Age of Taurus. Sometimes Mithra can be found represented inside of the zodiac *and* killing the bull.

Figure 34 -Mithra stabbing the bull

When working our way backwards through the zodiac in the *precession* of the equinoxes, we could possibly begin with Gemini, the twins, as they are represented by Adam and Eve in Genesis.[133] Both male and female stand equally together in harmony. Christians claim the world is approximately 6000 years old and when we look at the following chart, we see that the age of Gemini, or the Age of Adam and Eve, was approximately 6400 to 8600 years ago, and likely explains this *story* of the so-called *Age* of the world.

---

[133] Gemini is often represented by either male twins, or male/female twins.

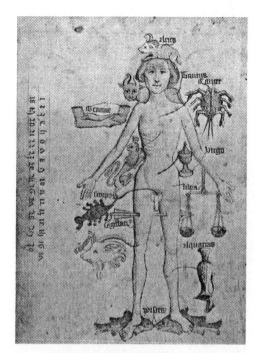

- Capricorn - Goat Fish - Knees (21,638 $_{BCE}$*)
- Sagittarius - Man Horse - Thighs (19,488 $_{BCE}$*)
- Scorpio - Scorpion - Sexual Parts (17,388 $_{BCE}$*)
- Libra - Scales – Pelvis (15,188 $_{BCE}$*)
- Virgo - Virgin - Womb (13,038 $_{BCE}$*)
- Leo - Lion - Heart (10,888 $_{BCE}$*)
- Cancer - Crab - Chest and Breasts (8738 $_{BCE}$*)
- Gemini - Twins - Arms (6588 $_{BCE}$* – Adam & Eve)
- Taurus - Bull - Neck and Throat (4438 $_{BCE}$* - Apis)
- Aries - Ram - Head (2288 $_{BCE}$* - Moses)
- Pisces - Fishes - Feet (138 $_{BCE}$* - Jesus)
- Aquarius - Waterman - Lower leg (2012 $_{CE}$* - Knowledge)

* Listed only as approximate dates.

Figure 35 -The Tiny Universe

Figure 36 - Pisces

Following the Precession of the Equinoxes, the next house of the Zodiac after Aries the ram, is Pisces. Though claimed to have been written in a previous Age of Aries, in the book of Genesis, Abraham (the Father of Christianity) was told by God to sacrifice his son Isaac as a burnt offering. Abraham had just "stretched forth his hand, and took the knife to slay his son"[134], when an angel spoke to him and told him not to go through with it.

Genesis 22:13 (KJV)
And Abraham lifted up his eyes, and looked, and behold behind him a ram caught in a thicket by his horns: and Abraham went and took the ram, and offered him up for a burnt offering in the stead of his son.

---

[134] Genesis 22:10; Today, when people hear voices and commit acts of violence, they are considered schizophrenic.

Just as Mithra kills the *bull* to usher in the Age of Aries, Abraham kills the *ram* of Aries to usher humankind into the next Age—the Piscean Age. Pisces is represented by the symbol of two fish. Jesus is known as the Fisher of Men and the stories tell of him feeding the masses with two fish. Was he feeding the masses actual fish, or was this character symbolically feeding the masses the teachings and knowledge of the Age of Pisces? Christians today often put a fish symbol on the back of their cars with the letters "IXOYE" inside of the fish. IXOYE directly translates into *FISH* in Greek (the original language of the New Testament). When depicted like this, you have the *word* fish contained within the *symbol* for a fish, thus making two fish, representing the Age of Pisces (Figure 37).

Figure 37 - IXOYE/Fish Emblem

The fish was often considered a symbol of abundance, domestic felicity, and prosperity. Eating fish on *Friday* likely came from the belief that eating fish promoted lustfulness and virility.[135] The goddess Freya (where Friday is derived) was the goddess of marriage (therefore associated to virility and possibly why fish were eaten on Friday.).[136] Fish symbology is quite common in pre-Christian iconography.

Figure 38 - Oannaes the Fish Man

This is the Babylonian god Oannes (the fish man, or "King Fish"), who, like his Sumerian counterpart Ea, came from the sea to teach humankind the greatest story ever told. Notice the way that he is dressed, it is almost as if he is a mermaid of sorts with a fish head as his hat. Joseph Campbell argued that John the Baptist is a remake of this ancient Sumerian/Babylonian god.[137] The first incarnation of Vishnu was that of a fish, Dagon wears a fish head as a hat, the Pope's miter is also a fish head.[138]

Commenting on the costumes that the priests of Oannes/Dagon's cult wore, well-studied occultist Fred Gettings commented that "the curious fish-like headgear is said by some to be the origins of the papal headdress, which does indeed have all the appearance of being a huge fish mouth gaping at the skies—the symbolism pointing to the idea that the pope is a high initiate.[139]
~ Chris Bennett & Neil McQueen

---

[135] *Symbols, Sex, and the Stars*, by Ernest Busenbark, pg. 174.
[136] Ibid.
[137] *Occidental Mythology*, by Joseph Campbell.
[138] See *Matrix of Power*, by Jordan Maxwell for more of these Papal headdresses (or Miters), looking exactly like fish heads representing the Age of Pisces.
[139] *Sex, Drugs, Violence and the Bible*, by Bennett & McQueen, Pt. 2, pg. 41, ft. 103 quoting Gettings, 1987.

However, Christianity is the newest extension of these "fish-headed priests." Oannes pre-dates Christianity by more than 5,000 years, but its symbolism is blatantly reflected in Christian symbolism and still remains prevalent today. Simply put, the symbolism of the fish was extracted from older myths and repackaged to mark the Age of (the fish) Pisces.

One of the best books we have found for understanding Gematria and religious symbolism, such as the yoni or vesica piscis in the macrocosm, is David Fideler's book, Jesus Christ: Sun of God.

Figure 39 - Portrait of William Warham, Archbishop of Canterbury - 1527

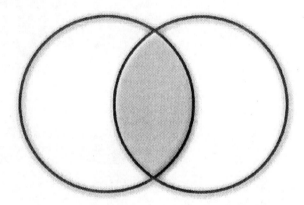

Figure 40 - The *vesica piscis (vessel of the fish)*.

Religious deities are often shown inside the vesica piscis in artwork, as if they are looking into this world from another.[140] You have probably seen this symbol often. One common place to find this symbol is in the MasterCard logo, or on Kool cigarettes (where the two O's are joined), it can be found in the symbol for the Olympics, and it conveniently served as a backdrop for the television game show, The Newlywed Game. The vesica is a symbol of the spiritual portal, which emerges from the harmonious balance the Great Polarities: intuition and intellect, knowledge and practice, yin and yang, heart and mind, heaven and earth, spirit and science, male and female, etc. The vesica piscis is literally a spiritual portal. It is through this portal that we enter into this dimension. This spiritual portal is the yoni (the female delta, the vulva, the vagina). Without this portal, we have no life. There is no other entrance into this world but through this portal.

Figure 41 - Vision of St. John the Evangelist - Jacobello Alberegno (circa 1370)

---

[140] David Fideler, *Jesus Christ, Sun of God.*

Virgin Mary or Lady of Guadalupe is painted in a very cryptic manner to represent female genitalia including the clitoris and the labia. This is blatant symbology of female genitalia and the regenerative process that women are part of in the existence of life and creation. She stands on a crescent of the moon symbolizing the moon's control over the female cycle.[141]

Figure 42 - Lady of Guadalupe positioned to represent the Yoni[142]

Figure 43

A primitive ritual of baptism often involved being physically drawn through a giant yoni structure. Those who underwent this ceremony were said to be *born-again.*

By simply turning this vesica piscis on its side, the Jesus-Fish is revealed. It is often said that the traditional two cupped hands joined in prayer was originally a symbol used by pagans to represent the Great Mother's yoni. Christians use this same symbol today when worshiping Jesus. This symbol derived from sex and fertility rites as well as sacred geometry.

---

[141] This crescent may also represent the planet Saturn (a.k.a. Joseph), see chapter 5. The moon was often associated with the female (menstrual), as the sun is associated with the male.
[142] Artist unknown.

Revelation 22:3 (KJV)
And there shall be no more curse...

Revelation 22:17 (KJV)
...And whosoever will, let him take the water of life freely.

Figure 44 - Aquarius

Now we have the promise of a new Age, the Aquarian Age. There are wonderful reasons to think this coming Age signifies emergence from several Ages of darkness. The role reversal in the symbolism is one clue. The men in the community have not fetched water for over two millennia, that's constantly been a "woman's job." So, the symbol in itself shows a man taking on the burden of what has always been a woman's unpleasant task.

During the last supper, the twelve disciples ask Jesus where they should prepare for the next Passover. This would be their first Passover without Jesus because Jesus was soon to be arrested and crucified. The disciples are asking where they should prepare for the Passover in the next Age—the Age after Jesus. Jesus, always speaking in parables, tells them (Luke 22:10) that when they enter the city, they will meet a man bearing a pitcher of water; they were to follow him into the house that he enters in.

> Luke 22:10
> And he said unto them, Behold, when ye are entered into the city, there shall a man meet you, bearing a pitcher of water; follow him into the house where he entereth in.

The symbol for the house of the zodiac that follows Pisces (in this precession) is that of a man bearing a pitcher of water. That symbol represents Aquarius. The Age of Aquarius is the Age of enlightenment. This is the Age when the waters of life (knowledge) flow freely onto humankind. We must learn from our ancestors. We are obligated to usher in this Age of Aquarius rather than resist the changes that seem taboo or foreign to us. Jesus, the Piscean sun god, is still leading many people today, but just as the bull-worshipping followers of Moses learned the hard way, it is essential that we welcome the new Age and not resist change.

Another important symbolic representation of the Aquarian Age is the symbol of the celestial deity pouring the *Waters of Life*, acting as the *Fountain of Living Waters*. The Water Bearer makes another transition into the supernatural in the esoteric interpretation of the Waters of Life and the symbolic pouring of this water onto the earth. The symbolic act of pouring the waters of Life into or onto the earth represents the knowledge of the plants and the heavens returning to earth. This is quite literally a second coming. The gifts of the gods are once again being given to humanity.

This concept of the Waters of Life will all be discussed later as we study the dualistic natures of these symbols. Symbols are subject to a wide variety of interpretation according to those select groups who choose to utilize them. Symbols may be true on a variety of levels simultaneously. However, the interpretation of the symbols in this book would be that as used by the entheogenic and astrotheological undergrounds throughout history. These gnostics, philosophers, sun worshippers, witches, heretics, even simple farmers—were all burned in the fires of the Pharmacratic Inquisition for hinting at the methodologies used to directly attain this non-verbal knowledge.

~ Etymology ~

Mark 4: 11-12 (NIV)
He told them, "The secret of the kingdom of God has been given to you. But to those on the outside everything is said in parables so that, "'they may be ever seeing but never perceiving, and ever hearing but never understanding; otherwise they might turn and be forgiven!'"

Before we move on, we are going to look into Etymology for a few pages, so that we can acquire a deeper understanding of the hidden meanings of language. Etymology[143] is the art of understanding the history and origins of words and what they mean to us today. It is the origin and the historical development of a linguistic form, revealed by determining its basic elements. 'Etymology' in Greek means 'the *logos* of the truth,' from *etymon*, 'true.' Below are a few examples, mostly pertaining to the topic of Astrotheology:

Amen – from Amen (Amon) Ra, one of the earliest Egyptian sun gods. The word Amen has a couple of meanings. Christians will say amen at the end of a prayer and they are told that it means, "So let it be." What this actually means is "So let it be *hidden*."[144] Amen Ra is an Egyptian sun god and the stars in the night's sky tell the greatest story ever told. Consequently, when the morning sun (Amen-Ra) rises, the stars disappear – "so let the story of the stars be hidden."

> The sun, in the sign of Aries, was personified in Jupiter Ammon, as well as in Christ. Ammon signifies the secret or concealed one, and sacred had originally no other meaning than secret.[145]

Of particular interest here, is the usage of the word amen at the end of a prayer (the Christian version of a spell). A definition of amen in the *Oxford Dictionary* reads, "A solemn expression of concurrence in, or ratification of, a prayer, or wish; Be it so really!" We see why the *amen* is there and how it adds additional empowerment to the spell.[146,147] For instance, Revelation 1:6 reads, "And hath made *us* kings and priests unto God and his Father; to him be glory and dominion forever and ever…" When we say *amen* at the end of this, it ratifies the spell giving the Pope[148] authority (*dominion*) over us, forever and ever. This is a *spell* in the truest sense. It is likened to a Christian version of "Hocus-Pocus" or "Abracadabra." We are no longer in the Age of "so let it be hidden." Humankind is collectively breaking the spell that has kept the truth from light.

Easter – is likely a compression of the words *Eastern* and *star*.[149] The star that rises or resurrects on the Spring Equinoctial point is again, the sun. In order to know when Easter is, we simply watch the sky. You will know that it is Easter by waiting until the vernal equinox, and then waiting again for the first paschal full moon.[150] Easter is celebrated on the following 'Sun-day.' God's sun survived three days in the tomb during winter, and with the passing of winter and the arrival of spring, the sun's return from the tomb is celebrated.

Horizon – the zone of Horus rising in the eastern sky. Horus is risen on the horizon.

---

[143] We thank the following for the majority of the words in this etymology section: Jordan Maxwell; Michael Tsarion; Acharya S.

[144] Acharya S., Jordan Maxwell, Robert Brown, James Arthur, Jack Herer.

[145] *Christian Mythology Unveiled*, Anonymous (circa 1840), pg. 59; *Suns of God*, by Acharya S (2004), pg. 448.

[146] James Arthur – interview on *Coast to Coast radio* with George Noory.

[147] Notice that when we *spell* a **word**, we are *spelling* (casting a *spell*). The **word** is the logos of God, inseparable (as Spess pointed out) from *Soma*.

[148] Although this prayer is used by all churches today, it was originally an interpolation by the Catholic Church to give it dominion specifically.

[149] Oxford (to paraphrase) suggests the word Easter is derived from the word from ôstara and Eostre; the name of a goddess whose festival was celebrated at the vernal equinox. Her name, "*austrôn*," is cognate with the Sanskrit *usrā* and means "dawn" or "dawn-goddess" (the rising of the morning sun, a star), which is related to the east. Furthermore, S.B. Roy relates: "The Semitic group of words Ishtar, Ashtar, Ashtarte, originate from the root STR. This root "str" connotes both a female (Skt. Stri), as well as a star. Thus, the primary mother goddess was a the female of the stars, and obviously she had a deep connection with the stars…" *Prehistoric Lunar Astronomy*, pg. 106-108; quoted in *Suns of God*, by Acharya S, pg 32. Ishtar and Ashtar as well have strong ties to fertility practices with the end of winter at the Vernal Equinox fertility festivities.

[150] The Paschal full moon is the first Ecclesiastical full moon after march 20th.

Hour – denotes the name of the sun god, Horus who was portrayed as the Hawk, wearing a solar disk. He was the rising sun. When anyone wanted to know what time it was, meaning where the sun was, they may have asked, "what Horus is it."

Israel – a composite word from ISIS, RA, and EL. **Isis** - the goddess revered throughout the ancient world and the mother of the Egyptian god Horus. **Ra** was the Egyptian sun god. **El** which is Elohim, and actually refers to several gods... El Ma'al, El Shaddai, El Neqamah, and the planet Saturn, to name a few. This is where we derive words like Elder, Elite, Elect, and Elevate.

Luna – means Moon. The Moon was also called Min (Minute), or Mon. The Spanish today still say Lunes for Monday. Anyone caught worshiping the moon by Christians of old, were labeled *lunatics*.

Minister – *Min* was the common name for moon, and *ister* (Aster), is Star. By referring to someone as a Minister, we are in fact referring to someone who studies the moon and the stars.

Monastery – from Mon (or moon) and Aster (a star), a place of the moon and stars. Monasteries were also called "houses" and typically had 12 monks, representing the 12 signs of the Mazzaroth, residing inside.

> Luke 11:9
> And I say unto you, Ask, and it shall be given you; seek, and ye shall find; knock, and it shall be opened unto you.

Month – a periodicity of the moon.

Nun – one of the earliest goddesses of stellar worship. She was also associated with the fish, (*Nun* means fish in Aramaic. Joshua Ben Nun, Moses' successor, means Jesus, son of the Fish.[151]). This refers to the vesica piscis (vessel of the fish).

Pastor – *Pa* and *Astor* (aster or star). The first syllable is the root of the word for the father, elder, a great. The latter stands for star.[152] The father star, or sun, guards his flock of stars as the "shepherd of the heavens," just as the pastor is said to do with his flock of religious followers, directing them to "God's son on Earth." People even call their children "kids," a derogatory name for a human child as being related to baby goats, as well as being related to a pair of stars in the Auriga constellation.[153] Regarding this, Acharya S further relates:

> There is also a reason pastors (pastoral, pasture) are "shepherds" with "flocks" of "sheep," as the attitude of the priesthood/brotherhood towards the sheeple has been consistently derogatory.
> [154]

Sol – means the sun (personified[155]), and the sun is single or alone. Solitude, solitaire, solo, solace and solar, etc. most every word that begins with "sol" relates to the sun.

> Matthew 28:20 – (KJV)
> Teaching them to observe all things whatsoever I have commanded you: and, lo, I am with you always, **<u>even unto the end of the world</u>**.

> Matthew 28:20 (NIV)
> and teaching them to obey everything I have commanded you. And surely I am with you always, **<u>to the very end of the age</u>**.

---

[151] "Nun is a Hebrew letter represented by a glyph symbolizing a fish, which indicates that Joshua was a "son of Fish," or more precisely as a 'son of Dagon'." *Sex, Drugs, Violence and the Bible*, by Bennett, pg. 70.
[152] This could also refer to the Passover star.
[153] *Oxford English Dictionary* – See kid.
[154] Suns of God –by Acharya S. pg. 498
[155] *Oxford English Dictionary* - O.E.D.

The end of this Age is not the final Judgment Day or the end of the world. It is simply the end of the Age of Pisces. Luke 18:30 mentions this Age and the "Age to come" (Ephesians 1:21 and Hebrews 6:5 speak of this coming Age as well).

Churches and governments have encouraged the idea of the end of the world in order to control the masses with fear, but the timeline that they have provided has expired and the true nature of the deity has been revealed. The word Apocalypse in the ancient Greek of the New Testament means "to reveal something hidden." Therefore, as you sit reading this book, you are actually having your own "Apocalypse."[156]

> Thomas 5
> Jesus said, "Recognize what is in your sight, and that which is hidden from you will become plain to you. For there is nothing hidden which will not become manifest."

---

[156] *Oxford English Dictionary* - Apocalypse: Any revelation or disclosure. *Strong's* Gr. # **602:** apokalupsis ap-ok-al'-oop-sis from 601; disclosure: appearing, coming, lighten, manifestation, be revealed, revelation.

Part II
The Pharmacratic Inquisition

Figure 45 - The Burning of Katherine Cawches, and her two Daughters in the Isle of Garnesy

Figure 45 is a sketch drawing of the burning of Katherine Cawches, and her two Daughters in July of 1556. This was in the town of St. Peter Port, on the island of Guernsey. Three women were tied to stakes to be burned alive for heresy, and for their denial of Romish doctrines of Transubstantiation and the Church's so-called "Real Presence." One of the daughters was pregnant at the time of the burning, and while being burned alive, she gave birth (some accounts say that the baby burst from the mother's womb, as shown in the figure above). The baby boy was quickly pulled from the flames and laid on the grass, but the Romish persecutors ordered it to be thrown back into the fire to be burned alive with its mother, aunt and grandmother. Consequently, the little baby was both born and died a martyr. Foxe, the great martyrologist, describes the Guernsey Burnings as:

> ...a spectacle wherein the whole world may see the Herodian cruelty of Popish tormentors.

This barbaric behavior proliferated as the Catholic Church desperately tried to gain control of the entire world. This example is merely one of the countless atrocities committed by the Catholic Church, inhumanities that would soon become the foundation of the Pharmacratic Inquisition.

> The Pharmacratic Inquisition:
> The Christian persecution of archaic religions based on the sacramental ingestion of entheogenic plants and the consequent personal access to ecstatic states; whose first great victory was the destruction of the Eleusinian Mysteries at the end of the fourth century; which then reached a gruesome climax in the persecution of witches in the middle ages; and which continues in today's Pharmacratic state in the guise of the public health 'War on Drugs.'
> ~ Jonathan Ott

The Pharmacratic Inquisition has been and still is suppressing the knowledge of the drugs, plants, our sexuality, *and* brain function. The inquisitions were not merely intended to suppress so-called pagan cultures. Pagan, as we mentioned, is a word that simply means rural—the country folk—who were the shamans, and the goal of the shaman is to increase consciousness. Most of these people were already "suppressed." It was the knowledge of the plants and the stars that these people possessed that was important for the Church to suppress and destroy (even if it meant killing people who had this knowledge). Anybody accused by the Inquisition was guilty until they could prove their innocence. The Inquisition has been in effect since *at least* 415$_{BCE}$, during the time of the Eleusinian mysteries.[157] More likely, however, it has been in effect since 621$_{BCE}$, with the *"discovery"* of the so-called Book of Law.

---

[157] "C. Kerenyi, working with Dr. Albert Hofmann, suggested that Mentha pulegium may have been responsible for the Eleusinian vision: *Eleusis: Archetypal Image of Mother and Daughter* (Pantheon, New York, 1967, translated from the German manuscript, revised by the author from publication in 1960 and 1962), Appendix 1. Dr. Hofmann, however, now claims that

The reforms Jeremiah represented as a member of the cabal that formed around the forged Book of the Law [Deuteronomy?], were clearly unpopular and had to be forced upon the people by threat of death for non-compliance. [...] In this telling passage [Jermiah 44:1-23], we learn so much about the Biblical roots of prohibition.[158]
~ Chris Bennett & Neil McQueen

Deuteronomy 12:1-3
These *are* the statutes and judgments, which ye shall observe to do in the land, which the LORD God of thy fathers giveth thee to possess it, all the days that ye live upon the earth. <u>Ye shall utterly destroy all the places, wherein the nations which ye shall possess served their gods, upon the high mountains, and upon the hills, and under every green tree: And ye shall overthrow their altars, and break their pillars, and burn their groves with fire</u>; and ye shall hew down the graven images of their gods, and destroy the names of them out of that place.

In the eyes of the Catholic Church, people are either secular or non-secular, the world is either Christian or pagan. This is similar to the mindset of creating a separation between military and civilians or Jews and Gentiles. The most negative connotation attributed to the word pagan that we can find is "*illiterate* country folk." Considering that the Church effectively banned reading for nearly 1000 years, it is no wonder that the "pagans" could have been illiterate.[159] Certainly the term "pagan" had no negative connotation before it was picked up by Rome and used in a negative context because simply calling someone a resident of the countryside (pagan) does not label one as evil. Lumping all beliefs and religions that are not Christian together and classifying them as *pagan*, is the same technique being used to lump all sacred plants into the singular derogatory category of illicit "drugs."

A "shaman," in many ways, is similar to what we more commonly refer to in America as a "medicine man." The term "shamanism" originated in Siberia[160] where the local shaman was the oracle of the community. Nothing of importance happened in the community without the okay from the shaman. The shaman would also hold very strong plant knowledge and they often used medicinal plants for healing and powerful entheogenic substances in ceremonies. The word shaman likely derived from an ancient Tungusic word *saman*, which means 'the one who knows.'[161] Plants to a shaman are food, clothing, shelter, *and* their link to spirituality. In this modern society, most of us do not provide our own healthcare. We go to a doctor instead. Rarely do we grow, kill, or even cook our own food, and we certainly do not have control over our own pharmaceuticals (without breaking the law). We have given the control of these and many other things over to institutions that do not always seem to have our best interest in mind.[162]

What we are contending is that not only did the elite constituents in the Vatican and some Christians (non-Catholic) at the highest levels of the Church use entheogenic substances, they suppressed the *knowledge* of this true **religious experience** throughout the world, hence, the term *Pharmacratic Inquisition*.

Kerenyi overstated the psychoactive properties of *Mentha pulegium*, and, in any case, <u>this mint is clearly not strong enough to have warranted those instances of profane use and attendant severe penalties that were occasioned during the great scandal of 415 _{BCE}</u>. The inclusion of *blechon* in the Eleusinian potion had a symbolic significance, as explained below." *Persephone's Quest* – by Carl Ruck Pg. 162 footnote #4.

[158] *Sex, Drugs, Violence and the Bible* –by Chris Bennett and Neil McQueen Part 1 pg. 188-9.

[159] The reference to illiterate was found in *The Christ Conspiracy*, by Acharya S. No evidence of illiterateness being associated with the word pagan was found in the *Oxford* or *Webster's* dictionaries.

[160] The word shaman is of Ural-Altaic origin and therefore a shaman is someone who uses the Amanita muscaria mushrooms, as did the original shamans of Siberia.

[161] John Allegro suggests the word shaman (saman/simon) is 'semen.' Considering the phallic representations of mushroom use, this is highly probable. See *The Sacred Mushroom and the Cross*.

[162] For more information, please research Jon Rappoport, Dr. Leonard Horowitz, Dr. Boyd Graves, Dr. Gary Null, Dr. John Yiamouyiannis. Also search "Urine Therapy."

~ Chapter Four ~
The Holy Grail

THE DIRECT RELIGIOUS EXPERIENCE

Christians partake in a ritual known as communion, whereby the body and blood of their god is symbolically consumed by way of two placebos: a cracker and grape juice (in some denominations, wine is used). The sacred meal is not native to Christianity although it is quite difficult to find records of ceremonial ingestion of a placebo in antiquity. In addition, ingesting a holy plant sacrament in a ceremonial setting is not a ritual practiced solely by the Native Americans with their cactus, peyote. The phenomenon of people ingesting entheogenic plants to achieve enlightenment is global and archaic. Each culture used different indigenous entheogenic substances. Whatever was available to increase or expand consciousness, people found and made use of it. The plants were smoked, eaten, snuffed (insufflated), drunk, made into an oil and applied topically. Any way the plants could be utilized, the shaman found the way.

In Europe, Siberia, Asia, and North America, one of the primary entheogens used (which remains legal) was the *Amanita muscaria* mushroom.[163] In the Amazon jungle and the Peruvian basin, one of the sacraments commonly imbibed is a brew called ayahuasca ("Vine of the souls"). This contains the *Banisteriopsis caapi* vine, which contains several beta-carbolines (monoamine oxidase inhibitors–MAOIs) and is the primary plant in this entheogenic brew. Other admixture plants are used with this base plant that contain several active alkaloids, the most common being *Psychothria viridis* and *Diplopterys cabperana*, both containing tryptamines including DMT (N,N-Dimethyltryptamine). The MAOI acts as a preservative, preserving the DMT from being destroyed in the gut, allowing absorption into the bloodstream. Otherwise, DMT is not orally active.[164,165]

The brew has been in use for thousands of years and, along with the sacred mushrooms, is probably the most widely used entheogen known.[166] Modern science has yet to figure out exactly how these ancient people discovered the use of an MAOI in order to make the brew orally active.[167] In the East, a similar brew that is used contains two admixture plants with the same active components. Syrian rue contains the beta-carbolines and Acacia provides the tryptamines. The effects are identical because the active ingredients are the same even though they are totally different plants from different continents of the world. Somehow, the local shaman from two different parts of the world found the correct ingredients to make this brew. Ask the shamans how they learned of the ingredients and they will look you in the eyes and tell you that the plants they ingest tell them about other plants. They will tell you that they learned the recipe from Mother Earth.

Consuming a sacred plant and/or drink is a worldwide phenomenon that has withstood the test of time and it continues to this day. In the Middle East, Asia and Africa, cannabis and opium were favorites among other plants (including the mushrooms). Certain frogs are another source for these substances. Consequently, we find frogs in a lot of symbology and folklore. The Bufo Alvarius toad emits something close to DMT, called 5 methoxy N,N DMT. For people in Africa, one of the preferred entheogens used is Iboga.[168] In the pacific islands, Kava is imbibed. There is now evidence to suggest that all over the Americas, Asia, and Europe people used *Psilocybe* mushrooms. Peyote is famous to cultures in North America and Datura is famous to cultures in Europe, India, and North America. In Oaxaca, Mexico, *Salvia divinorum* is well-known. There are also plants like morning glories, mandrake, belladonna, henbane, wormwood, nymphaea, nelumbo and many others that have a history of use and are still being used as sacraments throughout the world.[169] Today, shamans, for the first time in history, have the entire pharmacopoeia of sacred plants at their disposal.

---

[163] Often referred to as the "Fly Agaric."

[164] For a complete list of plants used in Ayahuasca and their active compounds, see *Pharmacotheon*, by Ott 1996.

[165] *Ayahuasca*, ed. By Ralph Metzner.

[166] Ibid, pg. 3.

[167] *The Cosmic Serpent, DNA and the Origins of Knowledge*, by Jeremy Narby and *The Holographic Universe*, by Michael Talbot, give plausible explanations. As well, a mixture of plants in a sort of salad could have caused the discovery.

[168] The extract from Iboga, Ibogaine has been proven therapeutically effective in the treatment of extreme drug, alcohol and tobacco addiction, but remains illegal in the U.S. source: DRCnet, www.stopthedrugwar.org.

[169] *Plants of the Gods*, by Richard Schultes; *Persephone's Quest*, by Wasson, Ruck, Kramrisch, Ott; *Shamanism and Tantra in the Himalayas*, by Müller-Ebeling, Rätsch, Shahi; *Soma the Divine Hallucinogen*, by Spess; *Food of the Gods*, by McKenna.

It is important to understand that in increasing or expanding consciousness some cultures used different plants than other cultures. Trading and bartering in plants and spice was more than just common, it was the norm—mainly because these particular plants did more than nourish the body, they nourished the mind as well. These shamanic cultures anthropomorphized their sacred plants in hopes that their stories, songs, and lore would encourage the knowledge of these plant substances to be passed down to future generations. This plant knowledge was combined with the astrotheological stories of the heavens that told them when to plant their crops, harvest and when to prepare for winter, etc. Today, these stories have been twisted into literal history and the *essence* has been spun as evil and demonic.

A lot of misunderstanding occurs when we stereotype "magic mushrooms" or other consciousness expanding plants or fungi as "drugs" that we should wage war against. These plants have been ingested throughout history and throughout the world. This is not a new concept. The people that are stumbling upon this knowledge now are rediscovering ancient techniques. This is the *Archaic Revival*.

These archaic shamanic techniques allow a direct communication with the spirit worlds. Anyone saying that they can achieve these altered states without the use of sacred plants should be thoroughly investigated.[170] Too many people today claim to have all the answers, or claim special abilities. What is being presented in this book is a set of techniques that will allow you to ask and answer these questions for yourself. Many impostors out there want nothing more than your money. "New Age" scammers and neo-shamans learn tricks such as motivational speaking (televangelist, salespersons, etc), or they bend spoons with sleight of hand, or they may pretend to talk to your dead grandmother or pet. These are just glamorized parlor tricks that do nothing for the process of ushering in this new Age, shifting the paradigm, or furthering human evolution.

> Every season is a fresh season. We are in a fresh season. What you gave last year will not reap anything this year. What you gave even a few months ago is gone...
> ~ Benny Hinn, televangelist
>
> What profit has not that fable of Christ brought us!
> ~ Pope Leo X

You must have the plant in order to have the experience. How can someone claim to have a communication with a plant spirit while omitting the plant? One will never have a peyote experience after ingesting mushrooms and one will never have an ayahuasca experience by smoking *Salvia divinorum*. The spirits of each plant are unique. If you do not believe there are plant spirits that communicate with us via these plants, think again...it all comes back to it being a matter of individual courage. This *is* something that can be proven by the *individual*. An experience like this is not something that you can acquire or understand from a book or from television. It also isn't something that one can achieve by sitting on a pillow for hours at a time or chanting a mantra all day long. These techniques work well in combination with the entheogens, but they are not often, if ever, successful alone. One will not see a priest or a monk shaking at the knees as they enter their temple to meditate or pray because they know of how terrifying and profound their prayer or meditation is about to be. But if inside that temple there were *Psilocybe* or *Amanita* mushrooms, dried and ready to eat, or if in front of the meditating guru on a pillow sat a pipe containing DMT or a glassful of ayahuasca, they would be fully overwhelmed with the spiritual experience that they were about to receive. This is what is missing in our society today, the experience. Terence McKenna called it the "felt presence of immediate experience"... an experience that is so profound that although it lasts only a matter of minutes or hours, it may take years or even a lifetime to process.

> That is why, on all these accounts, we have so little time for philosophy. Worst of all, if we do obtain any leisure from the body's claims and turn to some line of inquiry, the body intrudes once more into our investigations, interrupting, disturbing, distracting, and preventing us from getting a glimpse of the truth. We are in fact convinced that if we are ever to have pure knowledge of anything, we must get rid of the body and contemplate things by themselves with the soul by itself.[171]
> ~ Plato

---

[170] It should be noted that there are some—"shamanic" tribes use only drums, bodily mutilation, sleep deprivation, etc., to achieve ecstatic states. Dr. Strassman's work shows that this would likely effect endogenous DMT levels in the brain.
[171] Plato: *The Last Days of Socrates* - The Last Conversation: Phaedo

THE DEFAMATION OF ALLEGRO

In the first part of this book, we talked about "that which is above" (astrotheology) and how the sun, stars, and moon became part of today's religious dogmas. Now we are going to be discussing "that which is below" and about the plant substances, the holy sacrament, the flesh of God, or what can be called God's son (or God's children) on earth. These spiritual substances provide access to ecstatic states of consciousness when consumed. We will start with a brief bibliography and history of this area of research.

When the Dead Sea Scrolls were discovered in 1947, there was immense anticipation from Christians everywhere. This was thought to be a guarantee for the Church to **prove** Christianity correct. It appeared as though the only thing left to do was to read and interpret the scrolls and Christians would have all the proof they needed. The Dead Sea Scrolls were written in Semitic in the language of Aramaic between 250_{BCE} and 136_{CE}, which was the era that the Jesus character was said to be walking the earth. To find scrolls written in "His language" during the period of time in which he was said to be living, was a major finding and Christians everywhere were very excited about this. However, today we do not hear about this much at all, and for good reason. The information contained within the scrolls was exactly what the select, privileged few in the Church knew all along.

Figure 46 - John Marco Allegro[172]
(1923-1988)

John Marco Allegro was a researcher in philology who had graduated with a first-class honors degree in Oriental Studies from Manchester University in England. He had earlier begun training for the Methodist ministry, but had left to pursue the degree course when he found that studying biblical languages was making him question the foundations of his Christian beliefs. While working towards a doctorate at Oxford, he was invited to join the original Scrolls-editing team in 1953. In 1954, he became an assistant lecturer at the University of Manchester. Considered an up-and-coming philologist in regards to middle-eastern and Mediterranean languages, Allegro was the only agnostic on the international team of translators of the Dead Sea Scrolls. Most of the other members of the "international" scrolls team were ordained Catholic priests, including Father de Vaux and Father Josef Milik of the *École Biblique* (the library publication/research arm of the Vatican), Father Jean Starcky, Father Maurice Baillet, and Monsignor Patrick Skehan. They were joined by Frank Cross of the McCormick Theological Seminary and the Albright Institute, Claus-Hunno Hunzinger from Gottingen and later, John Strugnell from Oxford.[173]

The work of this team, organized by Father de Vaux, was originally supposed to be published as soon as possible and open to scholarly interpretation. John Allegro was the only member to publish all his translations in learned journals as soon as he felt they were ready to be laid open to scrutiny. The other members tended to hold onto their allocations for so long that some people–including Allegro from time to time, in moments of extreme exasperation–suspected a cover-up and suppression of the research. Scholars who attempted to question the orthodox view (as Allegro found out) had their careers destroyed.

In 1956, Allegro gave a series of talks on BBC radio in which he suggested that elements of Christianity derived from the beliefs and practices of the Qumran community and probably from some of the events in the life and death of the Essene Teacher of Righteousness as depicted in the Scrolls. In other words, Christianity was, in part, a derivative religion. This caused outrage among some members of the team. By 1957, he believed their anger had subsided and returned to Jerusalem unaware of anything awry in his relationship with the other members of the International team. He was soon to realize that the other members had clearly separated themselves from him because of his public statements and interpretation of scroll information.

---

[172] This previously unpublished photograph is courtesy of Judith Anne Brown, and the Allegro Estate.
[173] *The Dead Sea Scrolls Deception*, by Baigent and Leigh; *John Marco Allegro: The Maverick of the Dead Sea Scrolls*, by Judith Anne Brown.

A long, heated debate between John Allegro and the other research members of the Dead Sea Scrolls editing team ensued for decades. They held that Allegro had prematurely released information from the scrolls, particularly the Copper Scroll, with mistranslations. Allegro came to think that the other researchers were holding back information contained within the scrolls to promote their careers and to hide anything that might shake up the orthodox view about the origins of Christianity and Judaism.[174] Allegro pointed out that it was of utmost importance to release the scrolls as he translated them, even with possible errors, so that the rest of the research community would have access to the portion of the scrolls under his jurisdiction for peer review. The others wanted to wait until they had completed a definitive edition of the scrolls they were translating–an attitude that looked like possessiveness or secrecy from the outside. The conflict in approach came to a head over the Copper Scroll. Allegro's interpretation differed fundamentally from the official line. He held back the book in which he offered his "provisional" translation (*The Treasure of the Copper Scroll*, 1960) for over three years to enable Father Josef Milik to publish his version. Milik had in fact published an unofficial translation in English and French in July 1959, and expected the official edition to be out before 1960. At the last minute, it was delayed at the printer's and Allegro's book came out first. Because of this unintentional pre-emption, Allegro was condemned for piracy by most of the establishment figures of scrolls research.[175]

> ...[W]hen Allegro went ahead with his own publication [of the *Treasure of the Copper Scroll*], he found himself in the embarrassing position of seeming to have pre-empted the work of a colleague. In effect, he had been manoeuvred into providing the international team with further ammunition to use against him—and, of course, to alienate him further from them.... Allegro displays no propensity for either secrecy or self-aggrandisement. If he is conspiring, he is conspiring only to make the Dead Sea Scrolls available to the world at large, and quickly enough not to betray the trust reposed in academic research. Such an aspiration can only be regarded as honourable and generous.[176]
> ~ Michael Baigent and Richard Leigh

By 1968, Allegro completed and published all of his translations of the Cave 4 scroll fragments assigned to him and began work on a book that he was certain would explain the religious foundations of Christianity and Judaism. In the fifteen years since the international team was put together in 1953 to decipher the scrolls, Allegro was the only member to finish his assigned duty.

Because of Allegro's so-called errors in his translations and his willingness to release the translations with errors for other scholars to review (for the purpose of finding and eliminating errors), he came under the attack of his team replacement, John Strugnell. Though they had been friends, Strugnell later turned against Allegro and tore apart most of his translations, the effect of which was to further destroy Allegro's credibility amongst his peers. Michael Baigent and Richard Leigh made an explosive indictment of Strugnell and his so-called team of experts in *The Dead Sea Scrolls Deception*, published in 1991, though not all their inferences have been soundly substantiated. Baigent and Leigh suggest that there *was* a cover-up by Strugnell and the other members of the team, and it was deeper than Allegro had originally imagined.

---

[174] In letters to friends in 1957 and 1959 Allegro did voice suspicions about why de Vaux and the others appeared to be delaying publication of the Scrolls, but it would be putting it too strongly (as Baigent and Leigh did) to imply that he publicly alleged a conspiracy at this time. In angry moments, he may well have wanted to do so, but he did not have solid proof, nor enough backing from government officials and, in later years, acknowledged that the delays were more likely caused by mismanagement, coupled with reluctance or inability to think about the New Testament story in anything other than its orthodox interpretation. –Judith Anne Brown, daughter of John Allegro.

[175] See *John Marco Allegro: The Maverick of the Dead Sea Scrolls*, by Judith Anne Brown.

[176] *The Dead See Scrolls Deception* –by Baigent and Leigh, pg. 55-6-9.

Strugnell attacked Allegro's ability to translate because of the early releases that Allegro was willing to put up for debate. In 1970, Strugnell wrote a "rebuttal" against Allegro entitled *Notes in the Margin*.[177] This was one of only three pieces Strugnell was ever to write (not publish) in his 30-year career with regards to the scrolls.[178] The rest of the research team refused to release any of their own translations for nearly four decades, thus hiding any of their own possible errors.

In 1983, Dr. Robert Eisenman[179] of California State University, Long Beach, launched his attack against Strugnell and the other research members of the team. In 1985, Dr. Philip Davies of the University of Sheffield and other international scholars also joined Eisenman's forces, as did the *Biblical Archaeology Review* (BAR):

> The team of editors has now become more an obstacle to publication than a source of information.[180]
> ~ Biblical Archaeology Review

Three years after Allegro's death, in 1991, Strugnell was, with the approval of the Israeli government, dismissed from his position. The Huntington Library in San Marino, California decided to settle the dispute by releasing all their copies of original photographs of the Dead Sea Scrolls, thus ending the scroll monopoly by the remaining team members. This act of heroism caused the remaining members, who had not released the scrolls under their jurisdiction in nearly four decades, to scream "scholarly thievery." Interestingly, after 35 years of suppression, Dr. Eisenman published fifty of the Dead Sea Scrolls documents just one year after the release of the photographs.[181]

We must remember that Allegro was the only non-Christian member of the research team. All of the other researchers had the predetermined idea, based on flimsy or *no* evidence, that a man named Jesus Christ really existed.[182] Allegro argued that they had predetermined what they would find in the scrolls. From the start, Allegro and the other researchers never agreed. Since the other researchers did not release their research for nearly four decades, we will never know what they found in the interim.

Allegro's campaign for open access to the Scrolls was won by other scholars after his death. However, during the late 1960s, the continuing disagreements over publication and interpretation between Allegro and the Establishment arm of Scrolls scholarship meant that he had plenty of enemies.[183] When his brilliant work, *The Sacred Mushroom and the Cross,* came out in 1970, it pointed out that the foundation of Christianity and Judaism is not only derived from astrotheology, but much of the mythology surrounding these religions is firmly rooted in fertility cults and psychedelic mushroom and drug use as well. The establishment seized the opportunity to destroy his reputation once and for all.

> [Allegro], once a promising young scholar, has been turned into a babbler of sciolistic bawdry by an overdose of the hallucinogenic mushroom *Amanita muscaria.*
> ~ John Strugnell

---

[177] *Notes in the Margin* is 113 pages of Strugnell's criticism of Allegro which Dr. Eisenman calls "A hatchet-job" strictly to destroy Allegro's reputation; see *The Dead Sea Scrolls Deception* by Baigent and Leigh, pg. 51.

[178] On August 1st, 1997, and only after Eisenman and Vermes had released their full translations, did Strugnell finally publish *Qumran Cave 4 XV: Sapiential Texts (Discoveries in the Judaean Desert)*. It took Strugnell well over 40 years to publish his first work.

[179] See Robert Eisenman, *James the Brother of Jesus: The Key to Unlocking the Secrets of Early Christianity and the Dead Sea Scrolls* and *The Dead Sea Scrolls Uncovered: The First Complete Translation and Interpretation of 50 Key Documents Withheld for over 35 Years*, with Michael Wise.

[180] BAR, July/August 1989, pg. 18; *The Dead Sea Scrolls Deception*, by Baigent and Leigh, pg. 87.

[181] Dr. Robert Eisenman and Michael Wise, *Dead Sea Scrolls Uncovered: The first Complete Translation and Interpretation of 50 Key Documents withheld for over 35 Years* (1992, Penguin Books).

[182] GA Wells, John Allegro, Charles Waite, Jordan Maxwell, Acharya S., Gerald Massey, Kersey Graves, etc.

[183] See *John Marco Allegro: The Maverick of the Dead Sea Scrolls*, by Judith Anne Brown.

Jack Herer, author of *The Emperor Wears No Clothes*, spent eight months fact-checking Allegro's work in *The Sacred Mushroom and the Cross* in the 1980's. Herer had this to say about the book: "He [Allegro] has not made a mistake, excepting a few minor errors."[184] Herer still stands behind this statement twenty years later, and will soon publish his evidence.

> [W]e discussed Allegro when I was in graduate school in the late 1960's. His scholarship is not respected and his conclusions are fanciful. He should really write science fiction.
> ~ Dr. John Pilch, Biblical Scholar – Georgetown University

Many Christian organizations and other groups, who had not read *any* of Allegro's work, including those who believe the theory that Jesus was a shaman,[185,186] spent a lot of time and effort to discredit John Allegro's integrity as well. Instead of taking the time to sit down and research Allegro's work, to find out what he was referring to, they decided to attack his personality and his integrity. Based on false accusations and lies and with the help of Strugnell and the International team, they misconstrued the facts in order to make it appear as though Allegro was only out to profit from publishing the scrolls and *The Sacred Mushroom and the Cross*.[187] Jonathan Ott quotes Wasson extensively on page 352 in his argument against Allegro in *Pharmacotheon*:

> Allegro's book was originally serialized in an English tabloid of sensationalist stripe (The News of the World[188]), a far cry from the peer-reviewed scholarly literature he normally favored. Allegro never addressed his theory to fellow specialists in Biblical philology. Allegro was paid the princely sum of £30,000 for first serialization rights (Wasson in Forte 1988) and at the time was apparently hard-pressed to pay some debts (Wasson, 1977). It is difficult to escape the conclusion that he wrote *The Sacred Mushroom and the Cross* to make a fast buck. As Wasson later commented, "I think that he [Allegro] jumped to unwarranted conclusions on scanty evidence. And when you make such blunders as attributing the Hebrew language, the Greek language, to Sumerian—that is unacceptable to any linguist. The Sumerian language is parent to no language and no one knows where it came from" (Wasson in Forte 1988). This and several other points were made in the reviews of Jacobsen and Richardson (1971); see also the criticism of Jacques (1970). Nevertheless, Allegro's specious theory continues to be taken seriously by some students of entheogenic mushrooms (Haseneier 1992; Klapp 1991), and a recent German anthology on the fly-agaric (Bauer et al. 1991) was dedicated to John Marco Allegro.[189]
> ~ Jonathan Ott

> The enquirer has to begin with his only real source of knowledge, the written word.[190]
> ~ John Allegro

Unfortunately, when Ott published *Pharmacotheon* in 1993, he had not realized that Strugnell and his team of "scholars" had lost all credibility by 1991. Allegro had felt unable to submit anything for peer review for years, as he knew biblical scholars would attack him on principle. Baigent and Leigh think scholars were strong-armed by the Vatican's Ecole Biblique, which they went so far as to suggest is a direct arm of the Pontifical Biblical Commission, the Congregation for the Doctrine of the Faith, formerly known as "The Holy Inquisition" office of the Vatican.[191]

---

[184] The errors discussed were in reference to the growth cycle, effects and "bitterness" of *Amanita muscaria*, and the fact that Allegro overlooked some references to both *A. pantherina* and *P. cubensis*, and wrongfully classified Rue as an "abortifacient," not recognizing Acacia and Rue as an *Ayahuasca analogue. The Sacred Mushroom and the Cross*, pg. 67-68, 105, 163-166. Considering Allegro was a philologist, and not a mycologist, these errors are "minor."

[185] There is not one shred of historical evidence to suggest a man named *Jesus Christ* ever lived. Most who believe the notion of a historical Christ have no knowledge of astrotheology. Read Acharya S., GA Wells, Kersey Graves, Gerald Massey, Ernest Busenbark, Jordan Maxwell, and their many references.

[186] Jesus' human corruptible body was a question from the beginning of Christianity until *The Infallibility Bull* of July 18, 1870, where the Pope declared Jesus the son of God and the argument of Homoousian and homoiousian ended under penalty of blasphemy. It took one thousand eight hundred years to squelch the argument of Jesus being the same as or just like the father, as opposed to, or other than just like the father. Either Jesus was the same substance (being) as God, or he was of different substance. —Jay Lynn

[187] See *John Marco Allegro: The Maverick of the Dead Sea Scrolls*, by Judith Anne Brown.

[188] The article and four part series actually ran in the Sunday Mirror on Feb. 15, and April 5, 12, 19, 26 of 1970.

[189] *Pharmacotheon*, by Jonathan Ott.

[190] *The Sacred Mushroom and the Cross*, by John Allegro, Introduction xix.

[191] We did not verify if this claim is true. See: *The Dead Sea Scrolls Deception*, by Baigent and Leigh, Ch. 7.

Jonathon Ott's one remaining item against Allegro is, *"And when you make such blunders as attributing the Hebrew language, the Greek language, to Sumerian—that is unacceptable to any linguist."*

On page 334 of *Pharmacotheon,* Ott admits:

> The only evidence Allegro offered was linguistic. Since I am not an expert in Biblical philology, I will not attempt to evaluate his arguments. It should be noted, however, that specialists in the study of Biblical languages have unanimously rejected Allegro's thesis...
> ~ Jonathan Ott

When we began to research this scandal in the summer of 2004, we originally believed that it would be necessary to *prove* whether these arguments against Allegro's "language bridge" to Sumerian were in fact incorrect. We soon realized that this could require a lifetime of research to accomplish. After contacting many philologists, we often received much of the same blind condemnation against the idea that Allegro had endured.

During our research, however, we were able to find scholars who were willing to hint toward their agreement with Allegro. We contacted Dr. Philip Davies of the University of Sheffield, who was among those fighting John Strugnell and the International Team over scholarly access to the Scrolls. Dr. Davies stressed that he is not specifically a Sumerian palaeographer, there are few. However, he is a leading Hebrew, biblical and Dead Sea Scrolls scholar. He had this to say about Allegro's ideas of the development of Alphabets[192], which may also give credence to Jay Lynn's work (See Appendix B), and the so-called "language bridge":

> What Allegro said [pg. 11-13 of *The Sacred Mushroom and the Cross*] is almost certainly correct. That Cuneiform became stylized from an originally more pictographic script is true - the same happened in Egypt as Hieratic and then Demotic script developed from hieroglyphic. The letters of the Semitic alphabet can be shown to undergo the same development - the letter Aleph developed from an original depiction of a bull's head into various forms in other Semitic languages, while in Greek it was turned 90 degrees clockwise to form the now familiar 'A'. And so in many other scripts too.
> ~ Dr. Philip Davies

Since the time Allegro published *The Sacred Mushroom and the Cross*, much new research in the area of fertility cults and their relationship to entheogens, and especially mushrooms, has surfaced.[193,194] Finding a Sumerian philologist who possesses a knowledge of entheogens and fertility cults is next to impossible. However, during our research we learned of one highly accredited Sumerian philologist, Anna Partington. Partington is a former associate of Allegro, who also possesses a deep understanding of entheogens and fertility cults. Though not in *complete* support of his views, this is what she had to say regarding Allegro:

> Most people come to the field of Sumerian studies with a background in several early Mideastern languages. Although John was of a previous generation, he was, in common with most Orientalists, perfectly well equipped to deal with cuneiform languages. He found comparative linguistic study especially interesting; but early in his career the finding of the scrolls by the Dead Sea led him to specialise in translation of these Hebrew and Aramaic documents.
>
> Unfortunately, the comparative philological work presented in *SMC* [*The Sacred Mushroom and the Cross*] uses a number of hypothetical Sumerian words not attested in texts. These are marked with an asterisk following philological convention. This is akin to proposing there is a word in the English language 'bellbat' because the individual words 'bell' and 'bat' are known to exist separately. Then again words of different languages are gathered together without the type of argument which would be expected in order to demonstrate possible relationship.
> ~ Anna Partington

---

[192] *The Sacred Mushroom and the Cross*, by John M. Allegro pg. 11-13.
[193] See *Mushrooms and Mankind*, by Arthur; *Magic Mushrooms*, by Heinrich; and *Apples of Apollo*, by Ruck, Heinrich, Staples
[194] We will be covering fertility cults in our next book. For those interested in more research into fertility cults, see B.Z. Goldberg, O.A. Wall, Sanger Brown, Sha Rocco, Clifford Howard, etc.

We must also point out that both the Allegro family and their associates have informed us that the mushroom origins of religion were a serious area of study for John Allegro. There is no evidence to support the accusations that he was seeking revenge (as some have suggested), or out to make a fast buck. In May, 2005, John Allegro's daughter, Judith Anne Brown, published *John Marco Allegro: The Maverick of the Dead Sea Scrolls*, which proves, from Allegro's personal archives, that the attacks against him are unfounded.[195]

> ...Allegro's suggestion that "Jesus" was a mushroom god is not implausible, considering how widespread was the pre-Christian Jesus/Salvation cult and how other cultures depict their particular entheogens as "teachers" and "gods." However, this mushroom identification would represent merely one aspect of the Jesus myth and Christ conspiracy, which, as we have seen incorporated virtually everything at hand, including sex and drugs, widely perceived in pre-Yahwist, pre-Christian cultures as being "godly.[196]
> ~ Acharya S

David Spess, an expert in ancient Sanskrit (a member of the Semitic language group), has discovered that there is a direct correlation between Middle Eastern religions including Judaism, Christianity, and Gnosticism, and the Rg Vedic Soma use. Spess argues rather successfully that all Indo-European/Mediterranean religions are really a development through Indo-Aryan/Iranian cultures and Soma use in the Rig Vedas. Spess is not the only one to make this suggestion. In 1927, Ganga Prasad wrote *The Fountain-Head of Religion: Being A Comparative Study of the Principal Religions of the World and a Manifestation of Their Common Origin from the Vedas*, which covers this same topic in detail.

> Again it is this Soma, or <u>its two varieties called White Homa, and the Painless Tree which became the prototype of the Biblical "Tree of Knowledge," and the "Tree of Life"</u> supposed to have existed in Paradise.[197,198] [underline—ours]
> ~ Ganga Prasad

Indeed, Allegro re-discovered entheogens in the Bible.[199]

With these new facts, we can finally throw out the false indictments claiming, *"specialists in the study of Biblical languages have unanimously rejected Allegro's thesis"* and begin to move toward a more mature approach in looking at these ancient religions. Allegro's ideas were ahead of his time, and it is still very difficult to *prove* linguistic links to the Sumerian language.

Because this book is not a study of ancient languages, we intend to reveal the truth behind many of Allegro's ideas through other means. Furthermore, new evidence may suggest that both "Mesopotamian" and Rg Vedic religions are developments from the Ural-Altaic (Siberian) peoples, as Wasson suggested in 1968[200], thus, making arguments about the Mesopotamian origins of religion questionable.[201] It would be interesting to discover if there are possible links to Sumerian, Sanskrit, Hebrew, and Greek from the Ural-Altaic language groups, though we must admit we are not qualified to undertake such research.[202]

---

[195] See *John Marco Allegro: The Maverick of the Dead Sea Scrolls*, by Judith Anne Brown, 2005.
[196] The Christ Conspiracy, by Acharya S, pg. 294-295.
[197] *The Fountain-Head of Religion: Being A Comparative Study of the Principal Religions of the World and a Manifestation of Their Common Origin from the Vedas*, by Ganga Prasad, pg. 156.
[198] We will discuss more about these "two" varieties of soma later in the book.
[199] Wasson had earlier suggested it, but later retracted this notion.
[200] See *Soma: Divine Mushroom of Immortality*, by R. Gordon Wasson, and *Pharmacotheon*, by Ott, pg. 333.
[201] See Chapter 3 on the death of the sun above the 66.5° latitude.
[202] A connection between Sumerian and the Ural-Altaic language group has been suggested. See Polat Kaya, M. Sc. E. E. 1997 – "5. SUMERIAN AND URAL-ALTAIC KINSHIP: The Ural-Altaic languages are related to the Sumerian language. According to Hymes list of 100 common root words of Ural-Altaic and Sumerian languages used as tests for comparing these languages, any language that has 47% of the root words given in the list can be considered a direct descendant of the Sumerian language.... This test takes into account the fact that Sumerian and the present day Ural-Altaic languages are separated from each other in time by a duration of five thousand years. Turkish and Hungarian both pass this test with results far better than 50%, hence can be considered as direct descendants of Sumerian. In view of the Hymes test, the proto-Ural-Altaic language and Sumerian must have been one and the same."

An entire book could be written based solely on those who have wrongfully attacked Allegro.[203] Surprisingly, the most ruinous attacks to his career came from *within* the psychedelic research community. Many of the arguments against John Allegro seem to have stemmed from R. Gordon Wasson who admitted to never having read Allegro's work! How can an entire research community base its contentions against Allegro on a man who never read his work? Had any of these researchers had an understanding of fertility cults, archaeoastronomy, and philology, many of Allegro's theories would not have been heavily contested.

In scholarly circles, word spread that Wasson did not believe that John Allegro's work was correct.[204] In 1984, after Jack Herer spent eight months researching many of Allegro's references, he called Wasson to ask him personally why he felt Allegro's work was incorrect. Wasson informed Herer that he had actually been too busy to read Allegro's work himself and that two respected friends, a Jewish Rabbi and a Catholic Monsignor reviewed Allegro's work and reported back to him that "there was not one single word of truth in the book whatsoever." This blunder in Wasson's judgment had a huge impact on Allegro's credibility in psychedelic research circles which must be set straight. Allegro fell under disrepute among chemists, pharmacologists and psychedelic researchers because he quoted Andrija Puharich[205] (who quoted erroneous pharmacology[206]) in regards to the chemicals present in the *Amanita muscaria*. Puharich had not verified the chemical composition himself, and this reflected badly on Allegro. This is a minor error in comparison to the wealth of philological information Allegro contributed.

Wasson, in *Persephone's Quest* (published posthumously), stated:

> I once said that there was no mushroom in the Bible. I was wrong. It plays a major hidden role (that is, hidden from us until now) in the best-known episode of the Old Testament, tale of Adam and Eve and the Garden of Eden. I suppose that few at first, or perhaps none, will agree with me. To propose a novel reading of this celebrated story is a daring thing: it is exhilarating and intimidating. I am confident, ready for the storm.[207]
> ~ R. Gordon Wasson

Fortunately, for Wasson, Allegro had already weathered the storm. In 1972, Wasson also stated:

> I do not suggest that St. John of Patmos ate mushrooms in order to write the book of the Revelation. Yet the succession in his vision, so clearly seen and yet such a phantasmagoria, means for me that he was in the same state as one bemushroomed.[208]
> ~ R. Gordon Wasson

Christians will typically block out new information that invalidates their contention that Jesus was a real man because the validity of their entire religion hinges on that single argument. When discussing other theologies, no matter how similar to Christianity they may be, the Christian will recognize these other theologies as "myth," while denying vehemently the same possibility for their own *Savior*.

The fact is that no one else in the research community had ever seriously considered the idea that Jesus Christ was an anthropomorphism of the mushroom.[209] For Allegro to go out on such a limb is proof of his personal integrity to bring us the truth.

---

[203] In May 2005, Judith Anne Brown, John Allegro's daughter, released her new book entitled: *John Marco Allegro – The Maverick of the Dead Sea Scrolls*. This fantastic book is dedicated to debunking the wrongful attacks against Allegro and his research. *A Christian View of the Mushroom Myth*, by John C. King, and *The Mushroom and the Bride*, by John H. Jacques, are two books dedicated to making unjust attacks against Allegro and his research.

[204] Interestingly, it was Wasson who first proposed that the Bible was based on entheogens in *Soma*, though he later retracted this statement. Allegro took the idea, being a biblical expert, and ran with it.

[205] *The Sacred Mushroom: Key to the Door of Eternity*, by Andrija Puharich.

[206] Wieland & Motzel, 1953.

[207] *Persephone's Quest*, by R. Gordon Wasson, pg. 74.

[208] Wasson 1972a:196; see also *Hallucinogens and Culture*, by Furst, pg. 85-6.

[209] At the Societe Mycologique de France in 1910, the idea was briefly entertained.

When we dig deep into John Allegro's work, we find exactly why it was so important for the Church and others to attempt to discredit him even while building careers from his work. Many people had jobs on the line and if the majority of Allegro's work was shown correct at the time, which it is, they would have been out of a job. More importantly, if Allegro's work had found its way to the mainstream media, Christianity as we know it would have come to a screeching halt. Decades after the release of *The Sacred Mushroom and the Cross* and many years after his death, many of John Allegro's theories are being corroborated by different kinds of non-linguistic evidence. It is unfortunate for Allegro that he did not live to see this day. Such is the life of a martyr. Now is the time for John Marco Allegro to be awarded his due respect.

DISCIPLES OF THE MICROCOSM

John Allegro paved the way for researchers in many fields of study and validated those who came before him. Some researchers denied his findings while others embraced them. Other disciples of the microcosm include R. Gordon Wasson. R. Gordon Wasson was the father of ethnomycology and entheomycology. You can find his personal library maintained at Harvard University's botanical museum and more information about Wasson (biography, etc.) on Harvard University's web site.[210] Gordon Wasson spent his life researching the history of entheogenic mushrooms and their associations with different cultures. He was originally an international banker and in 1926, he married a Russian woman, Valentina Pavlovna. One day while on a walk through the woods during their honeymoon, Valentina ran off into the forest as she excitedly discovered and picked various types of mushrooms that she would later fix for dinner. This startled Wasson and the two began to research why their two cultures (Russian and Anglo-Saxon) had such juxtaposed stereotypes regarding mushrooms.[211]

Excerpt from: *Seeking The Magic Mushroom*, Life Magazine, May 13, 1957:

> It was a walk in the woods, many years ago, that launched my wife and me on our quest of the mysterious mushroom. We were married in London in 1926, she being Russian, born and brought up in Moscow. She had lately qualified as a physician at the University of London. I am from Great Falls, Montana of Anglo-Saxon origins. In the late summer of 1927, recently married, we spent our holiday in the Catskill Mountains in New York state. In the afternoon of the first day we went strolling along a lovely mountain path, through woods criss-crossed by the slanting rays of a descending sun. We were young, carefree and in love. Suddenly my bride abandoned my side. She had spied wild mushrooms in the forest, and racing over the carpet of dried leaves in the woods, she knelt in poses of adoration before first one cluster and then another of these growths. In ecstasy she called each kind of by an endearing Russian name. She caressed the toadstools, savored their earthy perfume. Like all good Anglo-Saxons, I knew nothing about the fungal world and felt that the less I knew about those putrid, treacherous excrescences the better. For her they were things of grace, infinitely inviting to the perceptive mind. She insisted on gathering them, laughing at my protests, mocking my horror. She brought a skirtful back to the lodge. She cleaned and cooked them. That evening she ate them, alone. Not long married, I thought to wake up the next morning a widower.
>
> These dramatic circumstances, puzzling and painful for me, made a lasting impression on us both. From that day on we sought an explanation for this strange cultural cleavage separating us in a minor area of our lives....

---

[210] http://www.huh.harvard.edu/libraries/wasson.html.
[211] *Persephone's Quest*, by R. Gordon Wasson.

Maria Sabina was a Curandera shamaness from Mexico and because of Wasson's research and interest, Robert Graves guided Wasson in her direction based on the original discovery of Mazatec entheogenic mushroom use by Weitlaner in 1936.[212] Subsequently, Wasson traveled south to visit the so-called "mushroom cult" in the 1950s. Wasson went to Mexico and asked Maria Sabina if she would allow him to partake in this experience. She agreed. You can find an article about this in the May 13, 1957 edition of *Life* magazine (still available in libraries today). Here is what Wasson had to say about his experience with the mushroom:

Figure 47 – Maria Sabina

The visions were not blurred or uncertain. They were sharply focused, the lines and colors being so sharp that they seemed more real to me than anything I had ever seen with my own eyes. I felt that I was now seeing plain, whereas ordinary vision gives us an imperfect view; I was seeing the archetypes, the Platonic ideas, that underlie the imperfect images of everyday life. The thought crossed my mind: could the divine mushrooms be the secret that lay behind the ancient Mysteries? Could the miraculous mobility that I was now enjoying be the explanation for the flying witches that played so important a part in the folklore and fairy tales of northern Europe? These reflections passed through my mind at the very time that I was seeing the visions, for the effect of the mushrooms is to bring about a fission of the spirit, a split in the person, a kind of schizophrenia, with the rational side continuing to reason and to observe the sensations that the other side is enjoying. The mind is attached as by an elastic cord to the vagrant senses.
~ R. Gordon Wasson

Wasson later had this to say about his mushroom experience.

...religion pure and simple, free of Theology, free of dogmatics, expressing itself in awe and reverence and in lowered voices, mostly at night, when people would gather together to consult the Sacred Element.[213]
~ R. Gordon Wasson

Wasson's description of his experience with the mushroom was the first known mushroom "trip report" in the modern world. The CIA was paying close attention to this and soon learned of Wasson's plans to return to Mexico and collect some mushrooms to bring back home.

During the intervening winter, James Moore [CIA agent] wrote Wasson—"out of the blue," as Wasson recalls—and expressed a desire to look into the chemical properties of Mexican fungi. Moore eventually suggested that he would like to accompany Wasson's party, and, to sweeten the proposition, he mentioned that he knew a foundation that might be willing to help underwrite the expedition. Sure enough, the CIA's conduit, the Geschickter Fund, made a $2,000 grant. Inside the MKULTRA program, the quest for the divine mushroom became Subproject 58.[214]
~ John Marks

Wasson later felt angst over revealing the secrets of Maria Sabina and the Mazatec peoples to the world for what he believed to have destroyed their culture. He failed to recognize that the opposite was true. Today, because of Maria Sabina, Gordon Wasson, Terence McKenna, and others, the mushroom experience is known world-wide, and, in reality, the "Mexican cult of the mushroom" has beckoned the return of this ancient lost knowledge for the rest of the world.

---

[212] *Hallucinogens and Culture*, by Peter T. Furst, pg. 83.
[213] Wasson, 1968; Wasson, et al., 1986.
[214] *The Search for the Manchurian Candidate*, by John Marks.

[T]he Mazatecs spoke of the mushrooms as the blood of Christ, because they were believed to grow only where a drop of Christ's blood had touched the earth; according to another tradition, the sacred mushrooms sprouted where a drop of Christ's spittle had moistened the earth and because of this it was *Jesucristo* himself that spoke and acted through the mushrooms.[215]
~ Peter T. Furst quoting Albert Hofmann

Gordon Wasson and his wife Valentina founded the field of Ethnomycology primarily when doing the research for *Russia Mushrooms and History* (1957). Wasson attributed the first in a series on Ethnomycology (Entheo-Mycological Studies No.1) into his most famous work *Soma, The Divine Mushroom of Immortality*. In this book, he lays out the foundation of the Rig Vedas in which he discovered that the basis of Soma in the Rig Vedas (at least in part) is in fact this bright red and white, *Amanita muscaria*, psychedelic mushroom.[216]

We (among others) contend that Soma in the Rig Vedas was often an admixture of *Psilocybe* mushrooms and other psychoactive ingredients as well.[217] We should point out that the argument regarding Soma is no longer concerning *if* Soma was an entheogen, but rather *which* entheogen Soma was. Wasson himself admitted to never having a successful experience with *A. muscaria*, but upon further investigation, we realized from his 1965 and 1966 publications that he ate the mushrooms raw, drank the juice, and had the juice with milk. Wasson's own research states the *A. muscaria* is always consumed dried: *"There is no aspect of the fly-agaric on which there is more testimony than this..."* He later stated that consuming them raw was in error.[218,219] Was his friend Imazeki the only one who properly prepared the mushroom by roasting? It also appears that Wasson never recycled his urine while conducting personal experiments with the *Amanita* even though he criticized anthropologists for not doing the same.[220] This is customary of cultures that use the *Amanitas* and will be discussed at the end of this chapter. Wasson concluded at the time, that Caucasians may not be able to experience the mushroom's effects.[221,222] Reviewing all of the ideas laid out by Wasson[223], McKenna[224], Flattery & Schwartz[225], Spess[226], and Bennett[227] brings us to the conclusion that all are partially right, and wrong. None have provided substantial evidence enough to refute the others, bringing us to the conclusion that "Soma"[228] is probably a generic term describing preparations in singular or combination of *Amanita, Psilocybe*, syrian rue, *nymphaea, nelumbo, cannabis*, opium, ephedra, and/or other psychoactive ingredients.[229,230]

---

[215] *Hallucinogens and Culture*, by Peter T. Furst, pg. 85.

[216] Wasson later presented more evidence in *Persephone's Quest*, which was contested by McKenna in *Food of the Gods,* ch. 7.

[217] See chap. 5 regarding combined mushroom experiences.

[218] *Soma*, by Gordon Wasson, pg. 154-155.

[219] Eating raw *Amanita muscaria* mushrooms has been reported (see *Soma,* by Hawk). The shaman *can* build up a tolerance to the toxins in this mushroom. However, the dosage needed for the shamanic death and rebirth experience is difficult to obtain before the shaman has a full belly. Amanita mushrooms do not greatly decrease in potency when dried. Drying the mushrooms out first would allow the shaman to ingest higher quantities and intensify the experience.

[220] *Soma*, by Gordon Wasson, pg. 25.

[221] The thousands of published and online "Trip reports" of the *Amanita muscaria* as well as our own experiences with the *Amanita muscaria* also disprove this theory.

[222] McKenna argues in *Food of the Gods* against A. m. citing that it contains Muscarine. Ott in *Pharmacotheon* shows that Muscarine is only found in trace amounts at 0.0003% in European species. McKenna admits to only eating 5 grams of roasted A. muscaria his first attempt (far too little), and the second time he consumed them raw. He never consumed his urine.

[223] See *Soma*, by Wasson. Heinrich, Ruck, and Staples also argue in total favor of the Amanita muscaria in *Apples of Apollo* and Heinrich in *Magic Mushrooms*.

[224] *Food of the Gods*, by Terence McKenna.

[225] Flattery & Schwartz argue in favour of *Peganum harmala*, the seed of the Syrian Rue plant in *Haoma and Harmaline, Near Eastern Studies, Vol. 21, 1989*.

[226] *Soma: The Divine Hallucinogen*, by David Spess, arguing in favor of Nymphaea, and Nelumbo, first proposed by Chapman Cohen.

[227] *Burning Shiva: Has the Soma Question Been Answered?* www.pottv.net; *Green Gold the Tree of Life, Marijuana in Magic and Religion;* and *Sex, Drugs, Violence and the Bible*, by Chris Bennett.

[228] One definition of "Soma" in *Webster's 3rd New International Dictionary*: akin to L tum ere to swell – more at THUMB; suggesting that Soma is a mushroom.

[229] See also *Mushrooms & Mankind*, by James Arthur.

[230] Spess argues that Soma is seven compounds and seven elixirs. *Soma: The Divine Hallucinogen*, pg. 138. He also argues that Nymphaea and Nelumbo are the only two plants used in Soma, thus, appearing to contradict himself. To Spess' credit, this contradiction in his research was due to the editors of his publishing company, and not by his own research and writing.

Soma was probably nothing more than a generic term (taxon) that was used in the same way as the words "drug," "entheogen," "psychedelic," or "psychoactive substance" are used today.[231]
~ Rätsch, Müller-Ebeling, Shahi

Soma was one of the most important anthropomorphized deities in the Hindu pantheon. On the surface, *Soma* can be confusing because it represents so many things. Soma is a plant, Soma is the word or logos ('vac'), Soma is a drink, Soma is a drink made from a plant[232], and the psychoactive urine of the priest who had ingested the plant.[233] Consequently, Soma has characteristics of plants and of gods as well. Soma, in the stories, married the daughter of the sun and is often referred to as the sun itself. The anthropomorphism of Soma embodies the sun, the plant, the god and the elixir made from the plant. The red and white-spotted *A. muscaria* mushroom can be seen as a red, sun-like ball with the white clouds crossing in front of it (representing the sun and the plant together),[234] and this sacred mushroom has been associated with a number of deities, as one shall soon see.

Jack Herer is the author of the book *The Emperor Wears No Clothes: Cannabis and the Conspiracy Against Marijuana.* He is an ethnobotanist and historian and is considered "the father of the hemp movement." Herer is responsible for reintroducing all of the suppressed information on industrial hemp, medical marijuana and the entire history of this plant's use throughout time. While Herer and his best friend "Captain Ed" Adair were researching hemp, they came across substantial information, including the works of John Allegro, which sent them on another path of research – ethno and entheomycology. Herer has spent over twenty years researching this information.

Herer has received many awards for his active role in bringing back the hemp plant. He and Adair (Adair died in the early 90's) are fully or partially responsible for the return of industrial hemp to over 50 nations. Herer maintains a $100,000 challenge to the world to prove his information on industrial hemp wrong.[235] This challenge originally started at $10,000 and has grown over the years. Even though this information has been public for nearly twenty years, we still do not find Herer's information in the mainstream media very often. You can read the entire book *The Emperor Wears No Clothes* for free on his website, www.jackherer.com.

Clark Heinrich has written two books, one of which is *Strange Fruit* that later evolved into *Magic Mushrooms in Religion and Alchemy.* This book is an excellent resource and is full of wonderful pictures. In regard to mushrooms in alchemy and Hinduism, this book is fantastic.

Heinrich was the first to attempt a decipherment of the Bible based on the *Amanita muscaria*[236] since Allegro.

> Let it be repeated: if even one only of the mushroom references of the cryptic phrases of the New Testament text were correct, then a new element has to be reckoned with in the nature and origin of the Christian religion.[237]
> ~ John Allegro

If Heinrich was indeed able to decipher correctly any information in the New Testament about the *A. muscaria*, then John Allegro, too, is validated. Heinrich is one of few researchers to give John Allegro any credit at all:

> John Allegro was an Oxford-educated philologist and Hebrew scholar, one of the original team of scholars (and the only humanist) who began working on the Dead Sea scrolls, first found at Qumran in 1947. In 1956, Allegro alienated most of the other members of the scrolls team by claiming in a BBC interview that the scrolls proved Christianity to be, at best, a derivative religion.... Allegro claimed that this was the proto-Jesus, reinvented and restructured circa 30 CE to appeal to the gentiles.... These stories, Allegro said, were the work of a revisionist group that took an older story, updated and embellished it....[238]
> ~ Clark Heinrich

---

[231] *Shamanism and Tantra In the Himalayas*, by Rätsch, Müller-Ebeling, Shahi, pg. 178.
[232] *Soma: The Divine Mushroom of Immortality*, by Wasson; *Magic Mushrooms in Alchemy and Religion*, by Clark Heinrich.
[233] *Pharmacotheon*, by Jonathon Ott, pg. 332.
[234] Clark Heinrich brought this to our attention during a lecture in 2000.
[235] See www.jackherer.com, or *The Emperor Wears No Clothes*, by Jack Herer.
[236] *Magic Mushrooms in Religion and Alchemy*, by Clark Heinrich.
[237] *The Sacred Mushroom and the Cross*, by John Allegro, pg. 194.
[238] *Magic Mushrooms in Religion and Alchemy*, by Clark Heinrich, pg. 23.

As we have shown, Christianity most certainly is a derivative religion.[239] Notice that this BBC talk was in 1956. Twelve years before Wasson published *Soma* in 1968, Allegro had postulated that the Christian story was based on Essene sectarian beliefs. Later, he began researching etymological links between Essene terms and the languages of ancient fertility cults. In 1956, he hadn't yet connected Essenism and early Christianity to an ancient fertility religion. This proves that Allegro had already been investigating the history of Christianity while a lecturer in Old Testament Studies at the University of Manchester and as an "Oxford-educated philologist and Hebrew scholar." Heinrich continues:

> ...Allegro sealed his fate in 1970 when he published *The Sacred Mushroom and the Cross*, a book that claimed on linguistic evidence, <u>real and imagined</u>, that <u>Jesus was the head of a cult that took psychedelic mushrooms</u>, namely the fly agaric or "penis mushroom.[240] [underline—ours]
> ~ Clark Heinrich

Actually, Allegro suggested in *The Sacred Mushroom and the Cross* that Jesus *is* the mushroom. As well, Heinrich's own work in the book *Magic Mushrooms in Religion and Alchemy*, is one of the best for substantiating the "penis mushroom" theory in Christianity and other religions.

> ...Allegro was attacked on every side and ridiculed mercilessly, as if his hypothesis [*The Sacred Mushroom and the Cross*] were more ridiculous than believing, for example, that a human being created the universe, revived from a horrible death, and floated bodily up to heaven. <u>Actually, his contentions are far more reasonable than the accepted versions of Christian and Jewish mythology, but there were few who would concede even this much</u>. The numerous mistakes he made about the mushroom itself, its life cycle and effects, didn't help matters, nor did the fact that he never tried the mushroom.[241] [underline—ours]
> ~ Clark Heinrich

Indeed, Allegro also missed some possible associations to both *Amanita pantherina* and *Psilocybe* mushrooms, and overlooked important aspects of astrotheology, just as Heinrich and many other have. Often, pioneers in a new field have much lower accuracy, and later researchers, using this new foundation, begin filling the in gaps (as Heinrich did). Allegro was a pioneer no doubt. He *was* wrong about the active compounds and effects of the mushroom, and it has yet to be proven sufficiently to us that all of Allegro's Sumerian interpretations were wrong. We still have no doubt he had some (or even many) errors. He stated himself that many of his interpretations were speculation and needed further research.[242] However, this is no reason to discredit entirely all of Allegro's work. If Allegro had taken the mushrooms, his theories would have been more reasonable. But he was not experienced with their effects. Because of the work of Heinrich, Herer, Ruck, Staples, Wasson, Wilson, Spess, Arthur, Merkur, Bennett, and this book, we are now forced to admit that Allegro was more right than wrong and he understood much, as Heinrich showed by writing two books that reinforce Allegro's research.

> It isn't crucial to me if the name Jesus means "mushroom" in some long-lost tongue, although I will consider it to be quite significant if it happens to be true.[243]
> ~ Clark Heinrich

---

[239] Chapter 3 and Acharya S., Jordan Maxwell, Kersey Graves, etc.
[240] Clark Heinrich in *Magic Mushrooms in Religion and Alchemy* argues that the *Amanita m.* is the penis mushroom.
[241] *Magic Mushrooms in Religion and Alchemy*, by Clark Heinrich, pg. 24.
[242] "It is now possible to propose combinations of known root elements with a fair degree of assurance; nevertheless the asterisk will appear frequently in the following pages and serve to remind us that such reconstructions, however probable, must find adequate cross-checking through the cognate languages if they are to be anything but speculative." *The Sacred Mushroom and the Cross*, by John M. Allegro, pg. 16.
[243] *Magic Mushrooms in Religion and Alchemy*, by Clark Heinrich, pg. 25.

If Jesus was not a real person, then this changes *everything*! In fact, we interpret Docetism[244] as the *key* to the Bible. Interpreting the stories cannot be properly accomplished with the false, Euhemerist conclusion that "Jesus of Nazareth" (the divine son of God) was a real man. Surely, there were "holy-men" who lived during this period, but the divine Son of God, with the characteristics discussed earlier, is 100% allegory. In understanding that Jesus was/is not a physical man[245] with divine attributes, but rather an anthropomorphism of the male phallic, the sun, the mushroom (and drugs), and entheogenically infused oil, all of the stories (as we will show) completely unfold.

Another book by Clark Heinrich is *The Apples of Apollo: Pagan and Christian Mysteries of the Eucharist*, which was co-written with Professor Carl Ruck of Boston University, and Blaise Stables, Ph.D. This is an excellent book for delving into the origins of Greek mythology and the Eucharist in Christianity. This book also strengthens the research of Allegro.

Another book written by Gordon Wasson, Carl Ruck, Jonathan Ott and Stella Kramrisch is *Persephone's Quest: Entheogens and the Origins of Religion.* This is an important book in looking at the very foundation of Maya, Hindu, Santal, Buddhist, and Christian theologies, the Eleusinian mysteries, and ancient philosophy. This book is available from Yale University Press.

Jonathon Ott has written a number of books on Entheogens, and is probably one of the most respected entheogenic researchers in the world today. Among his most important works are *Pharmacotheon* (Drug Gods), which is an amazing entheogen desk reference guide, and *The Age of Entheogens and the Angel's Dictionary*, in which he attempts to establish standard shamanic/entheogenic terminology. The term "Pharmacratic Inquisition" (discussed in the introduction to this section) is attributed to Ott from his *Age of Entheogens and the Angel's Dictionary*.

Christian Rätsch, Ph.D., is a world-renowned anthropologist and ethnopharmacologist who specializes in the shamanic uses of plants. He is the author of *The Encyclopedia of Psychoactive Plants: Ethnopharmacology and Its Applications*, *Marijuana Medicine* and co-author of the second edition of *Plants of the Gods* with Dr. Albert Hofmann (the discoverer of LSD) and Dr. Richard Evans Schultes of Harvard's Botanical Museum. He co-authored *Witchcraft Medicine* with Claudia Müller-Ebeling and Wolf-Dieter Storl, fantastic for looking at the female use of Wicca (witchcraft), its shamanic and healing plants and practices throughout Europe and, most importantly, its suppression. He also co-authored *Shamanism and Tantra in the Himalayas* with Müller-Ebeling, Ph.D., and Surendra Bahadur Shahi. *Shamanism and Tantra in the Himalayas*[246] is a beautiful and fantastic book for delving into the shamanic cultures existing in Nepal today and for understanding how more than one plant has always been used in Hindu mythology.

> There is said [to] be a total of 108 psychoactive plants that are consecrated to Shiva and are sacred, and that transport the shamans into a trance.
> ~ Müller-Ebeling, Rätsch, Shahi

Chris Bennett has co-authored two books, one of which was *Green Gold: The Tree of Life*, co-authored with Lynn and Judy Osburn. His latest book is *Sex, Drugs, Violence and the Bible*, co-authored with Neil McQueen. Bennett has approached the entheogens in the Bible issue from a new perspective, one with cannabis as the main sacrament. He has shown successfully that the mistranslated biblical "calamus" from the Hebrew *qaneh-bosem*, is actually marijuana or cannabis (q'aneh), an ingredient in the anointing oils. His interpretations sometimes lean slightly more toward literal than we agree with, and he barely touches on astrotheology. However, his books are well researched and make for fantastic, in-depth reading and are highly recommended.

---

[244] From the *Oxford English Dictionary*: Docetae – An early sect of heretics, who held that Christ's body was not human, but either a phantom, or of real but celestial substance. [underline—ours]

[245] We must note that the Essenes applied much older archaeoastronomical, shamanic, and fertility cult mythology to their "Teacher of Righteousness." (Bennett argues such a character [i.e. 'Jesus'] applied the mythology to '*himself*'!) The Church further amplified all three in the canonization of biblical texts trying to historicize two (until now unknown) mythological anthropomorphisms on top of one political/religious fanatic leader, Joshua. However, the Essenes themselves saw this Joshua, who died in 88 BCE, as yet the latest incarnation of a repetitive history – first with Joshua, son of Jehozadak, then to Joshua, Son of Nun, and ending with The Teacher of Righteousness. See *The Dead Sea Scrolls and the Christian Myth*, by John Allegro, ch. 14.

[246] *Shamanism and Tantra in the Himalayas*, by Müller-Ebeling, Rätsch, and Shahi, pg. 151. They also point out that "108" is a symbol for completeness, and claim to have discovered 88 of these plants used by shamans thus far. Pgs. 151-155.

David Spess is a microbiologist and former research mycologist for the FDA. He taught at the University of Colorado and studied Sanskrit at the Naropa Institute. He has written an interesting book called *Soma: The Divine Hallucinogen*, in which he argues that Soma is a combination of plants, particularly Nymphaea and Nelumbo. Spess does not argue sufficiently against other candidates for Soma.[247] However, for acquiring a deep understanding of the origins of the Middle Eastern and Mediterranean religions, alchemy and philosophy through Soma use in the Rig Vedas, this book is outstanding. His work is probably one of the most important for showing the origins of Judaism, Christianity, Gnosticism, etc., as a slow development from Indo-Aryan/Iranian cultures.[248]

Peter Lamborn Wilson is a well-known "underground intellect." He has written many books, but his largest contribution to this field comes from his book, *Ploughing the Clouds: the Search for the Irish Soma*. In this book, for the first time in entheogenic research, Wilson brings sufficient evidence to the table to show the use of mushrooms and other entheogens in Celtic cultures, especially in Irish folklore and tradition. Wilson also contends that Irish Soma use came through the traditions of the Rig Vedas by migratory movements of Indo-Aryan peoples to Ireland. Wilson brings new, startling theories to the table, such as his hypothesis that the spread of empire started over the chase of Soma by agricultural peoples who had lost the Soma traditions to the more natural woodland tribes. Wilson also argues sufficiently to suggest that Soma was generally acquired by purchase or theft in many cultures, and was considered taboo to harvest by the group who intended to use it. This idea, which he supplies ample evidence for, if correct, would make other arguments against mushrooms as Soma and Manna in desert regions, obsolete.[249, 250]

There are many other excellent researchers in this field and we would like to mention them all, though we have limited the scope to those whose work most pertains to our current study.

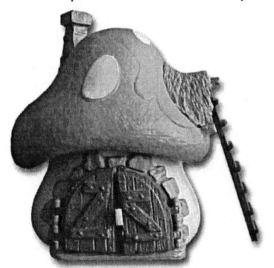

Figure 48 - Smurf Cabin

THE AGE-OLD ICON

Millions of children all over the world saw this mushroom in the Smurfs cartoon during the 1980's. Sears and Roebuck had an entire series of plateware with this mushroom on it. From postcards to video games like Super Mario Brothers, to cartoons such as Fantasia (which depicts two different kinds of mushrooms, both will be discussed in this book), these mushrooms are found everywhere. One will find that mushrooms often associated with Christmas and mushroom ornaments on the Christmas tree are not rare. Some of the oldest Christmas ornaments that one will find are red and white-spotted mushrooms.

---

[247] We contacted David Spess and he informed us that this was in no way his belief, but the doing of his publisher by uninformed editors.

[248] We agree with Spess that Judaism and Christianity derived from the Rig Vedas, however, we now believe that the Rig Vedas and Soma use may be of Ural-Altaic (Siberian) origin.

[249] Recent mushroom Hieroglyphs found in Libya also show that mushrooms grew in "the now desert" regions at least until the Neolithic period. See Ripinski-Naxon (1993). Those who contest the mushroom (A. muscaria) theory include Bennett (2001, pg. 53 ft. 115): "It is hard for me to understand how so much valuable research time by such intelligent men has been misspent trying to document a forest mushroom as the main sacrament of the desert people." Bennett also omits associations such as the message of Jevohah received by Abraham under the oak, likely to be *A. pantherina*, and the cedars of Lebanon that would most likely be in reference to *A. muscaria*. Both Allegro and Heinrich also overlooked this. Other associations are better suited as cubensis and will be discussed in the Ch. 5 section "What is This?" Evidence of climactic changes that would have effected available entheogenic sources in the biblical time frame can be found in *Saharasia* –by DeMeo.

[250] Wilson derived this idea from Gordon Wasson's *Soma: The Divine Mushroom of Immortality*, pg. 23-24.

Merry Christmas and Happy New Year: This is the same holiday just split into two days, New Year's and Christmas. We know this because both celebrations are founded upon the winter solstice, the death and birth of the sun. Making two separate holidays (holy-days) gives the Church their Christian celebration while everyone can still celebrate the New Year festivities. Once it has been pointed out, this red and white mushroom will be seen repeatedly in New Year's and Christmas icons as well as in places that one would never think to look.

Figure 49 -Holiday Card

It seems as though an important Christmas tradition is to never question the origin of the traditions themselves. Why do we bring a tree into our house to celebrate Christmas? If it is a Christian holiday, then, where in the Bible does it say to bring a tree into our house? In addition, why does it have to be a pine or other coniferous tree? Why do we decorate it? Why are the Christmas colors red, white, and green? Why do we put red and white presents *under* the tree? Why do we hang stockings on the hearth of the fireplace? Who is this Santa character and why does he do the strange things that he does? Did a man in a red and white suit *ever* crawl down someone's chimney with a sack full of goodies?

> According to Rogan Taylor, perhaps the most amusing hint of *amanita*-based shamanism may well be enshrined, perhaps by accident, in the popular contemporary image of Santa Claus. The figure of Father Christmas evolved over centuries out of pagan traditions, but the modern image of Santa owes most to the elements cobbled together in the 1820's by Professor Clement Clark Moore of Albany, New York, along with illustrators Thomas Nast and Morits von Schwind, both of Germanic descent. Taylor feels that some traditional elements got drawn into their version, perhaps from the professor's wide reading, or from the illustrator's Old World links—or both. He points out that Santa's robe of red, edged with white, contains the colors of *Amanita muscaria*, and that the idea of Santa clambering down the chimney evokes the entry via the smoke hole into Siberian yurts during winter. Moreover, the reindeers that pull the sleigh can be seen as a link to the reindeer-herder tribes who took the magic mushroom. And the magic flight of Santa Claus through the midwinter night sky is a superb expression of the basis of all shamanism— ecstasy, or the flight of the spirit.[251]
> ~ Paul Devereux

Dr. Patrick Harding of the University of Sheffield, Roger Highfield, James Bursenos and James Arthur have all furthered the research into the symbolism of Christmas (both pagan and modern), and answered many of these questions, as well as others that one may have never thought to ask regarding Christmas traditions. We repeat the same traditions every year, but are too busy to stop and question the origin of some very peculiar things that we do, things that might appear very silly to an outside viewer. However, there are not many outside viewers. Christmas is a worldwide celebration. The traditions and names may vary from place to place and from country to country, but the *template* of the Christmas story can almost always be found. "As above, so below," the Christmas template, is found above us in the stars as we discussed in the first part of this book and the Christmas template can also be found right below our feet.

---

[251] *The Long Trip: A Prehistory of Psychedelia*, by Paul Devereux, pg. 72.

In some mycology books, you still can find this mushroom listed as "**Not to Be Eaten**," or "**poisonous**." Both authors of this book have eaten this mushroom and we are alive and well. You do have to be careful in ensuring that you have the correct mushroom. In addition, the *Amanita* needs to be prepared correctly or you *may* get sick, and even proper preparation is not a guarantee that you will not get sick. We want to be clear that no one should pick any mushrooms without doing research and taking a class in mycology in order to better understand and identify exactly what you're about to ingest. Many people die each year by consuming deadly mushrooms mistaken for psychedelic or edible ones.

Figure 50 - *Amanita muscaria* **growing under a pine tree**

WHICH CAME FIRST–THE MUSHROOM OR THE SPORE?

The *Amanita muscaria* goes through a very particular growth cycle and this growth cycle is used in many mythological stories to help locate and identify these mushrooms. The growth cycle is very similar to the life and death of the mythological bird, the Phoenix.[252] This connection will be explored further in a moment, but first let's continue with the Christmas tree and explore the growth cycle of this magical mushroom.

The Christmas tree is not just a symbol for eternal life, which is what many Christian children are told. It is *literally* the Tree of Knowledge from the Garden of Eden.[253] Metaphorically, Jesus "comes from the trees" by saying that his father was a carpenter.[254] The *Amanita* is the *fruit* of this Tree of Knowledge/Life[255,256] because neither the *A. muscaria* nor the *Amanita pantherina* can grow without a tree as their host. The *A. muscaria* mushrooms flourish under pine trees and other coniferous trees such as spruce, larch, cedar, and fir. Also, they flourish under betula trees such as the Birch. These trees *remain undisturbed summer and winter*. The *A. pantherina* prefers to grow under quercus trees like the oak. The major differences between these two are that *A. pantherina* is smaller, blackish in color, is 4X more potent than its *muscaria* cousin, and prefers oak trees. These mushrooms are quite literally the fruit of the tree because of the mycorrhizal partnership that they have with the roots of these particular types of trees. Just as Mother Nature needs trees to grow apples, she also needs trees to grow these sacred *Amanita* mushrooms (the "pine-apples"[257]). *This* is why the worship of these trees is so profound in ancient mythology.

Further evidence to support John Allegro's theory is found in the parallel gods of the ancient world. We mention them here, because all happen to be associated with trees.

The Babylonian/Sumerian god Tammuz (Damuzi or Damu) was known as ***Attis*** to the Phrygians, ***Adonis*** to the Greeks and Syrians, ***Atunis*** to the Etruscans, ***Adoni*** ("my lord") to the Phoenicians, and ***Adonai*** ('lord' or 'YHWH'; *pl.* of Adonis) and ***Tammuz*** (Thomas) to the Hebrews.[258] Scholars attribute these name changes to cultural evolutions of the same god. In most of these legends, this god dies young and his birth and death are honored on his birthday at the winter solstice (Christmas).[259] In the case of Attis, the celebration was held at the winter solstice, or the vernal equinox (Easter). In Phrygia, pine trees were sacred to Agdistis (Gr. Cybele), the lover/mother of Attis. Attis tortures himself, cuts off his own penis and then turns into a pine tree, creating the fruit (mushroom) under the tree.

In Roman mythology, Rhea/Cybele turns Attis into a pine. Adonis is born from the base of a myrrh tree, which was an ingredient in psychedelic oils (see Appendix B) and probably was earlier associated with the pine. Adonai creates the fruit of the tree. Most of their religious rituals involved cutting down a young evergreen (Christmas) tree as a way of commemorating the premature death of Tammuz.

> Ezekiel 6:13
> Then shall ye know that I *am* the LORD, when their slain *men* shall be among their idols round about their altars, upon every high hill, in all the tops of the mountains, and under every green tree, and under every thick oak, the place where they did offer sweet savour to all their idols.

---

[252] *The Sacred Mushroom and the Cross*, by John Allegro, pg. 95.

[253] The packages that appear magically overnight under the Christmas tree, and the fruit of the Tree of Knowledge appear to be synonymous with the growth and appearance of *A. muscaria & A. pantherina*.

[254] *The Sacred Mushroom and the Cross*, by John Allegro, pg. 102 (see also Ott, *Pharmacotheon*, pg. 333, regarding the fly-agaric and the Tree of Life being the progenitor of today's religions).

[255] Dan Merkur makes a strong argument that the Tree of Life and the Tree of Knowledge were one in the same. See *The Mystery of Manna*, pg. 32-33. We feel there is also the possibility that the Tree of Life and the Tree of Knowledge are two different types of mushrooms or other entheogens consumed as an admixture; see ch. 5. Both theories are probably, in part, correct.

[256] *The Apples of Apollo*, by Ruck, Staples and Heinrich, pg. 51.

[257] See chapter 5, *The Song of Songs*.

[258] We thank Marcel Battle and Jay Lynn for their input here.

[259] Many scholars will argue that Adonai is not related to the other gods, but their likenesses are undeniable. Jewish theology, in its attempt to separate itself from older religions, no longer worships Adonai on the birthday of Adonis, Dec. 25.

Other associations to trees include:

- Dionysus, whose devotees wore foliage from pine trees.
- Baal, a Phoenician god whose followers made sacrificial offerings under the oak.
- Abraham (in Sanskrit, Brahma), who in Jewish mythology encountered the "Angel of Jehovah" under the oak tree.
- The oak tree, for Socrates, was an Oracle tree. The oak tree is worshipped in all Druidic rites (Druid means 'oak').
- Shiva, who has his penis severed in the forest, where it returns each year.
- Artemis, the "Lady of the Forest."
- Eve, in Gnostic texts, turns into the tree of "acquaintance" (knowledge).[260]
- Joseph Smith, who in Mormon mythology, discovers the golden plates atop pillars in the forest, no doubt under a tree, and so on (dried *Amanita* is often a very bright gold in color).

The number of forest/tree related myths is countless.[261]

> *Upon the pillars rested the plates which shone like bright gold.* I saw also lying in the box a round body, *wrapped in a white substance*, and this I knew to be the *ball* or directors, which so many years ago guided Lehi and his family to this land. The top stone of the box was smooth on the inner surface as were the others, but *on the top it was rounded....* From the bottom of the box, or from *the breast-plate*, arose *three small pillars* composed of the same description of *cement used on the edges....* But these three pillars were not so lengthy as to cause the plates and the *crowning stones* to come in contact.... [italics–ours]
> ~ Joseph Smith

THE GROWTH CYCLE

Figure 51 - White Mushroom Spore Greatly Enlarged

Tiny spores rain down onto the pine needles surrounding the mushrooms that release them. Deep down into the ground, these spores become the mycelium that will attach itself to the roots of this particular tree. These mushrooms live in what is known as "mycorrhizal symbiosis," with the tree as their host. In fact, these living organisms (mushrooms) are taxonomically classified as a *mycorrhizal symbiont*. This is different from parasitizing another life form, in that the host is helped and in fact improved by the presence of the *symbiont*, whereas a *parasite* hurts and drains the life force of its host and may even kill it (e.g. honey fungus or mistletoe). The explanation for why these mushrooms are found growing only under particular types of trees is because they have a relationship with the roots of these particular trees. Without these specific trees, these mushrooms cannot grow. Consequently, these mushrooms can be seen as the fruiting bodies of the tree and, because of their psychedelic qualities, they have been anthropomorphized into gods.

> The mass of the mycelium of the fungus envelopes the roots of the tree in effect greatly increasing the soil area covered by the tree root system. The fungus aids the tree in absorbing water from the soil, increases the stability of the root system, and protects the roots from drying out and the effects of heavy metals. In return the tree provides sugars and starches to the fungus that the fungus uses in its metabolism.... It's possible trees and forest, as we know them today could not exist without the mycorrhizal relationships between trees and fungi.[262]
> ~ Dr. Robert W. Poole and Dr. Patricia Gentili

---

[260] On the Origin of the World, *The Nag Hammadi Library*.

[261] We would also like to remind the reader of the tree's macrocosmic association to the Axis Mundi. For further research, see *Hamlet's Mill*, by de Santillana & von Dechend.

[262] Dr. Robert W. Poole and Dr. Patricia Gentili, who have over fifty combined years in research and teaching at the university and government level, founded Nearctica.com.

One thing often seen when mushroom hunting is something that resembles small white stones near the *Amanita* flushes. These small white stones are actually more *Amanita* mushrooms that are in the egg[263] stage of the growth cycle. They, too, are the mushrooms, although they have yet to spring up out of the ground. This is the first time that we can really see (in nature) the mushroom in its first stage of growth—a small white stone.

Thomas 19
Blessed is he who came into being before he came into being. If you become my disciples and listen to my words, these stones will minister to you. For there are five trees for you in Paradise which remain undisturbed summer and winter and whose leaves do not fall. Whoever becomes acquainted with them will not experience death.

Figure 52 - The egg stage of the growth cycle – *Amanita muscaria*

This *Amanita's* first growth stage is similar to an egg shape, giving the mushroom its bulbous base. It also appears that this mushroom has been born from a tiny pot. One of the sons of Shiva was born of a pot that Shiva ejaculated into. There are quite a lot of sex worship and fertility rites involved with mushroom history. This is in part because mushrooms themselves are the phallic organs of the organism.[264]

The mushrooms are the reproductive part of the actual "body" of the organism. The mushrooms spring up to reproduce by releasing their spores. The actual body of the organism is a fine network of mycelia which is a growth of hair-like fibers throughout the soil. These networks of mycelia (when describing many mushrooms containing psilocybin) can be many acres in size and may have many more connections than exist in a human brain.[265]

Michael Talbot pointed out in his book, *The Holographic Universe*,[266] that memory, vision and quite possibly the entire universe itself exist as a hologram. If a holographic film containing an image of a dog is broken into 10 pieces, there will then exist 10 different images of the same dog. Mycelia, having more connections than the human brain, are interesting because the argument exists that these mushrooms contain information (or have a memory). When these mushrooms are ingested, it could be suggested that the data contained within these mushrooms is transferred into the user. Many people who have eaten psilocybin mushrooms acknowledge that the mushroom actually speaks to them.

---

[263] The word egg is where we derive the word ego, and ego is the *inner sun*. The egg when cracked open looks like the sun, with the yellow yolk.
[264] See Appendix C.
[265] See Appendix C.
[266] Based on the research of Alain Aspect and David Bohm.

Three feet under the forest floor in Malheur National Forest in eastern Oregon exists a 2200-acre mycelial network of the *Armillaria ostoyae*, ranging 3.5 miles across and consuming the equivalent of 1665 football fields. This is the largest and oldest living organism known to the world. Estimates of its age range between 2400 to 7200 years old.[267]

John von Neumann (contributor to game theory, quantum mechanics, and functional analysis) once calculated that over the course of the average human lifetime, the brain stores approximately 30 billion gigabytes of information. Imagine the size of Mother Earth's *brain* and the information contained over the course of millions of years. If the human brain (and the universe) could function as a holograph, so too could these networks of mycelia, the body of the mushroom. The mycelial network is worldwide. It is so vast that it would take the destruction of the planet to destroy it. The information contained within this network goes *much* deeper than guidance for personal transformation. We suggest the possibility that this information is the history of the cosmos and this holographic-like information has been broken into more than just a few pieces. This information has been separated into billions of regenerating fragments, called *mushrooms*.

> Thomas 113
> ...The kingdom of the father is <u>spread out upon the earth,</u> and men do not see it.

Figure 53 - Easter Card

The gnome is often associated with the mushroom and the hare with eggs (and mushrooms as well). It seems odd not to question why we use a rabbit to symbolize eggs at Easter when rabbits do not lay eggs. Even stranger still would be to not question *why* we include *eggs* in the Easter celebration. Traditionally, the brownish hare symbolized fertility *and* the brownish *Amanita pantherina* mushrooms. The fiery red Phoenix symbolized the bright red *Amanita muscaria*[268] and as we discussed earlier, the first stage of the mushroom's growth cycle is this egg shape. The tradition of Easter egg hunting found its way into modern times because our ancestors provided their children with baskets and sent them into the woods to look underneath the trees and shrubbery for the sacred sacrament: the often egg-shaped mushroom used in many tribal rituals.

---

[267] Dr. Catherine Parks, a scientist with the USDA Forest Service's Pacific Northwest Research Station, led the research in discovering the fungus in cooperation with Oregon State University. The fungus is calculated to be about 2400 years old, although it could be two to three times older.

[268] See *Magic Mushrooms in Religion and Alchemy*, by Heinrich, pg. 148, 175-76; *The Sacred Mushroom and the Cross*, by Allegro, pg. 95.

Figure 54 - Speculum Veritatis

The symbolism of the egg is important to mythology. The sun represented a great yolk inside the "Cosmic egg." On the microcosm, the concept of the ego is based on this same principle of the sun/egg where the soul is the yoke (sol = the sun. The word *soul* often signified the *ego*, which is derived from the word 'egg'. Metaphorically speaking, one must crack the ego to find his or her soul. The letter u in 'so-*u*-l' was a fertility symbol that was a later addition to alphabets.).

In a theory of creation found in India, Egypt, Phoenicia, Greece, and among the modern Polynesians and Finns, the whole universe came from a cosmic egg. In the version known at Memphis, in Egypt, Ptah (the opener) broke the egg from which the sun and moon came forth.[269]
~ Ernest Busenbark

Further down the microcosmic ladder, the egg is symbolized by the early stages of the mushroom's growth.[270] Today, most people no longer use these mushrooms in their ceremonies, but Christians still symbolize it with their ritual of sending children on an Easter egg hunt in the morning time, symbolic of the shaman's children gathering the colored mushrooms before the *sun waxes* hot. The spring feast and intoxicating celebration in the evening (symbolic of the shaman consuming the intoxicating mushrooms) would complete their ritual, a ritual that remains exemplary to this very day.

Figure 55 - *Amanita muscaria* - the colorful hidden egg

Describing the growth of the mushroom (boletos), Pliny says: "The earth... produces first a 'womb' (vulva)...and afterwards (the mushroom) itself inside the womb, like a yolk inside the egg; and the baby mushroom is just as fond of eating its coat as is the chicken. The coat cracks when (the mushroom) first forms; presently, as it gets bigger, the coat is absorbed into the body of the footstalk (pediculi)... at first it is flimsier than froth, then it grows substantial like parchment, and then the mushroom... is born.[271]
~ John Allegro

---

[269] *Symbols, Sex, and the Stars*, by Ernest Busenbark, pg. 101.
[270] "Before the vulva breaks, the fungus[*] looks somewhat like a pigeon's egg half-buried, or like a small phallus 'egg.'" J. Ramsbottom, op. cit., p.39, quoted by John Allegro, *The Sacred Mushroom and the Cross*, pg. 54. *Amanita phalloides.
[271] *The Sacred Mushroom and the Cross*, by John Allegro, pg. 54.

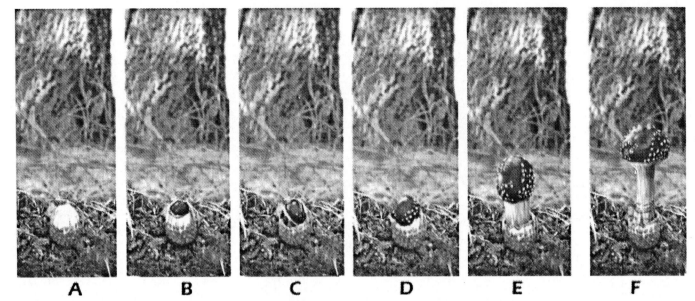

Figure 56 -*Amanita* Growth Cycle

These images show the growth cycles or the stages of the development of the mushroom. It starts egg-shaped (A), and soon the universal veil begins to peel away (B & C) as the red cap begins to separate itself from the base (D). Next is the dumbbell stage (E) where, symbolically, the moon is represented by the white bulbous base and the sun represented by the round, red cap. In this stage (E), you can see the phallic representation of the mushroom. The dots on top of the mushroom cap grow further and further apart as the mushroom grows. When the mushroom was in the egg stage, the spots were connected, forming the universal veil. This universal veil covers the entire mushroom, wrapping it in "swaddling clothes" (A). The universal veil attaches itself to the rim of the mushroom cap (pileus) as well as the stalk (stipe), covering the gills of the mushroom (F).

As the mushroom grows further, the cap begins to open. In the next stage of growth (Figure 57), the outer rim of the mushroom cap begins to separate itself from the universal veil, exposing the gills and releasing its spores. This universal veil is still attached to the stipe of the mushroom as it peels away from the underside of the cap. The previous stage of growth was the last time the mushroom would appear to be the adult male. The universal veil is beginning to peel away from the cap. This stage of the mushroom's growth could be, at least in part, the source of the male circumcision ritual, though most cultures do not circumcise.[272]

Figure 57 - Cap separating from universal veil

---

[272] This theory originates from *The Sacred Mushroom and the Cross*, by John Allegro, pg. 59, and is maintained by Heinrich, Ruck, Staples, and Herer, and others. However, there appear to be conflicting reports by James DeMeo, in *Saharasia*, and others, that will be brought together and explained in another volume. Bennett (2001), suggests this was done as serpent worship, pg. 69. However, Bennett overlooks the obvious associations of the serpent to the mushroom, which will be discussed in the following sections.

As the mushroom expands further, the universal veil separates itself completely from the underside of the cap, falls, and hangs on the stipe of the mushroom like a skirt. Because the tips of the universal veil were once touching the red part of the cap, the very tips of this skirt become colored amber or gold. In addition, another important thing to point out is that the cap of the mushroom is now becoming a canopy or *eave* of the mushroom. This will be discussed further in a moment.

Figure 58 - *Amanita muscaria* **- Canopy stage**

Figure 59 - *Amanita muscaria* **– Table stage**

Figure 60 - *Amanita muscaria* **- Cup Stage**

The *Amanita* will then continue to grow upward, flattening itself into a small table (Figure 59). One may wish to keep in mind that the Knights of the *Round Table* were the keepers and protectors of the *Holy Grail*.

From the table stage of the mushroom, the cap continues to upturn and the cap becomes somewhat of a cup or a chalice (Figure 60) and will often hold the morning dew (Figure 61). When the morning dew collects in the cup of the upturned mushroom cap, some of the psychedelic substances are drawn out of the mushroom and into the water. Consequently, the water is colored red, like blood. The bright red pigment originates in the mushroom's cap and "bleeds into" the water. This will fade the mushroom from a bright red into an orange-like or golden cup. Although the psychedelic effects would not be as intense as a belly-full of mushrooms, one could literally take this golden, chalice-shaped mushroom from nature and drink the blood of "Jesus" from the Holy Grail.[273,274]

---

[273] The philosophers' stone of alchemy and the Holy Grail, as well as Aladdin's famous magic lamp, are all considered metaphors for the Amanita muscaria. *Pharmacotheon* –by Jonathon Ott (Bauer 1991A; Heinrich 1995) and Arthur 2000.
[274] The story of the Holy Grail was started by Chretien de Troyes in the late 12th century in *Li Conte del Graal* ("The Story of the Grail"). Chretien also wrote the stories of King Arthur and the Knights of the Round Table based on Templar lore and older religious (pagan, Christian, and otherwise) stories of the cup and Eucharist worship.

Figure 61 - The Holy Grail - *Amanita muscaria*

74

We would like to call your attention back to the icon of Krishna and/or Jesus being crucified. The next stage of the mushroom is a table or (Tao) cross stage. The Tao cross (**T**) is the origin of the cross that Christians use today. The *Amanita* mushroom has a crown of thorns on top, a sash, and it is standing on one leg. The Christ character, or Krishna in this image (Figure 62), also stands with his arms up, a crown on his head and a sash around his waist.

Figure 62 - Crucifixion in Space

Figure 63 - Amanita muscaria - The Holy Grail

The opened cap represents the "female" portion of the mushroom--or the mushroom with one breast--or the red menstrual (*menstrual* from moon and star) blood. This is also the unison of intercourse with the white "male" stalk (stipe) of the mushroom which represents the white semen being secreted into the female cap, thereby creating all life. Before the scientific understanding of fertility, it was thought that the mixture of semen and menstrual blood, incubated in the blackness of the womb, is what created life.

The mushroom then continues up into the table stage, and finely into the cap, resembling a cup, as the mushroom raises its "arms" to form the *Holy Grail* (illustrated in Figure 63). This mushroom was and is symbolized often. Each characteristic of it was anthropomorphized from every perspective, from every stage of its growth cycle, and from every possible angle.

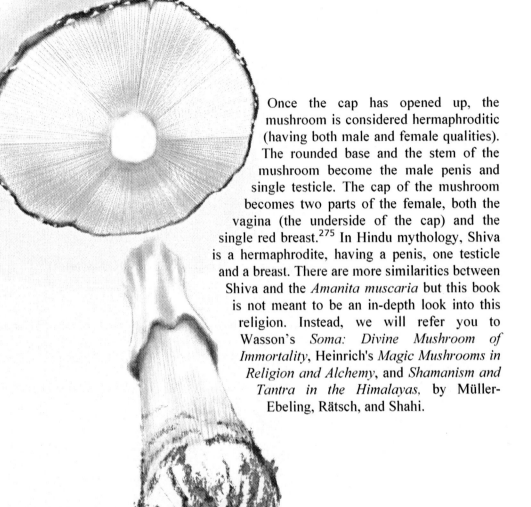

Once the cap has opened up, the mushroom is considered hermaphroditic (having both male and female qualities). The rounded base and the stem of the mushroom become the male penis and single testicle. The cap of the mushroom becomes two parts of the female, both the vagina (the underside of the cap) and the single red breast.[275] In Hindu mythology, Shiva is a hermaphrodite, having a penis, one testicle and a breast. There are more similarities between Shiva and the *Amanita muscaria* but this book is not meant to be an in-depth look into this religion. Instead, we will refer you to Wasson's *Soma: Divine Mushroom of Immortality*, Heinrich's *Magic Mushrooms in Religion and Alchemy*, and *Shamanism and Tantra in the Himalayas*, by Müller-Ebeling, Rätsch, and Shahi.

Figure 64 - Male and female qualities of the *Amanita muscaria*

---

[275] *The Sacred Mushroom and the Cross*, by John Allegro. The Bible makes several references to "red breast(s)" including Song of Solomon 4:5, "Thy two breasts are like two young roes that are twins, which feed among the lilies." In addition, Song of Solomon 7:3, "Thy two breasts are like two young roes that are twins." A roe is a red deer with white spots. See also Heinrich.

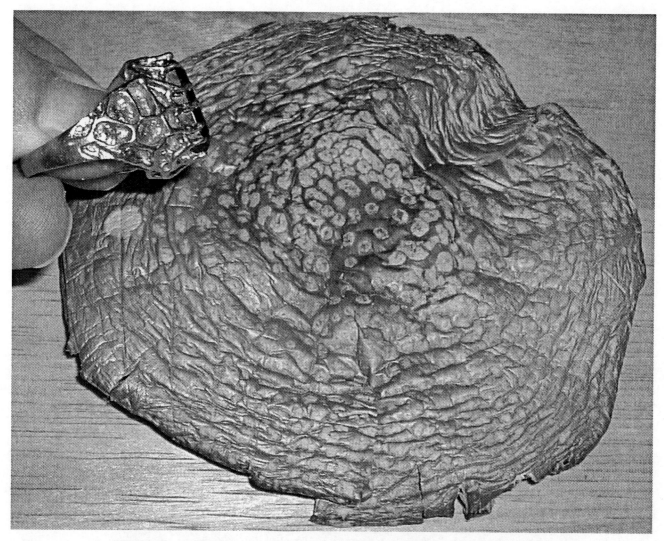

Figure 65 - Gold ring and a dried *Amanita* cap turning gold – Alchemical Gold

After the mushroom cap is upturned into its Holy Grail or chalice stage, it begins to die and rot away and one can see the different colors that it turns. It actually looks like the sun, like shimmering alchemical gold. The different colors range from bright metallic gold to a bleeding red. When the mushroom is found dried on the stem without rotting, it is the most prized finding by the shamanic cultures. Metaphorically speaking, Jesus is on the cross and his flesh is ready to be consumed.

The mushroom is Soma. In the stories, Soma is a bull. As the mushroom begins to dry, the leathery skin of Soma appears. These mushrooms turn brown and sometimes black when they are sun-dried. Most often, they resemble leather. At this stage, the mushroom can be reconstituted (or baptized in water, thus being "born again").[276]

As the Christian story goes, Christ, at the last supper, said to his disciples, "Take and eat, this is my body." Giving thanks, he then took the chalice and said, "Take and drink, this is the cup of my blood. Do this in *remembrance* of me" (Mt 26:26-27; 1 Cor 11:25). This interpolation of "remembrance" somehow gives the Church the right to hand out placebo crackers and grape juice (or a tiny shot of wine in some churches) instead of the real sacraments for their practice of theophagy.

Thomas 74
He said, "O lord, there are many around the drinking trough, but there is nothing in the cistern.

---

[276] *Magic Mushrooms in Religion and Alchemy*, by Clark Heinrich.

THE ORIGINS OF SACRIFICE

The words *sacrament* and *sacrifice* have the same origins and for good reason. When man decides to structure a society, he constructs laws and rules of conduct designed to mold the world into his image (or at least the image he wants it to be in). For the past 6000 years the laws in much of the world have been paternal, a society based on a male dominated social order.[277] The laws were made by man and for man, yet *not admittedly* by man. Instead, it is claimed these laws are authored by God <u>Himself</u>. Once the claim was made that the origins and authorship of laws was God, not man, there was no turning back. Humanity began a plummet into the abyss of guilt, fear, self-loathing, accusation and something called *eternal torment*. Therefore, the authorities realized that they needed to fabricate a way out. Once law was created, so came *sin* into the world. Along with sin, came guilt and the need for atonement. Sin against God must be punished by God. God created sin and the law. Consequently, it is God who must punish the sinner. This is all fantasy, but it becomes very real to the person who is experiencing the guilt of breaking *God's law*. Civilization cursed itself by the invention of these laws because they were not truly authored by God, but man. Man should never attempt to play God or claim to speak for God because that is a recipe for a disaster of historic proportions.[278]

The creation of law created the psychological need to be forgiven of sin, regardless of whether it is real or imagined. The first forms of atonement consisted of saying a prayer (reciting a spell) that would take all of the sins of the tribe and put them into a portion of their harvest. Then, they would burn it with fire. This burning of the sins somehow took them away. After a time, this sacrifice seemed inadequate. Their sins were too great. A living creature was given the sins and was slaughtered, one atonement each year for the tribes' sins. They invented laws such as the animal must be pure, without blemish, and other strange qualifications became part of the ceremony.[279] Soon, the insane leap of priestly wisdom ruled that the sacrifice of an animal was no longer adequate. The sins were too great. The sacrifice needed to be human! Following the origin of this abstract and abhorrent idea should make it clear that the concept is absurd and the social continuance of this crazy idea shows us how backward humans can be. Continuing in this insane direction, it only makes sense that the human sacrifice needed to be perfect, a virgin ("sinless"). Often, children were considered candidates for sacrifice because they were the most "unblemished" of all. This idea, some realized, had gotten way out of hand and so the idea developed that a god must incarnate and be put to death, taking upon himself the sins of the world *once and for all*. As silly as this concept is, it was readily accepted as a replacement for the yearly slaughter of children and loved members of the group. Years of a developing system geared humankind towards this and also sufficiently suppressed the logic that would normally cause one to object to the entire idea.[280] Kersey Graves in *The World's Sixteen Crucified Saviors* shows just how widespread this concept became. He explores 16 of these dying saviors and shows the similarities between them. It is baffling how popular such a bad idea became. When all is said and done, the true law of the universe is "love thy neighbor as thy self" because guilt for breaking this law is real. Only real remorse can receive true absolution. False guilt associated with false law can never be resolved because it is not real in the first place. It is a delusion. Whether talking about sin, guilt, or karma, all religions try to express the concept of setting oneself free. The big question is how to do it. We suggest those interested in further research to read *Saharasia*, by James DeMeo.[281]

---

[277] See *Saharasia*, by James DeMeo.

[278] Ibid.

[279] This is the origin of the Sacrificial Ram or Lamb. The peasants who could not afford these animals for sacrifice used goats as a replacement animal. Two goats were taken to a place of sacrifice. One was ritually slaughtered and the other was set free. The one that was killed was an offering to God. The other, the *escape goat*, carried away the sins of those who sacrificed it, hence the word scapegoat.

[280] For a deeper understanding of the underlying psychological and environmental issues at work here, see *Saharasia: The 4000 BCE Origins of Child Abuse, Sex-Repression, Warfare and Social Violence in the Deserts of the Old World*, by Dr. James DeMeo.

[281] Ibid.

SANTA CLAUS–CONDITIONING OUR YOUTH?

Figure 66

We would like to discuss for a moment how Santa Claus is being used as a key tool in the Christian conditioning of our youth.[282] It could be called brainwashing, but the ones who are doing the brainwashing think that they are doing the right thing.

Children are the churches' target audience and today's Santa is an ideal way to hook children into the God-fearing mindset. Santa gets kids mentally ready to accept an omniscient, omnipresent, and omnipotent God. This is something that would be very difficult to do without the proper conditioning at the proper age.

When kids ask what God looks like, they are often given a description of a man with a big beard, sitting on a throne in heaven. In the malls during Christmas time, one will likely find a man with a big beard, sitting on a throne. According to popular belief, Santa can do most of the things that "God" can do, and visa-versa..

Here is a Psalm (*139*) from the Bible that could easily describe Santa Claus:

> You see me, whether I am working or resting; you know all my actions.

Let us try to describe the Christian god in a way that may sound a bit more familiar:

> He sees you when you're sleeping. He knows when you're awake. He knows if you've been bad or good..." so be good or you'll go to hell and burn for eternity.

Santa has the ability to be everywhere at once. This is how he delivers presents to the billions of (good) children in the world in just one night. Therefore, God and Santa both have the power of omnipresence. God and Santa are also all-powerful (omnipotent) and have the ability to reward and punish. Santa rewards with toys and punishes naughty children by leaving them with nothing… or worse, a lump of coal.

The punishment drastically increases when the child graduates from Santa to the Christian god. Being naughty is then referred to as a sin and the punishment is much more severe than a lump of coal in their stocking.

However, according to Christianity, we are all naughty (or sinful). It is our nature. If you have been to a Christian church even one time, this following prayer should sound familiar. The church pounds this into the heads of millions of Christians as they chant this prayer together week after week, collectively brainwashing one another into believing that they are dirty sinners, in need of forgiveness:

> Most merciful God, we confess that <u>we are by nature sinful and unclean</u>. We have sinned against you in thought, word, and deed, by what we have done and by what we have left undone. We have not loved you with our whole heart; we have not loved our neighbors as ourselves. <u>We justly deserve Your present and eternal punishment</u>. For the sake of Your Son, Jesus Christ, <u>have mercy on us. Forgive us</u>, renew us, and lead us, so that we may delight in Your will and walk in Your ways to the glory of Your holy name.

---

[282] Ideas taken from an online article written by Gary Grassl.

Omniscience and performing miracles are the obvious similarities—both God and Santa know all of our actions, so in both cases we are to be good or will be punished. Furthermore, both God and Santa are the creators of the things for which we are most nostalgic. For a child, Santa, with the help of his elves, is the Creator of their toys. As we grow older and as we become more and more curious, children are told that Santa isn't real—but God is, and *He is* the creator of *everything*, the Great Architect of the Universe.

Teaching children to believe in Santa at a time when they believe everything that their parents tell them prepares their minds to accept this adult (male) god when they are older. Then children can easily be told that Santa is not real, but Jesus is, and their conditioned mind has no choice but to believe. We are not suggesting that there is no such thing as *God*. We are suggesting that the current concept of God is more than a bit twisted. The reality is that you are God. More on this later.

Often times, when parents tell their children that Santa is *not* a real person, they do this while assuring the child that Jesus *is* real, when in fact, the opposite is the truth. The actual story of Santa is very old, and almost everyone has heard of this character. Most countries today still include him in their winter solstice celebrations. Throughout the Ages, Santa was the shaman, and one can easily find many similarities between the shaman of the past and our Christmas traditions and holiday symbolism of today.

HOLIDAY SYMBOLISM

On many Christmas cards, you will find Santa Claus in a forest. Santa is said to live at the North Pole. What is he doing in a forest? Our traditions mention nothing of Santa Claus in a forest but we do bring a pine tree into our house and place red and white presents under it. So here is the connection to the forest, the mushroom, and Santa Claus.

When the *Amanita muscaria* is picked from the earth, the dirt or mud remaining on the base looks very much as though the mushroom has a single black foot.[283] The colors of the Great Work are red, white, and black. Santa Claus, this all-knowing and all-seeing deity for children, is red and white on top and he has black boots.

Figure 67 - The black foot of the *Amanita muscaria*

---

[283] *Apples of Apollo*, by Ruck, Staples, Heinrich, pg. 96-97; *Mushrooms and Mankind*, by Arthur.

Figure 68 - *Amanita muscaria* **Holiday Card**

The mushroom on this holiday card is winking, as if to convey a secret. Santa Claus is also often winking as if he too has a secret (or *is* a secret). The winking eye is very symbolic. On the macrocosm, the winking eye is the moon that appears to wink as it passes through its phases each month, the open eye being the sun.[284] On the microcosm, the winking eye is symbolic of a single eye, or the third eye inside your head.[285]

Odin, the holiest of the Norse gods, also "winks." Odin (also known as Othin, Wotan, Woden, Wuotan, Voden, or Votan) sacrificed one of his eyes so he could drink from the roots of the World Tree. Drinking from the roots of a tree will be discussed in the section entitled, "Living Water." Not unlike the winking Santa Claus, Odin is depicted as a man with long curly hair and a beard. This wink is symbolic of one eye looking out at the world while the other eye is looking into the soul.[286] This is a remarkable representation of shamanism: one eye looks into the heart or inner realms, while the other eye is used to navigate the world. The all-seeing-eye adopted by Freemasons and other occult orders also represents this internal vision.

Internal vision has puzzled humankind for a very long time. How is it possible to see inside one's mind when the eyes are closed? Dreams and visions are appointed religious significance because of their seemingly unexplainable and spontaneous occurrence. We now know that even spontaneous dreams and other visionary experiences are chemically induced. Naturally produced (endogenous) DMT is suggested to be one of these chemicals. The organ primarily responsible for many of these phenomena is suggested to be the pineal gland, or third eye.[287]

---

[284] *Symbols, Sex, and the Stars*, by Ernest Busenbark, pg. 52.
[285] See chapter 5.
[286] See James Arthur – radio interviews available online.
[287] See ch. 5, section on Opening the Temple Doors.

The person who designs the symbolic gowns that the Pope wears is an artist of sorts. On our web site[288], we have many pictures of popes wearing a white gown with a red cape draping over their shoulders. In one of those pictures, the pope is walking in the snow and the snow is making white spots on his red and white garb. Popes and Cardinals all throughout history have worn red and white clothes to be symbolic of their deity. When they would go behind the great curtain in the holiest of holies, and close the curtain off to the masses, we suggest that they were, at times, ingesting the mushrooms that they were anthropomorphizing with their garb and in other symbolism.

Figure 69 - Portrait of Innocent X - VELÁZQUEZ - 1650

This creates a separation between the people and the priests. It helps set the priests up on a higher level than the masses, and it allows them to wear intricate robes and big hats while making fancy claims that they are the only ones with a direct line to God. After all, if a Christian were in the hospital, which person would they rather have pray for them, their priest or their favorite actor? Somehow there is a false, indoctrinated psychology that a priest has God's ear more than you do. The question is, who benefits from this belief?

---

[288] http://www.gnosticmedia.com/eidetic.

Figure 70 - The Cardinal Infante (1639) and *Amanita muscaria*

Repeatedly, we see these Cardinals dressed like mushrooms, complete with a skirt, red (or black) cap and black shoes. Knowing that the *Amanita muscaria* mushroom is symbolized by the Phoenix, taking this a step further we know that the Phoenix is a red bird, Cardinals in nature are red birds and the "Cardinals" in the Catholic Church dress exactly like the *Amanita muscaria* mushroom. On the macrocosm, these Cardinals represent the four *cardinal* points. In ancient times, these points were marked by the stars Fomalhaut, Aldebaran, Regulus, and Antares and are now marked by the solstices as Capricorn in the winter, Cancer in the summer and at the Equinoxes (equal nights) as Aries in the spring, and Libra in the winter *without* regard to the actual constellations.[289] Again and again, we see these mushrooms (and the celestial bodies) being anthropomorphized by the same people who were trying to prophesize the teachings of the mushrooms and tell the story of the cycle of our cosmos.

---

[289] *Stellar Theology and Masonic Astronomy*, by Robert Hewitt Brown; *Symbols, Sex and the Stars*, by Ernest Busenbark.

Figure 71 - Ezekiel's Dream

Ezekiel had a dream after a thunderstorm and in this dream, he was told to eat something several times. "Eat this scroll" is what he was told to do.

Ezekiel 1: 1, 4-6, 15

1 Now it came to pass in the thirteenth year, in the fourth month, in the fifth day of the month, as I was among the captives by the river of Chebar, that the heavens were opened, and I saw visions of God...

4 And I looked, and, behold, a whirlwind came out of the north, a great cloud, and a fire infolding itself, and a brightness was about it, and out of the midst thereof as the colour of amber, out of the midst of the fire.

5 Also out of the midst thereof came the likeness of four living creatures. And this was their appearance; they had the likeness of a man.

6 And every one had four faces, and every one had four wings...

15 Now as I beheld the living creatures, behold one wheel upon the earth by the living creatures, with his four faces.

84

Ezekiel 3: 1-14

And he said to me, "Son of man, **eat what is before you**, **eat this scroll**; then go and speak to the house of Israel."

So I opened my mouth, and he gave me the scroll to eat.

Then he said to me, "Son of man, **eat this scroll** I am giving you and fill your stomach with it." So I ate it, and it tasted as sweet as honey in my mouth.

He then said to me: "Son of man, go now to the house of Israel and speak my words to them.

You are not being sent to a people of obscure speech and difficult language, but to the house of Israel—

not to many peoples of obscure speech and difficult language, whose words you cannot understand. Surely if I had sent you to them, they would have listened to you.

But the house of Israel is not willing to listen to you because they are not willing to listen to me, for the whole house of Israel is hardened and obstinate.

But I will make you as unyielding and hardened as they are.

I will make your forehead like the hardest stone, harder than flint. Do not be afraid of them or terrified by them, though they are a rebellious house."

And he said to me, "Son of man, listen carefully and take to heart all the words I speak to you.

Go now to your countrymen in exile and speak to them. Say to them, 'This is what the Sovereign LORD says, whether they listen or fail to listen.'"

Then the Spirit lifted me up, and I heard behind me a loud rumbling sound—May the glory of the LORD be praised in his dwelling place!—

the sound of the wings of the living creatures brushing against each other and the sound of the wheels beside them, a loud rumbling sound.

The Spirit then lifted me up and took me away, and I went in bitterness and in the anger of my spirit, with the strong hand of the LORD upon me.

Upon eating this mysterious *something*, the spirit of the lord lifted Ezekiel up and he then went to speak to the house of *Israel*.

Amanita mushrooms go through a chemical process as they dry. This process is necessary, for most people, before ceremonial ingestion. In other words, they *must* be dried in order for them to work. The reason that we want to dry the mushrooms out is that they contain Ibotenic acid, which is a mild toxin to the human body. By drying the mushrooms out, the Ibotenic acid is converted (decarboxylated) into muscimol, which is a psychoactive substance that our bodies can safely digest.[290]

Figure 72 - Dried *Amanita muscaria*

One of the practices of drying the mushrooms would be to place them in stockings and hang the stockings over the hearth of the fireplace overnight. What was poisonous or unusable that night becomes, by morning, a nice present after hanging over the warm fire, and is ready for consumption during the winter solstice celebrations.

The ancient shamans of Siberia would gather enough mushrooms for the entire *community* and have a *communion*. These ancient shamans would go to the houses of the people in the community in celebration of the winter solstice and deliver the mushroom to them and guide them through the experience... it was their yearly tradition. This is where Santa comes from. The shaman, often dressing in the red and white colors of the *Amanita* and carrying a huge bag full of the same red and white mushrooms that he or she had picked and dried during the previous season (enough for the entire community), would go door to door and give the community the mushroom experience.

When these mushrooms grow, they do so in flushes, many at a time, and the shaman would gather as many as possible because they do not grow all year round.

Figure 73 - Kamtchatka Shamaness - Photo by Manny and Jason Salzmann

---

[290] Hawk and Venus, the authors of *Soma Shamans*, recommend eating the *Amanita* raw. However, their ability to eat the mushrooms raw is likely due to tolerance buildup from near daily use over many years. Eating Amanita raw goes against the overall majority of anthropological research and science on *Amanita muscaria*. Their technique is NOT something we recommend for beginners, and we caution those who follow their work.

These mushrooms grow to be large and quite heavy when they are wet. The ideal practice would be to dry these mushrooms out in the field before bringing them home. This way, the mushrooms are not as heavy when they are carried, and those on the bottom of the bag or basket won't be destroyed by the weight of those on the top. After all, forty pounds of dry mushrooms are going to be much greater in quantity than forty pounds of wet mushrooms.

Figure 74 - *Amanita* drying on a pine tree

The mushrooms are dried in the sun before the shaman returns home with them. One way to do this is to find a tree in a central location and hang the mushrooms on the tree and let them dry out in the boughs or the branches of the tree while the shaman continues to hunt for more mushrooms.[291] After a period, all these mushrooms hanging in the tree resemble a decorated Christmas tree. It appears as though the pine tree is bearing fruit. It can even look as though candles have been placed throughout the tree, with the red cap representing the flame and the stipe, the candle itself. Today, like the modern Easter celebrations, most who celebrate Christmas do not use these mushrooms in their traditions, but they do continue to use the symbolism of the mushrooms in many ways. In the Middle Ages, when alchemy was at its peak, mystery plays often featured decorated trees. The church did not like this. Although they compromised at first, they soon forbade the tree ritual altogether. How they compromised was interesting, to say the least. They added holy Eucharistic wafers to the ornaments on the tree.[292] Just as the shamans did, they decorated the tree with their sacred meal.

[291] Arthur, 2002.
[292] *When Santa was a Shaman,* by Tony van Renterghem.

Figure 75 - Shaman entering yurt through the chimney

Once the winter solstice had arrived, the shaman would go out into the local community and deliver these dried mushrooms to each of the tribe members. Because of the cold Siberian climate, the main entrance into the Siberian homes (known as yurts) would often be snowed over, so everyone in the family must climb up to the roof and enter through the secondary or winter entrance, the chimney.[293] Santa Claus, or the shaman bearing the bag of goodies, would enter the yurt through the smoke hole. This is where the symbology originated.[294]

Figure 76

Santa Claus is not always red and white. Santa Claus or Father Christmas, or the shaman, would dress in clothing resembling the plants that were available in their local vicinity. The darker colored Santa Claus is actually representing a different mushroom. It is not the *A. muscaria* that this darker colored Santa represents, but the *Amanita pantherina*.

---

[293] See Patrick Harding for more information.
[294] *The Long Trip*, by Paul Devereux, pg. 72 (1997), referencing Rogan Taylor, 1980/1994 1-4; See also *Mushrooms and Mankind,* by James Arthur (2000).

Figure 77 - Ouroboros

It had no need of eyes, for there was nothing outside it to be seen; nor of ears, for there was nothing outside it to be heard. There was no surrounding air to be breathed, nor was it in need of any organ by which to supply itself with food or to get rid of it when digested. Nothing went out from or came into it anywhere, for there was nothing. Of design it was made thus, its own waste providing its own food, acting and being acted upon entirely within and by itself, because its designer considered that a being which was sufficient unto itself would be far more excellent than one which depended upon anything.
~ Plato

This is a description of one of the greatest mystical symbols in alchemy: the ouroboros. It needs nothing. It is a symbol of the eternal life. The word *ouroboros* comes from the Greek *"ouron"* (*to make water*), and is the source of the English word "urine," as well as the name of the constellation of Orion[295] on the macrocosm. The ouroboros is symbolized by a snake biting its own tail, and often it is represented as a winged dragon above a serpent, both biting one another's tails. In Norse mythology, the sea serpent "Jormungand" grew so big that he was able to surround the earth and grasp his own tail. In the heavens, the ouroboros is the Milky Way, appearing to wrap itself around the earth like a serpent. In this respect, the ouroboric serpent it is known as Leviathan.[296]

The symbol for the ouroboros can also be found in Christianity. What is interesting in Figure 78 is not that the All-Seeing Eye is representing God or that the Holy Spirit is the bird, but that Jesus is represented by a snake, the ouroboros.

---

[295] *Apples of Apollo*, by Ruck, Heinrich, Staples, pg. 74.
[296] *Suns of God*, by Acharya S.

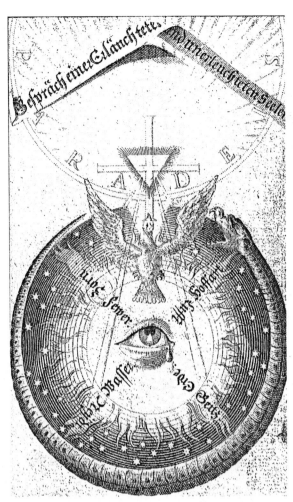

Figure 78 - Bohem – Amsterdam, 1682 [297]

The ouroboros and it biting its tail continues. On the macrocosm it represents the cyclic motion of the sun. In the winter, like a serpent shedding its skin and being "reborn," so too is the sun reborn on Dec. 25th. From Dec. 21st to the 25th, the sun is metaphorically "shedding its skin," like a serpent, to be born anew in the cycle of life. On the microcosm, the mushroom dies and is reborn of a virgin in its own ashes in the continuous cycle of the phoenix. Furthermore, as the cap of the *Amanita muscaria* pushes its way through the universal veil, it appears to be a red snake, shedding its white skin (Figure 56, plates B–D). Upon consumption of the body of this mushroom/deity and the waters of life (as described over the next few pages), one becomes "en-light-ened," or "brought into the light," as from the light of the sun and the light of knowledge, thus metaphorically ending the wheel (cycle) of life, and opening the third eye. The All-Seeing Eye of God is further depicted here as a solar eclipse with the light of the sun (the ouroboric serpent) illuminating from behind the moon (the eye). In this respect, the All-Seeing Eye of God peers down from the heavens.

The mythological dragon has its origin in Egypt. Winged serpents known as *cacodaemons* were associated with evil to the Babylonians and the Chaldeans, while the *agathodaemon* is associated with good fortune, life and health. It is obvious that there are good and bad serpents in philosophic dualism. In alchemy, the winged serpent represents the unity of "as above so below" and shows the accomplishment of the principal of unification. The dragon and the snake are both symbolic representations of the *Amanita muscaria* mushroom in alchemy and various mythologies. The proverbial *dragon slayer* is the victorious initiate over the mushroom experience.

In alchemical poetry, there is a story of a poisonous dragon which inhabits forests and that is exactly what the *A. muscaria* is, a poisonous dragon found at the forest floor:

A poisonous dragon inhibits the forest,
Yet lacks nothing:
When he sees the sun and its fire,
He scatters his poison and flies upward fiercely:

Neither can the Basilisk[298] master him,
For the dragon knows well how to kill the serpent.

It struggles with all and yet is nothing.
His color increases with death,
And from his venom can be made medicine.

He consumes the poison completely,
Devouring his envenomed tail.

This consumed,
The noblest Balm comments from within himself,
Providing the gift of youth.

This greatly pleases all the wise.
This surely is a great marvel and wonder,
when the best Balm flows from the dragon's ill.[299]

---

[297] Bohem, Amsterdam, 1682.

[298] The name basilisk comes from the Greek basileus, which means king. The basilisk was the King of the snakes and the most poisonous creature on earth. According to legend, it was able to kill with its breath or glance.

Mercury, precipitated and sublimated properly by chemistry, is dissolved in its own water and re-coagulated...the Greek god Mercury bears the symbol of the caduceus, which will be discussed in a moment.[300,301]

There is also a story in alchemical texts of two birds that are the colors of the *A. muscaria*, resemble the ouroboros, and become the Phoenix:

> There is a forest in India
> Where two birds are bound together;
> One is white, the other red.
>
> Together they bite themselves to death,
> And one completely devours the other.
>
> Both then change into a white dove,
> from this dove will be born the Phoenix.[302]

The dove is a *white* bird with *red* eyes, but more on the dove in a moment.

> Proverbs 5:15
> ...drink water from your own cistern. Running water from your own well.

> John 7:37-38
> ...in the last day, that great day of the feast, Jesus stood and cried, saying, if any man thirst, let him come unto me, and drink. He that believeth on me, as the scripture hath said, out of his belly shall flow rivers of living water.

What could this be talking about, where you *drink from your own cistern* and *running water from your own well*? We have rivers of living water flowing out of our own belly?

The Hebrew name "Moses" means "to draw out (of water)." It is the Hebrew word "Mosheh" and when one understands what it means to "draw out," you understand one of the fundamental basics towards becoming an alchemist.

The Siberian shamans were also reindeer herders. It is a little known fact that the reindeer's favorite snack is the *A. muscaria* mushroom. In Greek Olympic mythology, the sacred olive branch is said to derive from a reindeer's antler from the Hyperborians of the north, where the olive does not grow. As Ruck, Staples, and Heinrich suggest in *Apples of Apollo*, this could be a reference to the reindeer and the Siberian mushroom shamanism.[303]

Reindeer are known to do some interesting things when they are around the *A. muscaria*. One thing the reindeer are known to do, other than just eat the mushroom, is that they are known to go mad in order to get to the mushrooms. They are also known to drink the urine of other reindeer, and even the urine of the shaman after either has consumed these mushrooms. The shamans were even known to use the *A. muscaria* on the end of a stick (a proverbial carrot) to entice reindeer to work.[304]

---

[299] *The Modern Alchemist*, by Richard and Iona Miller, referencing *The Book of Lambsprinck*, a sixteenth-century alchemical text by the German mystic "Lambsprinck."
[300] *Alchemy & Mysticism*, by Alexander Roob.
[301] *Worship of the Serpent*, by John Bathurst Deane, 1830.
[302] *The Modern Alchemist*, by Richard and Iona Miller, referencing *The Book of Lambsprinck*, a sixteenth-century alchemical text by the German mystic "Lambsprinck."
[303] *Apples of Apollo*, by Ruck, Staples, Heinrich, pg. 32.
[304] Ibid, pg. 106.

Thomas 108
Jesus said, "He who will drink from my mouth[305] will become like me. I myself shall become he, and the things that are hidden will be revealed to him.

The shamans knew that the mushrooms contained a toxin (Ibotenic acid) that would make them sick. Once the mushroom has been filtered through the body, its undesirable properties are removed, leaving a higher potency of *Amanita* in the urine. By observing the practices of the deer, the shamans learned the practice of drinking their own urine. It is also very likely that the shamans themselves would drink the urine of the deer, because urine of the deer would have already filtered out the poisonous Ibotenic acid from the mushroom. Eating meat of a reindeer that had eaten *Amanitas* might prove to be another way mushroom inebriation was achieved. We suspect that "shamanic farming" techniques were common practice. Other proponents of this idea have included Heinrich, as well as a number of unpublished shamans.

This concept may not be limited to reindeer meat, but chickens (eggs included) and other farm animals (meat and milk) as well. All of this gives the shaman the option to eat the mushrooms, get the sweats and the shakes, feel sick and then re-uptake their urine for better results. Or the shaman could avoid the ill effects altogether and just drink the urine of the reindeer (or other shamans) that have all ready undergone this process.

Koryak, for example, learned empirically that the hallucinogenic effects of the mushroom pass into a man's urine. As a result, men waited outside a house where the plant was being consumed in order to collect the urine of a user in special wood containers. The process was repeatable for five cycles before the drug began losing its potency. It is possible that the Siberian herdsmen learned about the relationship between the mushroom and its lingering effects in urine from their reindeer.... Every Koryak man carries a vessel made of seal skin, which he suspends from his belt as a container to catch his own urine. This is done as a means of attracting refractory reindeer. Sometimes, a reindeer will run to the camp from faraway pastures to drink urine-saturated snow, which appears to be a delicacy for them.... When reindeer eat the fly agaric mushrooms, which is not an infrequent occurrence, they behave in a drunken fashion, falling into a deep sleep... if a Koryak encountered an intoxicated animal, he would tie its legs and not kill it until the drunkenness wore off. The Koryaks claimed that if one killed an animal while it was intoxicated, the effects of the fungus would be felt by all who ate the meat.[306]
~ Marlene Dobkin de Rios

It is well known that the urine of humans who have eaten Fly Agaric [*Amanita muscaria*] becomes in itself hallucinogenic. Among some Siberian populations it was customary to drink the urine of those who had drugged themselves with the mushroom to attain an even greater degree of intoxication, **reputedly more powerful than that achieved by eating the mushroom itself**. Even reindeer "go mad" for the urine of other reindeer or human beings who have ingested the hallucinogen. In fact, it would seem that the Siberian peoples discovered its inebriating properties by observing the behavior of the reindeer.[307] [bold—ours]
~ Giorgio Samorini

Reindeer, as it happens, have an inordinate fondness for *Amanita muscaria* and will eat it whenever they find it, either until there is no more or until they fall over in a trance, whichever comes first...Reindeer will also nearly trample one another to eat the *golden snow* created when, after eating their fill of mushrooms, they urinate.[308]
~ Ruck, Staples, Heinrich

It is muscimole that holds the pharmacological key to the urine-drinking custom. Muscimole, they [Eugster -1967, Waser 1967 & 71] discovered, is an unsaturated cyclic hydroxamic acid that secrets through the kidneys in basically unaltered form.[309]
~ Peter T. Furst

---

[305] Mouth – The opening to any cavity or canal in an organ or a bodily part.
[306] *Hallucinogens: Cross-Cultural Perspectives*, by Marlene Dobkin de Rios, pg. 32.
[307] *Animals and Psychedelics*, by Giorgio Samorini, pg. 39.
[308] *Apples of Apollo*, by Ruck, Staples, and Heinrich, pg. 51.
[309] *Hallucinogens and Culture*, by Peter T. Furst, pg. 93.

This process is also known throughout esoteric sciences as *alchemical transmutation* and *transubstantiation*. When the oxygen and carbon atoms are removed from a compound, it has been decarboxylated. This is exactly what happens in the body. When you decarboxylate this Ibotenic acid, the compound becomes muscimol (the psychedelic substance that the shaman is seeking). The first way to decarboxylate the *Amanita* is to dry it. Heating and drying cause decarboxylation, as the shamans knew that fresh mushrooms should not be eaten.

Otherwise, one may suffer the unpleasant effects of Ibotenic acid. This mushroom can be passed from one person to another by recycling (re-uptaking, drinking) the urine of someone who has eaten the mushrooms or consumed already active urine. The secret to alchemy and the consumption of the *Amanita* is the taking of the urine and recycling the mushrooms through the body. It is considered nothing short of miraculous by those interested in *Amanitas* that each time you recycle it, it becomes more desirable.[310] The heat and digestive process in the body also decarboxylates any remaining Ibotenic acid and each time you process it through your body, it is further purified into the perfect *elixir*. The ouroboros is the mushroom recycling through the body, represented symbolically as a snake eating its tail.

In recycling the mushroom-infused water, out of your belly flow rivers of *living* water. The shaman is quite literally turning water into wine. Now we understand this bizarre passage found in the book of John 7:38, "out of his belly shall flow **rivers of living water**." It totally puts into perspective "drinking from the roots of a tree," as the shaman is drinking an elixir produced from mushrooms, which attach to the roots of a tree. This understanding also sheds new light on "drinking from your own cistern." A *cistern* is a receptacle for holding water or other liquid. In anatomy, a *cisterna* is a fluid-containing sac or cavity in the body. This understanding sheds new light on the biblical story of the woman at the well. Jesus went to a well to fetch some water. He asked a Samaritan woman at the well, who was carrying a pitcher of water on her head, to give Him some water to drink:

> John 4:9-10 (KJV)
> Then saith the woman of Samaria unto him, How is it that thou, being a Jew, askest drink of me, which am a woman of Samaria? for the Jews have no dealings with the Samaritans. Jesus answered and said unto her, If thou knewest the gift of God, and who it is that saith to thee, Give me to drink; thou wouldest have asked of him, and he would have given thee living water.

The human organs separate toxins out of the body by expelling them through the sweat, breath and feces. Wedged into the fabric of dualism, our bodies separate the good from bad, as the beneficial substances like vitamins and antibodies are suggested to be filtered into the urine. Of particular interest is the fact that the organs send antibodies produced by the immune system to the urine. Urine is completely non-toxic, sterile. Since the urine contains antibodies, it is reported to give a specialized boost for an individual's immune system.[311] With the current trend of the emerging diseases attacking people from every direction, this practice, if correct, could be more valuable than ever, and this "drinkable gold" is infinitely more valuable to a sick person than the base gold could ever be. The human body is miraculous indeed in its design.

Armed with the knowledge of the shaman and alchemist, "living water" makes perfect sense. In this story, the Jesus character is an alchemist. The woman in the story goes on to ask Jesus, "you have nothing to draw with and the well is deep. Where can you get this living water?" He replies to her saying, "Everyone who drinks *this* water will be thirsty again, but whoever drinks the water I give him will never thirst. Indeed, the water I give him will become in him a spring of water welling up to eternal life."[312] It will become in him a spring of water welling up to eternal life.... Again, notice that the living water is *in you*. After consuming the mushroom (the body of Christ), the living water is in your own *cistern*, and "Out of your belly shall flow rivers of living water."

---

[310] It is said that this recycling process works at least 5 times before losing potency. See *Hallucinogens*, by de Rios, pg. 32.
[311] See *Golden Fountain : The Complete Guide to Urine Therapy*, by Coen Van Der Kroon and Volker Moritz.
[312] Jesus Talks With a Samaritan Woman – NIV.

THE CADUCEUS

Figure 79 - Goddess as Caduceus symbol

The Goddesses, as well as women in general, have been suppressed in this modern day, alpha-male-god society. This goddess[313] is depicted standing on top of a primordial mound, with her feet together and arms outstretched, two snakes climbing her body, wings on her back, and a crown with seven points on her head. This posture is exactly as other deities stand during their crucifixion. Her crown of *seven* is a representation of the seven chakras on the microcosm, the seven planets, and the seven stars of the Pleiades on the macrocosm. Often, Libertas will be seen with the symbol of a staff with snakes climbing it and wings at the top.[314]

> Amos 5:7-8
> Ye who turn judgment to wormwood[315], and leave off righteousness in the earth, Seek him that maketh the seven stars [Pleiades] and Orion, and turneth the shadow of death into the morning, and maketh the day dark with night: that calleth for the waters of the sea, and poureth them out upon the face of the earth...

This symbol (Figure 80) is called the **caduceus** and is the serpent-entwined staff that is used as a symbol for healing and drugs today. There are primarily two types of caducei—the single snake entwined around a simple staff, and the winged-staff entwined by two serpents. The symbols are also associated with the world tree, the Tree of Life, the Tree of Knowledge of Good and Evil, the Axis Mundi, the cross, and other symbols. According to Arthur:

> ...the caduceus is the symbol of pharmaceutical drugs and the Mark of the Beast. You must have the mark to "buy or sell" drugs. This is a worldwide system encapsulating all drugs, including the covert black market. The seal (mark) of God (also found in the book of Revelation) is also the caduceus. This represents all plants and drugs, especially the psychedelics. In particular, at the deepest level, the Seal of God represents both *Amanita* and *Psilocybe* mushrooms in the body at one time.... The seal of God delivered by the angel is exactly this; Taking *Amanita* and *Psilocybe* together.[316] [For more on this, see page 151.]

---

[313] www.jamesmuir.com.

[314] Arthur, *She Who Remembers* audio archives.

[315] Wormwood is used in the making of the psychedelic drink called absinthe as well as vermouth.

[316] See Arthur, *Mushrooms and Mankind* (2000).

Figure 80 - The Caduceus

The caduceus symbol has been notorious with thieves, merchants, and messengers. We're told thru our myths that sometimes the gods will communicate with us. And the medium thru which they do this is always Mercury. Mercury is the messenger[317] (logos) of the gods, just as the entheogens are. Mercury, carrying the caduceus, is said to be the patron of thieves and outlaws. This is not necessarily a desirable symbol for a doctor of medicine, but may explain why new casinos in Las Vegas place them above, or often near their main entrances.[318]

This caduceus symbol is the symbol for modern day medicine. Today, one cannot practice medicine without the authority of the symbol. Chiropractors and EMT's for example, are represented by the symbol of one serpent on the staff while a medical doctor's symbol has two. Those represented with one serpent on the staff cannot administer drugs to people, while those who carry the symbol with two snakes may.

It is important to know that the symbol of the caduceus (the symbol of drugs) is the same today as it was thousands years ago. We can find this same symbol representing drugs and representing the pharmacopoeia in nearly every society on earth. Whether it was the Native Americans, the South Americans, the Africans and the Egyptians, in the Middle East, in Asia or in Europe, this symbol for drugs was ubiquitous.[319] Often, when the caduceus itself was not represented, two cornucopias would take its place.

---

[317] The planet Mercury was called the "messenger" because of its rapid movement through the sky. Busenbark, pg. 280.
[318] In the summer of 2004 we took a trip to Las Vegas and found that nearly all new casinos (designed by large corporations) used the same symbology. The older casinos contain much less symbolism in comparison.
[319] Arthur, *Coast to Coast* radio interview with George Noory.

These horns-of-plenty (Figure 81) represent the entire bounty of plants. On one side, there are the plants that are harvested and consumed as food. On the other side, there are the plants that are used as medicines and for spiritual practices. For further reading on the cornucopia of pharmacy, a.k.a. "pharmacopia," we highly recommend, *Pharmako/Poeia: Plants Powers, Poisons, and Herbcraft* by Dale Pendell.

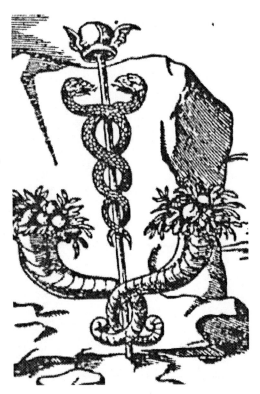

Figure 81 - Caduceus and Cornucopia

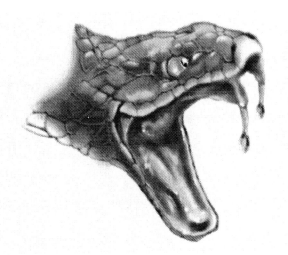

Snake venom is not strictly poisonous. There are reports about snake venom producing pleasant visionary experiences as well.[320] Snake venom has also been used medicinally for millennia. The caduceus is a perfect symbol for allopathic medicine because it is based upon poisons being taken into the body in the hopes that the medicine will kill the disease before it kills the host.

Figure 82 - Snake Venom

Poisonous creatures have long been assigned allegiance with evil through mythological stereotyping. These include spiders, scorpions, and especially snakes. The Egyptian god Apophis, the Celtic serpent gnawing away on the world tree, and the biblical "that old serpent which is the Devil and Satan" (Revelation 20) are but a few examples. Snakes permeate religious lore because they can kill with poison. Death and disease are associated with evil. Decay, decomposition and rot are similarly aligned. Molds, fungus, decomposing mushrooms and maggots also fall into this category. Since maggots eat decaying human bodies from the inside out, they have maintained a particular stigma. They resemble tiny snakes and Egyptians indeed regarded maggots as tiny serpents.

The venom of serpents has been used in healing throughout human history. In Persia, the forces of good and evil were depicted as two serpents locked in an eternal conflict fighting for control over the cosmic egg, the souls of man, and all of creation. These are the spirits of light and darkness engaged in an eternal struggle for control over the dualistic universe.

---

[320] *The Christ Conspiracy*, by Acharya S, pg. 186. Also the Bufo Alvarius frog emits a powerful psychedelic drug (5 methoxy N,N DMT) in its venom. *Shamanism and Tantra in the Himalayas*, by Rätsch, et al.

Mushrooms are also associated with serpents, particularly the *Amanita muscaria,* due to its habitat, poisonous qualities, shape, and white patches on the cap that resemble previously shed skin. These mushrooms are shaped like snakes that pop out of the ground, like snakes appearing out of holes in the ground. After the mushroom finishes its lifecycle and rots, it is eaten by maggots[321] and disappears as quickly as it came.

Job 7:4-5
When I lie down, I say, When shall I arise, and the night be gone? and I am full of tossings to and fro unto the dawning of the day. My flesh is clothed with worms and clods of dust; my skin is broken, and become loathsome.

Exodus 16:19-21
And Moses said, Let no man leave of it[322] till the morning. Notwithstanding they hearkened not unto Moses; but some of them left of it until the morning, and it bred worms, and stank: and Moses was wroth with them. And they gathered it every morning, every man according to his eating: and when the sun waxed hot, it melted.

As the mushroom "melts," the only things left behind are the spores and the hole where the mushroom formerly stood. Aside from their physical resemblance to snakes, mushrooms share another characteristic. They can kill with their poison or produce visions with their chemical makeup. If a snake bites you, you have one very important question on your mind: "Is it poisonous"? This is the same question one should ask when finding any mushroom in the wild that could be ingested… the very question that sent Gordon Wasson and his wife on a life-changing journey. Mushrooms, like snakes, have received quite a reputation around the world as a deadly thing that can also heal.[323, 324, 325]

Figure 83 - Minerva with Liberty Cap on chest

Figure 84 - Detail of Minerva's Liberty Cap

Figure 85 - Phrygian cap on coin - Circa 16th century

---

[321] *Apples of Apollo,* by Ruck, Staples, Heinrich, pg. 134.
[322] Manna.
[323] *Pharmacotheon,* by Jonathon Ott – The use of muscimol as medication in Germany.
[324] *The Sacred Mushroom and the Cross,* by John Allegro.
[325] *Soma; Divine Mushroom of Immortality,* by Gordon Wasson.

As a rule, the "Liberty Cap" is depicted as a long staff with what appears to be a Phrygian cap[327] hanging from the top. The Psilocybe semilanceata mushroom is also referred to as the liberty cap. That is a psilocybin-containing, entheogenic mushroom. These mushrooms are called liberty caps and they look exactly like the "Liberty caps" that Minerva is seen with.

Figure 86 - Psilocybe semilanceata - Liberty Cap mushroom[326]

We often find this same Phrygian cap in other symbols such as flags or military emblems, on coins and included in many statues over the centuries. The cap, torch, and serpent are all implements of the female personification of America, Libertas (lady-Liberty). The origin of the name *America* is Mayan, it comes from the word *Amaruca*, "Land of the Plumed Serpents."[328] A "plume" is a large feather or cluster of feathers. Thus, the "Plumed Serpent" is the "winged serpent," a.k.a. the caduceus.

Figure 87

---

[326] Photo by John W. Allen
[327] *Oxford English Dictionary*: Applied to a conical cap or bonnet with the peak bent or turned over in front, worn by the ancient Phrygians, and in modern times identified with the 'cap of liberty.'
[328] James Pyrse researched an article written in the Theosophical Society magazine entitled *Lucifer*, which gave insight into the word "America." James Pyrse says that the chief god of the Mayan Indians in Central America was Quetzalcoatl. In Peru, this god was called Amaru and the territory known as Amaruca. He states "Amaruca is literally translated "Land of the Plumed Serpents p. 45." – Dr. Lee Warren, B.A., D.D.; To this day, the tribe of Amaru exists in Peru.

~ Chapter Five ~
Climbing the Ladder to Godhead

Figure 88 - Nativity panel from Grabow Altarpiece – circa 1383, Bertram

Luke 1:27
> To a virgin espoused to a man whose name was Joseph, of the house of David; and the virgin's name was Mary.

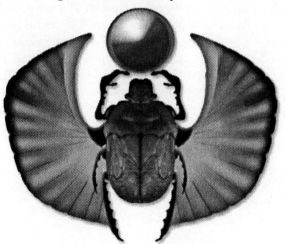

Figure 89 - Scarab Beetle

BORN OF A VIRGIN

Not only Christianity, but also most every ancient mythology and tradition teaches that each respective deity was born of a virgin. Below, we have described several examples of different types of virgins, these virgin types were often used interchangeably.

In Christian stories, Jesus was born of the Virgin Mary. Mary was a *virgin* in the most common usage of the word, meaning that she had not yet experienced coitus. Throughout antiquity, artists would try to show that Mary was a virgin without the use of words. One will often notice that Mary is a young girl and Joseph is often an old man with a gray beard. Why would this young girl be having relations with such an old man? The artists are utilizing psychology in their art to show Mary's virginity and to suppress the notion of sexual union as a prerequisite to pregnancy. The female virgin is the first and most obvious type of virgin.

This scarab beetle is also seen by many as having a virginal birth. In ancient times, people did not realize that the beetle mated before it created a ball of dung that it would roll around. The beetle would then impregnate this dung-ball with a single egg, which would feed on the dung until it hatched from the dung-ball. Its life of rolling this ball of dung on the ground is a microcosmic representation of the sun being pushed across the sky, a representation of the up-stretched arms of the Holy Grail reaching for the sun disk, also representing the mushroom, as previously described.

Now that you are aware of the macro/microcosm relationship in the symbology of the sun disk, notice the "feathers" or wings of the beetle representing the cap and striations of the mushroom. This is important symbology to notice as one continues with this research.

The microcosmic, dualistic nature of the scarab beetle (as a beetle and a as phoenix) also symbolically reveals the respective natures of the two primary mushrooms of worship, the *Amanitas* and *Psilocybe*. The scarab beetle rolls balls of dung, assisting in the proliferation of several species of dung-loving fungi. The phoenix, too, is associated with the sun and particularly, the *Amanita*/phoenix is the sun of the microcosm, the earthly embodiment of the solar orb – ruler of the macrocosm. The similarities between the scarab and the phoenix lead us to conclude that due to its relationship to dung, the scarab beetle is representative of the *Psilocybe*, while the fiery red phoenix is symbolic of the *Amanita*.

The phoenix also has a virginal birth, as it is born from ashes. The phoenix will never live to leave its nest, for as it lifts its wings in attempt to fly, it bursts into flames and engulfs itself, leaving nothing behind but its own ashes and the cycle continues. This whole story is a metaphor describing the detailed lifecycle of the mushroom, particularly the *Amanita muscaria* mushroom. When the *Amanita* mushrooms are picked carefully, the stipe and the bulbous base come out of the pine needles that have been surrounding it. It leaves behind what appears to be a nest after the mushroom is removed from the ground. This nest of pine needles appears to be covered with ashes (white mushroom spores), so is the nest of the Phoenix.[329] The ashes are actually the spores of the mushroom that are sprinkled all over the ground below the mushroom when the universal veil is torn and the gills are exposed. When the gills are exposed, they are symbolically the *wings* of the mushroom and the wings of the Phoenix. When these gills present themselves (or when the Phoenix first spreads its wings) the white ash-like spores rain on the pine needles below and like the phoenix, the mushroom's next stage is death.[330]

Another type of virgin birth is that of the pearl and shell. The pearl symbolized God's semen, which formed a pearl inside an Oyster shell. The "birth" of this rare pearl was seen as a virginal birth. The pearl is synonymous with the entire concept of the virgin and is quite common in Christian artwork and architecture.

> Job 28:18
> No mention shall be made of coral, or of pearls: for the price of wisdom is above[331] rubies.

Pearls are white, rubies are red and the *wisdom*, or the drug, comes *from out of* (above) the cap.

> Proverbs 3:13-14
> Happy is the man that findeth wisdom, and the man that getteth understanding. For the merchandise of it is better than the merchandise of silver, and the gain thereof than fine gold.

Figure 90

A common argument made by many researchers against the *A. muscaria* as the foundation of Christianity, Judaism, and Hinduism is that the mushroom does not cause bliss.[332] Bear in mind that most of them have not consumed the *Amanita* at all, much less in the traditional shamanic manner, which includes urine consumption. The entire history of entheogen use, especially that of the mushroom, is not only of a blissful experience, but the ups and downs of heaven and hell told in many stories throughout the world. Part of the heaven-like or blissful experience is realizing the totality of your being, the hell side of these experiences is the fear and ego driven "bad trips." These "bad trips" and "bad experiences" can be most important because they can teach the user the most about him or her self. As religion teaches us, all of this symbolism and ritual is about purification and transformation of the soul, to make ourselves better human beings. The purpose is *not* just to have a "blissful experience" or to party with your friends, but rather to help you grow spiritually and even mentally.

---

[329] See *Magic Mushrooms in Religion and Alchemy*, by Clark Heinrich for more information and examples.

[330] John Allegro was the first to expose the phoenix as a polymorphous representation of the Amanita muscaria in *The Sacred Mushroom and the Cross*, by John Allegro, pg. 95-96 & 134-135.

[331] *Strong's*: 4480 – <u>Above</u> in Greek means marker of a source or extension from a source: from out of, of... because of, from, etc.

[332] Chris Bennett and those in favor of a Cannabis theory as Soma base part of this on a wrongful claim by G. Wasson that *A. muscaria* may not affect Caucasians, or cause bliss (*Sex, Drugs, Violence and the Bible*, pt. 2, pg. 75, ft. 185); though Bennett has shown substantial evidence that cannabis was used as Soma as well. It is well known that cannabis is now used in the making of the sacred drink "Bhang." However, Bennett has not presented substantial evidence to debunk those portions of the Rig Vedas listed in this book; or in *Magic Mushrooms in Religion and Alchemy*, by Heinrich; or in *Soma: The Divine Hallucinogen*, by Spess; or *Shamanism and Tantra in the Himalayas*, by Rätsch, et. al. See Cf. Shrestha, 1998, pg. 134. "It has been convincingly verified linguistically by Flattery and Schwartz (1989) as well as other authors (Gelpke 1967, Li 1974, Rosenthal 1971) that bhang (or bhanga, bang, bangii, beng, etc.) is not only the word for hemp leaves and the drinks and delicacies made with them, but originally meant "drug" in general." *Shamanism and Tantra in the Himalayas*, by Müller-Ebeling, Rätsch, Shahi, pg. 17, footnote 21. Bennett admits this fact (*SDVB*, pt. 2, pg. 74, ft. 183 & pg. 75 ft. 186). We do, however, agree that the Sula Benet and Chris Bennett's qaneh-bosm theory in *Green Gold: The Tree of Life* (pg 87-96) and re-presented in *SBVD*, is likely correct. We also concur, in part, with Bennett's statements (*SDVB*, pt. 1, pg. 73, ft. 161) toward Allegro with regard to cannabis and Allegro's prejudiced "weary dotards" statement against it. See *The Sacred Mushroom*, pg. 188-9, by Allegro.

1 Corinthians 11:27-30

Wherefore whosoever shall eat this bread, and drink this cup of the Lord, unworthily, shall be guilty of the body and blood of the Lord. But let a man examine himself, and so let him eat of that bread, and drink of that cup. For he that eateth and drinketh unworthily, eateth and drinketh damnation to himself, not discerning the Lord's body. For this cause many are weak and sickly among you, and many sleep.

The sun in the sky is born under the constellation of the virgin, Virgo, on December 25th. As a result, the sun deity is born of a virgin as well. As the Age of Pisces began, its opposite sign in the zodiac, Virgo the virgin, was on the western horizon.[333] As we pointed out in chapter three, Horus was born of the virgin Isis-Meri on December 25th. Isis-Meri (Mary) was the Egyptian name for the constellation of Virgo. Meri (Mary)[334] also happens to be where words like marina and marine (references to the sea) come from because cultures who watch the sun rise over the ocean witnessed God's sun being born out of the ocean, and walk on water.

Let's look at Luke 1:27 again.

> To a **virgin** espoused[335] to a man whose name was Joseph, of the **house** of David; and the virgin's name was **Mary**.

Virgo married (or engaged) a man whose name was Joseph (Saturn[336,337]), of the house of David (Jupiter, their son[338]) and Virgo's name was Mary (Isis-Meri).

All of the above *virgins* are anthropomorphisms of both the mushroom (microcosm) and the sun and/or stars (macrocosm) in various cultures.

Figure 91 - PIERO della FRANCESCA 1472 -Madonna and Child with saints. Notice the shell and pearl above the deities.

Our final example of virgin symbolism is found in the mushroom. The mushroom was considered born of a virgin because the mushroom's spores (Figure 51), which are basically mushroom seeds, are too small to be seen by the naked eye. Prior to the invention of microscopes, it appeared that the mushrooms arose magically overnight, without seed.

---

[333] *The Jesus Mysteries* Freke, Gandy.

[334] Often, religious and alchemical artwork will depict Mary (or the female) standing on a crescent of or near the moon. The moon was often associated with the monthly female cycle because of its effects on the monthly flow of women, and tides or the flow of the ocean; the "marine."

[335] The *Oxford English Dictionary* defines espoused as: a betrothed person of either sex; also a newly-married person, a bride or bridegroom. *Strong's:* 3423 mnesteuo mnace-tyoo'-o from a derivative of 3415; to give a souvenir (engagement present), i.e. betroth: espouse.

[336] The word Saturn is possibly where Christians later derived the word Satan; many Satan worshipers were the "Saturn Worshipers" of the older religions, just as Lunatics were moon worshipers and primarily women.

[337] There is a conflict of information between Acharya S, *The Christ Conspiracy*, pg. 141, referencing Joseph to Sagittarius. Robert Hewitt Brown, *Stellar Theology and Masonic Astronomy*, pg. 68, says that Joseph is likely Saturn; the *Masonic Encyclopedia*, by A. G. Mackey, M.D., & C. T. McClenachan, pg. 1002, pub. 1910, confirms this.

[338] The house of David is often referred to as possibly being the planet Jupiter, son of Virgo. This is verified by *Stellar Theology and Masonic Astronomy*, by Robert Hewitt Brown, pg. 68.

To Pliny the fungus had to be reckoned as one of the "greatest of the marvels of nature," since it "belonged to a class of things that spring up spontaneously and cannot be grown from seed" ...One explanation for the creation of the mushroom without apparent seed was that the "womb" had been fertilized by thunder, since it was commonly observed that the fungi appeared after thunderstorms... Thus one name given them was Ceraunion, from the Greek keraunios, "thunderbolt." Another word in the Greek hudnon, probably derived from Sumerian *UD-NUN, "storm-seeded." It was thus uniquely-begotten. The normal process of fructification had been by-passed. The seed had not fallen from some previous plant, to be nurtured by the earth...[339]
~ John Allegro

Mithra was born of a virgin, Mithra was born of a stone and we have shown how the mushroom appears to be born of a stone, or the cosmic egg, and born of a virgin (no seed), so the anthropomorphism of the deity is also born of a virgin.

WINGS ABOVE/SERPENTS BELOW

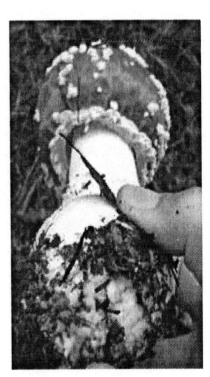

Here is Mithra (Figure 92) standing on top of the cosmic egg, or the primordial mound. Mithra has tail-feathers like the mushroom does (the annulus), and he also has wings at the top, on his shoulders. Mithra is the entwined caduceus. He has the entwined serpent around his body, making the caduceus and symbolizing drugs. Mithra is the drug itself, the mushroom.[340]

The *Amanita* mushroom is born from the primordial mound. Notice the primordial mound in Figure 93. When the cap opens up completely, the newly exposed gills become the wings on the shoulders of Mithra. As the universal veil falls around the stipe of the mushroom, the annulus becomes the wings on the back of Mithra.

Figure 93 - *Amanita muscaria* - primordial mound

Figure 92 - Mithra

[339] *The Sacred Mushroom and the Cross*, by John Allegro, pg. 54-55.
[340] Arthur, *Mushrooms and Mankind* (2000), pg. 56.

Tradition tells us to put wings on top of our Christmas tree by placing an angel on the top. The Christmas tree is the microcosmic representation of the world tree or a representation in the microcosm of the world tree – the axis of the earth (among other things). Tradition also tells us to entwine this tree with ribbons or stringed popcorn (most of the older Christmas tree ornaments were edible). Entwining the Christmas tree like this shows that the snake is climbing the column to the wings at the top. The Christmas tree is the caduceus, symbolizing the very drugs (mushrooms) that grow underneath it. Again, it is as above, so below.

Figure 94 - Symbolism of the decorated Christmas Tree

Figure 95 - Serpens (left) and Aquila (right)

A constellation along the southern horizon, Ophiuchus, is a combination of three different figures. *Ophiuchus*, the Serpent Bearer, is holding *Serpens Caput* in his left hand and *Serpens Cauda* in his right. These snakes are often depicted as a single snake, Serpens (pictured left).

The Greek god Asclepius could appear as a serpent and is often ichnographically depicted as a serpent (or with a serpent). The serpent-entwined staffs are the symbol of Asclepius. And he is also the Greek god of medicine, and his association with medicine is his association with the serpent. He can be the administer of medicine (venom) or can be the medicine himself. Gnostics associate Jesus with Asclepius due to the story of Jesus astonishing the Masters (physicians and astrotheologists) at the age of 12. Many connect him with other mythological healers as a great healer archetype. The staff of Asclepius has but one snake, but the myth involves two snakes, one that dies and one that appears and heals the other with plants. Ophiuchus saw this, and learned how to use herbs to cure people.

Snakes can be associated with good, healing, and wisdom. Asclepius is attributed all of these positive characteristics. Moses raised the serpent-entwined staff in the wilderness to heal the Israelites of serpent bites. Using a snake to heal someone from the venom of another snake mythologically demonstrates that snakes are both good and evil. And that venom (drugs) can harm as well as heal. Gnostics associate Jesus with the snake because of the passage in John (3:14) where it says, "...and as Moses lifted up the serpent in the wilderness, even so must the son of man be lifted up," and the Jesus Character was *lifted up* onto a cross. Many other myths associated the serpent with fecundity, procreation, wisdom, and good, rather than evil[341], including the original Garden of Eden tale that included the goddess Asherah, who was often depicted as a *tree*.[342] In the biblical account, for example, the serpent saved humanity from enslavement by teaching us to question authority and convinced us to eat the forbidden (enlightening) fruit.

In the heavens, near the North Pole is Aquila, Thor's bird (Figure 95), and Cygnus (or the Northern Cross). These constellations indicate some of the brightest areas of the northern Milky Way. The *wings above* are the wings of Aquila, representing the North Pole and the *serpent below* is Serpens, representing the South Pole.

As we have said, the Christmas tree is a (microcosmic) representation of the world tree axis, the surrounding (macrocosmic) stars and celestial constellations that can be seen when looking into the night sky. This is a way of preserving the hidden knowledge, hiding it **right in front of your face,** year after year.

> Thomas 113
> His disciples said to him, 'When will the kingdom come?' Jesus said, 'It will not come by waiting for it. It will not be a matter of saying 'here it is' or 'there it is'. Rather, **the kingdom of the father is <u>*spread out upon the earth*</u>, and men do not see it.**

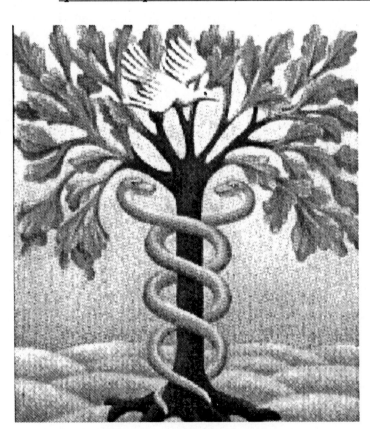

Figure 96 - Alchemical Caduceus

In alchemy and even in religion, the snake climbing the tree is a well-known symbol. Here is the snake climbing the tree. One can visualize the bird with the wings above the serpent, or the branches may be viewed as the wings above the serpent.

---

[341] *The Secret Teachings of All Ages*, by Manly P. Hall; *Symbols, Sex, and the Stars*, by Ernest Busenbark.
[342] *The Wisdom of the Serpent*, by Dr. Jay Williams.

THE STAIRWAY TO HEAVEN

In the story of Jacob's ladder, Jacob was lying with his head on a stone (the philosopher's stone?), and he had an out of body experience. Having an out of body experience is real and there is much to be learned about our reality and ourselves by going out of body and assessing our own state of affairs from a new perspective.

What we call *reality* could very well be quite different from what is actually happening. Nevertheless, we are surrounded with what is called *matter*. All matter is surrounded by, and in existence because of, things that science does not understand. We do not know what is "out there" but science is constantly seeking these answers. Our shamanic ancestors understood that the answers to these questions could not be found with telescopes and two-dimensional pictures. The universe must be *experienced* and entheogens that promote out of body experiences, and/or astral projection, have not remained in our traditions so prominently because they are only *slightly* successful. When one learns how to use them, they truly can send you *out of body* in the most literal sense of the term.

Climbing the ladder to the heavens, whether it is told in fairy tales, religion, or myth, is anciently symbolic of the shaman going out of body and connecting *that which is below* to *that which is above*.[343] The shaman has the advantage of taking a glimpse of the unknowable and reporting back to the community. Unfortunately, these experiences are often impossible to put into words. One theory that the shaman has successfully brought back to us repeatedly throughout history is that the entire universe, everything that we can imagine, is only a tiny part of what actually is. Just as we are connected to something beyond our understanding (our spirit or soul), so too is the universe.

The human body, the solar system, the universe, and space itself are identical in law and morality. The only difference is in size. Good reading on this subject matter can be found in the book titled *The 3-Pound Universe: from the Chemistry of the Mind to the New Frontiers of the Soul* by Judith Hooper and Dick Teresi.

The initiated shaman understands that under normal conditions, we humans can only perceive 4% of our reality. The plants that the shaman uses will increase this percentage dramatically (the dilating of the pupils is an indication of this). Unfortunately, shamanic research is multidimensional and does not fit into the realm of modern physical research.[344] Science generally only recognizes the physical universe as the Great Mystery, while this is only a small portion of it. With advancements in String Theory, hopefully this will change.

In his emerald tablets, Hermes suggests that the above is like the below, the superior is like the inferior, and the greater is like the lesser. All things follow one immense pattern, and if one can piece together this pattern at any particular point, the keys to unlock the entire mystery will be revealed. That is the purpose of the Aquarius Initiation: to provide the keys that will unlock new doors of understanding in your quest to find your *Self*. What is coming is a gradual development in understanding of these Great Polarities, the law of analogy, the harmonious balance of the macrocosm and microcosm. As above so below, as in the heavens so on earth, as in the sky so in the body of man. This can be visualized by considering musical octaves as they are the same note on different levels of harmony.[345] Connecting the macrocosm and the microcosm is symbolized by the ladder, and the ladder of Jacob, upon which the angels ascended and descended, is only one of many examples. The earth, in this example, is the foundation which Jacob's ladder rests upon. On the microcosm of this philosophy is man, and in our anatomy, the human spinal column is the great axis, the ladder leading to the brain.

---

[343] The ladder symbolism may have originated from the shamans climbing onto the roofs of their yurts to meditate on mushrooms. Mackey and McClenachan in *Encyclopedia of Freemasonry* admit the symbol is pagan and existed almost universally in antiquity (see pg. 373-75, 438-439).
[344] Dr. Rick Strassman was the first researcher allowed to do entheogenic studies in the U.S. in twenty years at the time his research began. *DMT: The Spirit Molecule*.
[345] Laws of harmony and geometry were often studied with the use of the musical instrument the 'monochord.' *Jesus Christ: Sun of God*, by David Fideler.

This picture comes from Fulcanelli's *The Mysteries of the Cathedrals*. The image is from a bas-relief on the Great Porch of Notre Dame in Paris. Notice the ladder climbing the body, leading to the Godhead. Fulcanelli was a master alchemist and after he wrote this book, he vanished. Nobody knows much more about him. In his book, he takes us through Notre Dame and shows the cathedrals and the mysteries within them, making a boast of his mastery of the Great Work.

Figure 97 - Bas Relief on the Great Porch - Notre Dame, Paris

The ancient mystery schools were the sacred institutions of knowledge. These mystery schools or "universities" (places to study the universe or uni (one) and verse (word), the word of God, whole and entire.) were not public schools whereby simply *anyone* could attend. These institutions would accept students by way of initiation. The initiate would symbolically work his way up the ladder of initiation, hopefully learning how to *use* knowledge rather than to *abuse* it. These mystery schools would often *perform* their teachings in allegory and dialogue. Mystery plays were quite well known and still exist today in passion plays, Christmas pageants, and within Masonic temples.

Jordan Maxwell covers in detail the relations between modern education's "12 grades" and "mortar boards" (worn at graduation) compared to Freemasonry and the levels (ladders) of initiation within the ancient mystery schools. There are many ladders in mythology, religion, and alchemy, all connecting the above with the below. Often symbolic for heaven above and hell below, the ladder is a representation of the two opposite extremes of the experience brought on by these entheogens.[346] In this regard, the mushroom is the ladder because it connects that which is below (the shaman) with that which is above (the heavens, via the out of body experience).

> Genesis 11:4-9
> ...Go to, let us build us a city and a tower, whose top may reach unto heaven; and let us make us a name, lest we be scattered abroad upon the face of the whole earth. And the LORD came down to see the city and the tower, which the children of men builded. And the LORD said, Behold, the people is one, and they have all one language; and this they begin to do: and now nothing will be restrained from them, which they have imagined to do. Go to, let us go down, and there confound their language, that they may not understand one another's speech. So the LORD scattered them abroad from thence upon the face of all the earth: and they left off to build the city. Therefore is the name of it called Babel; because the LORD did there confound the language of all the earth: and from thence did the LORD scatter them abroad upon the face of all the earth.

In Genesis 11, humankind was getting too close to what the Age of Aquarius may offer us: "the people is one," "nothing will be restrained from them." Even the possibility of telepathy and a mystical language of the 'bards' (birds) known to the Maya as '*Zuvuya,*' which is said to be possible for many students of entheogens such as DMT or Ayahuasca. This language is of pure understanding of the word (logos), and indeed the authors of this book have experienced similar phenomenon while on various entheogenic substances.

---

[346] Clark Heinrich, *Magic Mushrooms in Religion and Alchemy* (see ch. 14, "Heaven" and "Hell") .

Figure 98 - J Bowring - 1819

In Masonry, one will often find ladders as having the key, and adherents climbing the ladder to the heavens with the keys of enlightenment (represented in Figure 98). The mushroom has often been referred to as a key, the key that opens the doorways of eternity.

> Matthew 16:19
> And I will give unto thee the keys of the kingdom of heaven: and whatsoever thou shalt bind on earth shall be bound in heaven: and whatsoever thou shalt loose on earth shall be loosed in heaven.

Figure 99 - The Catholic Church uses a golden key and silver key crossed underneath the cosmic egg (left image), also making the skull and crossbones (right image). The golden key represents the key to enter the heavens, and the silver key represents the key to enter the earth.[347] These keys most likely represent *Amanita muscaria* and *Psilocybe cubensis*, at least to some degree, respectively.[348] The left image is the emblem found on the Vatican flag, with keys crossed below the cosmic egg making the Skull and Bones. In the center is the official seal of the Sede Vacante, the period between Popes. Notice the seal of the Sede Vacante is complete with crossed keys and a parasol[349] showing the mushroom reference. On the right is a Maltese cross with the skull and bones (a symbol for poison, *drugs*, and knowledge[350]) revealing the similarity.

> Luke 11:52
> Woe unto you, lawyers! for ye have taken away the key of knowledge: <u>ye entered not in yourselves</u>, and <u>them that were entering in ye hindered</u>.

Figure 99

---

[347] San Diego Museum of Art –"Saint Peter & The Vatican, The Legacy of the Popes."
[348] They do not represent the mushrooms themselves, but the inference is clearly present. The knowledge and understanding of these mushrooms (where they grow, how to prepare them, etc.) is also an important factor and can be considered "keys of understanding" alchemy and shamanism.
[349] The word Parasol ('chattra') in Sanskrit also means mushroom. *Soma*, by Gordon Wasson, pg. 63.
[350] The word skull is where we get words like skill and school. See Jordan Maxwell, William Henry.

Figure 100 - Jack climbing the beanstalk

In the story of *Jack and the Beanstalk*, Jack climbs an entwined ladder made from a giant beanstalk leading to the heavens. In the story, he steals from the giant (representing God) the golden egg of alchemy, the eggs in the basket, the *Amanita muscaria*. This can also be seen as the shaman climbing the world tree (Axis mundi) to the heavens where Cepheus is found. The connection between *stealing* these golden eggs and Jesus being crucified between two *thieves* is not a far stretch. In his book *Blue Apples*, William Henry writes:

> One of Moses' operatives, Joshua, an ancestor of Jesus, was called the "Son of Nun." Along with a companion, Joshua was dispatched to the valley of Eschol ('valley of the cluster' as in grapes) where he stole a cluster of grapes from the sons of Anak who were living there. He returned the grapes to Moses.
>
> Nun and the cluster of grapes later became cryptograms that were extremely important to the Essenes, the priesthood of which Jesus was a member[351], and the Gnostic Grail heretics that they held sacred and secret.
>
> The cluster of grapes symbolized the secrets of creation, the secrets of manipulating the mother substance and the symbol for the Grail.

---

[351] There is absolutely no evidence supporting the theory of Jesus existing as a man, much less as an Essene. The Teacher of Righteousness of the Essene community was only another recent (and many times repeated) application of this most ancient story. However, both Allegro and Josephus tout the Essenes' particular plant knowledge.

Figure 101 - Vision of the Throne of the Lord - 1400

Looking at Figure 101, the vesica piscis once again is shown with the deity in the middle. Below the vesica piscis is an angel with her wings spread, and the shape of the angel is very much the mushroom itself (probably the *Amanita pantherina* due to the coloring). The feathers are representing the gills or the striations of the mushroom. These are peacock feathers, which resemble the spots of the mushroom. To the left is a stairway with twelve steps, the thirteenth step is the vesica piscis.

Figure 102 is a panel taken from a plate of the Canterbury Psalter, Canterbury, England circa 1147 CE showing Adam and Eve in the Garden of Eden. Notice the serpent wrapped around the tree making it the caduceus, the tree here is actually shown as a mushroom. As we mentioned earlier, the caduceus is the symbol of drugs today, as it was thousands of years ago. The serpent is giving Adam and Eve something, or, the caduceus, the symbol of drugs, is giving Adam and Eve something to eat that will open their eyes and make them as gods, knowing good and evil.[352]

The Rig Vedas are full of sex worship, much more so than Christianity and more graphic as well. Shiva was having sex with his consort up on top of a mountain and they were having such passionate sex that the weight was compressing the air below into a solid. The gods were in panic and they came running to Vishnu to try to put an end to it, to save their own lives. As they run up the mountain, Shiva performs coitus interruptus and stands up (still fully erect) and says that they will stop having sex, but then asks who will take his seed. Who will eat it? At that, he ejaculated. The gods all looked to Agni and they said Agni is our fire god, he is the only one hot enough to handle this. Agni does and this causes him to have a great bliss. Therefore, we have the story of eating the red tipped, red capped, fiery red seed and having great bliss.[353]

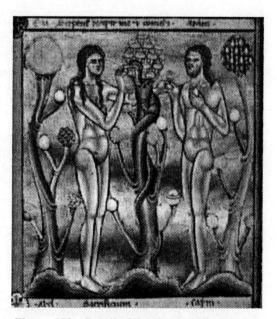

Figure 102 - Detail of the Tree of Knowledge of Good and Evil –
Canterbury Psalter - 1147 CE

---

[352] Thanks to Paul Lindgren for finding this image.
[353] Clark Heinrich, lecture, 2000.

Figure 103 - Agni drinking the seed of Shiva

What is happening in Figure 103 is that Agni (on the right) is drinking the seed of Shiva (on the left). Because semen and urine both appear to come from the same place, these two fluids were interchangeable in some stories. Here, urine is imbibed from the cup. Agni is impregnated by the seed of Shiva, who, like Jesus, is the mushroom (and the sun). For more information regarding this story as well as other Shiva and Agni stories, read Clark Heinrich's *Magic Mushrooms in Religion and Alchemy*.

We like to define alchemy as the art of concealment surrounding the shamanic arts of self-transformation by way of occult artwork and cryptic writing. By this definition, revealing the secrets of the Great Work to the masses is, in a sense, "anti-alchemy" because the alchemists were known for saying things such as "What we say we are doing, we are not doing." They were a secretive bunch and they would create artwork that showed exactly what they were up to, but their art was so cryptic that it could only be recognized and appreciated by fellow alchemists who also possessed these keys of understanding.

> This science transmits its worth by mixing the false with the true and the true with the false... and it endeavors to transmit the work obscurely and to hide it as much as possible.[354]
> ~ Hogheland, the Theatrum chemicum Britannicum

Many believe alchemy only to be working with changing the properties of metals. While this is true to an extent, David Spess has shown that this type of lab alchemy did not appear until the 1200s in Europe, whereas shamanic alchemy has been in practice since the earliest times of the Rig Vedas.[355]

> Early Indian alchemy, using Soma as the rejuvenative elixir, is primarily concerned with its spiritual side rather than the use of external mineral preparations... its central idea is of a white or luminous plant that grows from the primal waters of creation to become the living universe. This plant was the white haoma/Soma; it is an internalized plant that grows from the heart to form the pneumatic body of light.[356]
> ~ David Spess

---

[354] Quoted from *Magic Mushrooms in Religion and Alchemy*, by Clark Heinrich.
[355] *Soma: The Divine Hallucinogen*, by David Spess, pg. 64-5, (700 – 765CE). Geber is the founder of alchemical art, pg. 83.
[356] Ibid, pg. 153.

This is the fundamental nature of alchemy, not what most understand it to be. Alchemists danced with the devil and if they told what alchemy was really about, the *devil* surely would have burned them at the stake. This is the reason the secret knowledge of alchemy is encoded into cryptic symbolism. The same reasoning is given by Allegro as to the origins of the Gospels. Both initiates and adepts concealed the mushroom secrets as tales of people (Jesus and his disciples) in order to protect themselves from the Romans and Jews.[357, 358]

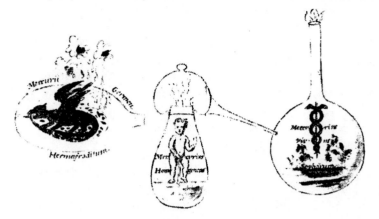

On the far left in Figure 104, the rain is falling into what looks like a spoon. Notice inside the spoon is the ouroboros biting its own tail, depicted with wings on top. Next to it, in the middle image, is the homunculus (or little man) urinating into the water and the (living) water is being boiled and recycled up. On the far right is the caduceus, completing the alchemical process of the drugs from beginning to the end.[359]

Figure 104

SEXUALIA

Ephesians 5:31
For this cause shall a man leave his father and mother, and shall be joined unto his wife, and they <u>two shall be one</u> flesh.

This couple is about to join together and join names in unification of marriage, or "holy matrimony."[360] The colors of the white dress and black tuxedo show the symbolic hermaphrodite, now the two are one. This unification can be seen as either sun-mother-moon, or Sun (male) joining with moon (female)—Sol and Luna. They will wear a wedding ring to represent the idea of two being joined as one, in the continuous cycle of the ouroboros. The ring also represents the planet-god Saturn and its rings.

The biblical creation story speaks of Adam as a hermaphrodite in Genesis 5:2, where it is written: "<u>Male and female created he them</u>; and blessed them, <u>and called their name Adam</u>, in the day when they were created." Eve[361] was later said to be born from the side of (or from the rib of) Adam, showing a separation of the hermaphrodite into two separate people. However, since we know that women bear children, why would these ancient stories tell us that Eve was born from Adam instead of the other way around?

Figure 105

There are indeed pre-Christian stories of Eve giving birth to Adam.[362] Part of the reason for this flip-flopping stems from the suppression of the female by the Church, the other part of it deals with the development or growth cycle of the mushroom.

---

[357] *The Sacred Mushroom and the Cross*, by John Allegro.
[358] *The Dead-Sea Scrolls & the Christian Myth*, by John Allegro.
[359] This image can be found in *Alchemy and Mysticism*, by Alexander Roob, and is described in *Magic Mushrooms in Religion and Alchemy*, by Clark Heinrich.
[360] "Maat" is the goddess of the unification of opposites, and where the word matrimony is derived.
[361] The name Eve gives a further clue to the origin of this myth. The word Eve (pronounced *Hawwa* in Hebrew), when aspirated, is the same as the Aramaic word *Hawwe*, denoting a serpent. The word *nagash*, written n-g-sh without vowels, also signifies a serpent in Hebrew and is pronounced almost exactly the same as the word n-c-sh, meaning sexual intercourse. The association of *Hawwa*, the woman, with *Hawwe*, the serpent (the cause of her "fall"), is, therefore, a play upon words, a practice which was very popular with Oriental myth makers. *Symbols, Sex, and the Stars*, by Ernest Busenbark Pg 186.
[362] *Nag Hammadi Library*, On the Origin of the World.

Mercury carries the caduceus and has wings on his helmet and feet. These wings signify the ability to travel between the heavens and the earth. Mercury is the messenger of the gods, tracing back the origins of angels leads the theologians and mythologists directly back to Mercury. The gods of the earth were, for thousands of years, the plants. The plants still reflect the names of the gods. The gods and the messengers of the gods are the same. Catholic descriptions of angels reflect this fact by their colors and symbolic folds in their robes. They are often decorated with oak leaves, indicating *Amanita pantherina*, golden red and white colors with pine trees in the landscape indicating *Amanita muscaria*, blue stains on white robes or bluing with golden tan indicating *Psilocybe* mushrooms, purple indicating ergot, and blue indicating morning glories and Lotus. In Christian belief, the angels are the messengers. To the shaman, the messengers are the plants, and the plants are the gods. Sometimes angel messengers show indications of the *Amanita/Psilocybe* combination as well. All of these simply reveal the true nature of the *real* messengers of the gods, the plants that connect humankind's consciousness with the heavens. Mercury/Hermes is precisely a plant messenger, as the attributes reveal. The hermaphroditic nature of angels reflects mushrooms because mushrooms look like sexual union of coitus. The stem is the phallus, it penetrates the cap as if it was female genitalia (Figures 64 and 107).

Religious symbolism all over the world often refers to the phallus of God and in many instances we have found a mushroom under the symbol. The hermaphrodite also reflects the mushrooms in symbolism of Hari-Hari in India, Chinrezee and Avalokiteshavara in China and Tibet. In Judaism and Christianity, the stem is the rib of Adam, and the cap the female body of Eve. In addition, as John Allegro pointed out, Esau is the cap, Esau meaning canopy, and Jacob is the stem—*Jacob* meaning pillar. The rebis of alchemy[363] gives us the most clues to unlocking the mysteries because the rebis is depicted in many ways, always related to mushrooms.

Figure 106

The Hindu god/goddess Hari-Hari or Hari-Hara is the East Indian form of the rebis and is depicted in *Tantra Asana* by Mookerjee, standing atop a spotted disk, surrounded by lotus peddles, with mushroom-looking lotus flowers growing on the ground beside it. The figure is male and female, colored blue, red, gold, and white. It's one of the most profound representations depicting *Amanita*, *Psilocybe*, and lotus together. Northern India, where mountains prevail and *Amanitas* are abundant, is mostly focused upon *Amanita* worship and Vishnu myths, but southern India where valleys abound is focused primarily on *Psilocybe* and Shiva worship. Southern India retains more of its traditional culture and art with thousands of temples dedicated to Tantric sexual yoga. However, Northern India is much more repressed due to Islamic/Saharasian influence.[364] Both northern and southern India also have deep roots in alchemy, along with ayurvedic herbal healing. The rebis is also associated with the Axis Mundi and the world tree, as the rebis stands at the center axis of all alchemical knowledge.

[363] See figure 119.
[364] For more information see *Saharasia*, by James DeMeo.

Much of ancient mythology was based on sex and fertility worship, and here is the hermaphroditic symbol of the unification of sex in the mushroom itself. The underside of the mushroom takes on the appearance of a vulva penetrated from below and supported by the male phallic. It has formed into a embodiment of *interfused duality*. The stem of the mushroom (representing the male phallic and the sun) is joined with the cap of the mushroom (the underside of the cap represents the female uterus and the top of the cap is symbolized as a single female breast and also the earth). Once the cap of the mushroom begins to separate from the stalk, it is no longer considered exclusively male. In the biblical stories, Adam existed before Eve. Metaphorically, Adam is representing the phallic stages of the mushroom, which occurs before the female stages of the growth cycle. Eve (the eave of the mushroom[365] and symbolically, the female portion of the mushroom), is born from the side of Adam. In nature, when the *Amanita's* cap separates to form the eave (canopy), it figuratively pulls a rib out of the stalk. We will discuss this *rib* of the mushroom more in a moment, but first, as an example of this mushroom's growth cycle, let's anthropomorphize it.

Figure 107 - Male and female qualities of the *Amanita muscaria*

Figure 108 - *Amanita muscaria* as a baby wrapped in swaddling clothes

Figure 109 - *Amanita muscaria*

The mushroom begins as a baby wrapped in swaddling clothes. The white, universal veil covers the red mushroom from head to toe.

Luke 2:12
And this shall be a sign unto you; Ye shall find the babe wrapped in swaddling clothes, lying in a manger.

---

[365] *The Sacred Mushroom and the Cross*, by John Allegro.

Figure 110 - *Amanita muscaria* – growth cycle

As the mushroom grows, it begins to stand erect, representing the male portion of the mushroom as a phallic symbol. If you can imagine a person standing upright with their arms to either side, representing the mushroom in this stage, the arms will begin to lift up into the air representing the cap of the mushroom expanding or opening, thus, exposing (or rather creating) the female part of the mushroom. In this example, as soon as we raise our arms up, forming the cap of the mushroom, the universal veil of the mushroom tears away from our ribs and drops down forming a skirt or (Freemasonic) apron. At this time, the eave of the mushroom appears to be 'born' from the rib or from the side of the male portion (stipe) of the mushroom.[366] The mushroom is born wrapped in swaddling clothes, and when it is on the cross (or rather, when it is at the cross stage of growth), all that remains of those swaddling clothes is the skirt and little thorn-like bumps on its "head," making the crown of thorns.

Eve, or the eave of the mushroom is being born from Adam. The cap continues to open up, raising its outer lip, just as if we raise our arms to the sun forming the Holy Grail in complete unification and representation of the cycle of life of the mushroom and fertility rites.

Figure 111 - Frans Floris - The Sacrifice of Christ protecting Humanity – 1562 (Louvre Museum, Paris)

In Figure 111, it should be totally clear why this posture or the stance is so important. We see Krishna, Sampson, Jesus, Libertas, and other deities who all stand with this posture, all standing like the *Amanita* mushroom. This figurative posture clearly represents the *Holy Grail*, the cup stage of the *A. muscaria* mushroom.

---

[366] Heinrich and others are in agreement with Allegro, in *The Sacred Mushroom and the Cross*, pg. 104; that the story of Adam and Eve represents the growth cycle of the mushroom.

Figure 112 - Dried *Amanita muscaria* cap - Photograph by Michael Hoffman, Egodeath.com

The body of Christ, bread of heaven, the shiny golden metallic Holy Grail made of neither bone nor metal nor wood.

Figure 113

Figure 114

This bas-relief in stone (above) is another excellent representation of the sex symbology of the mushroom. The macrocosm of this symbol is the sun above the obelisk. The microcosm of this symbol is the penis coming up and joining with the womb. Next to it is the exact same representation in the mushroom. The ancients looked at this mushroom, portrayed it from many different perspectives, and anthropomorphized those perspectives of the mushroom, as well as the celestial bodies, into the gods and deities of today.

115

Figure 115

Here you can see the hidden mushroom symbolism at the Vatican with the alignment of the obelisk, the spotted dome, and pediment representing the stem, spotted cap, and fallen annulus.

Figure 116 - Caravaggio - Madonna with the Serpent - 1606

This story (Figure 116) of the snake being crushed or the head of the snake being crushed, separating the tail from the head, is symbolic of the act of unification of the sperm cell penetrating the egg. At this point in our life, we are a hermaphrodite, or rather, it is not decided what sex we are going to be until 49 days after conception. During this period, we are either or both sexes, we are "undecided."

On the macrocosm, the constellation Virgo (Isis-Meri) appears to step on the head of Serpens (the constellation of the snake) with her right foot[367] just before the sun is born (rises) below her, on December 25th.

---

[367] The image above wrongly depicts Virgo (Mary) stepping on the serpent's head with her *left* foot.

116

Figure 117

This *cock* (pictured left), said to be a Dionysic amulet,[368] can be found in *The Christ Conspiracy* by Acharya S, and *The Sacred Fire* by B. Z. Goldberg. It is an outline sketch of an actual bronze sculpture hidden in the Vatican treasury.[369] Once again, the sun, mushroom and fertility are all represented by the phallic symbol. On the microcosm, this is a symbol of Saint *Peter* (the sex and/or phallic stage of the mushroom). The word peter (also petra, piedra, etc.) means both rock and penis, and the rock was another name for the early stages of the mushrooms.[370] Saint Peter is *Saint Mushroom* on the microcosm. On the macrocosm, St. Peter has connections to Jupiter, as is evidenced by the fact that the old Roman statuette of Jupiter in the Vatican was converted into "St. Peter."[371,372] It is actually a symbol of Saint Peter or (the planet) Ju-Peter. The inscription reads – "Savior of the World."

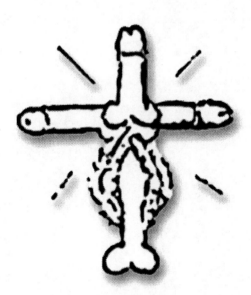

Figure 118 - The Rosicrucian[373] phallic cross

The Vesica piscis or the womb with the three penises is coming out on either side, with the testicles at the bottom of this Rosicrucian cross.

---

[368] *The Sacred Fire: The Story of Sex in Religion*, by B. Z. Goldberg, pg. 145.
[369] *The Christ Conspiracy: The Greatest Story Ever Sold*, by Acharya S.
[370] *The Sacred Mushroom and the Cross*, by John Allegro, pg. 40.
[371] *Jesus: God, Man or Myth?*, by Herbert Cutner.
[372] In regard to Peter or 'Cephus' of the Essene ('Physician') community at Qumran, Allegro states: "Some texts of the New Testament transcribe the name Caiaphas, and it now appears that the form Cephas, applied to the first apostle, was either a dialectal version of this variant, or adapted to fit the allusion to the Stone (Aramaic 'kepha') as the foundation of the Church. In any case, there can be little doubt now that Caiaphas/Caiphas and Cephas are, in origin and meaning, one and the same, 'Investigator', 'Prognosticator'. It is a very special <u>designation</u> of one who is credited with particular insight and the gift of prophecy." See *The Dead Sea Scrolls and the Christian Myth*, pg. 208-222.
[373] Ancient Mystic Order, Rosae Crucis – The Rosicrucian were actually several secret organizations or orders of the 17th and 18th centuries, all of them concerned with the study of religious mysticism and professing esoteric religious beliefs.

117

The term *hermaphrodite* relates us to the god Hermes, who was also sometimes half male and half female. Hermes and Mercury are simply the Greek and Roman names for the same deity. Sometimes, like Osiris and Horus, they are the Father and son (and the Father and son are one). The hermaphrodite that we are referring to is not the common type of hermaphrodite that we understand today. The hermaphrodite is the symbol for the rebis with the wings on its back, the male and female duality, the crown at the top, and the bulbous base. This description should sound familiar by now, as this symbolic hermaphrodite is representing the Holy Grail, the *A. muscaria*.

Behind the hermaphrodite in Figure 119, one will notice the Phoenix, representing the *Amanita*. Below are the snakes on the primordial mound. Inside the chalice, the snakes (representing poison and/or medicine) are ready to be consumed. Notice the yin/yang of the hermaphrodite, the positive and the negative, light and dark, male and female properties. Also, notice the thirteen suns in the tree, representing the sun in the form of a plant, showing the connection to the sacred plants, and the twelve constellations (as well as God's son on earth, Jesus with his 12 disciples, the *A. muscaria*). The lion also represents the constellation of Leo. The sun at its peak during ancient times was under the constellation Leo. Clark Heinrich suggests that Leo is the mushroom as well.

Figure 119 - The Demonstration of Perfection - Rosarium Philosophorum manuscript

Figure 120

Figure 121

If you strip away everything but the symbol from this image, you will notice the bulbous base with the skirt, the striations and the crown at the top the *A. muscaria*.[374]

---

[374] Clark Heinrich, *Magic Mushrooms in Religion and Alchemy*.

118

Figure 122 - Masonic Double-Headed Eagle[375]

In Masonic symbology, the double-headed eagle (or Aquila, with Pyramid or sun symbolically over its head) is standing on the rounded, bulbous base (often depicted standing on a globe). The wings are above the banner-entwined staff (representing the serpent) in an alchemical representation of the caduceus and the mushroom under Freemasonry.

In *Splendor Solis* (16th century), there is an alchemical depiction of Sol and Luna, the divine hermaphrodite. There are many layers of symbolism in this painting. Sol is always red, and Luna is always white. They have the red and white wings and they are exposing one leg in the forest under the tree. This painting is extremely symbolic of the *A. muscaria*. Around the waist is a skirt complete with the dangling gold at the bottom. This is the annulus of the mushroom whose tips are colored gold from the cap of the mushroom. The shield represents the sun, the cap of the mushroom, and the self-reflection that eating this cap brings about. In addition, the buttons running up the chest of Sol and Luna represent the ladder that is climbed to the heavens. As above, so below. Sol and Luna are the Sun and the Moon. Sol is the red cap of the mushroom and Luna is the white bulbous base. And what are they holding, but the cosmic egg? Maybe the Philosopher's Stone?

Heinrich points out the peculiarity of how the hand is placed around this egg. The fingers are making it into the shape of a mushroom. The position of the feet is also not insignificant. For a more in-depth look into this painting and much more symbolism regarding Alchemy and the *Amanita muscaria* mushroom, we cannot stress enough to read Clark Heinrich's book, *Magic Mushrooms in Religion and Alchemy*.

Psalms 84:11
For the LORD God is a sun and shield...

Figure 123 - Hermaphrodite with egg, Splendor Solis - 16th century

---

[375] Image from the cover of *Morals and Dogma,* by Albert Pike.

The *A. muscaria* and *Psilocybe* mushrooms are represented as male and female, Rebis, hermaphrodite, snake and bird, the colors red and blue, and many other various symbols or symbolic types. Symbols can have their multiple meanings, as in the two snakes or two dragons eating each other's tails, meaning the recycling of the mushrooms' active ingredients. Often one snake will have wings. This will be the *Amanita*, because it is the one associated with the heavens and the *Psilocybe* with the earth. Because its active substances are tryptamines, the *Psilocybe* is more closely related to human endogenous substances, whereas *Amanita* takes the initiate out of body and is seen as coming from above. The combination of both red and blue mushrooms is a key secret to alchemy. These colors represent *Amanita* and *Psilocybe*. Alchemy is rooted in this secret or some aspects of this secret. Many alchemical symbols elucidate this understanding and take it to new levels of actual practice.

THE PARADISE OF EDEN

Out of Adam's rib comes Eve, the female part of the mushroom. This is the part of the mushroom that is consumed. Out of the red portion of the mushroom (Eve) comes the enlightenment. Eve represents the active part of the mushroom. Eve, the female, the drugs, have all been suppressed by the combined effort of Church and State.

Figure 124 - Bible Moralisee (ca. 1250)

Adam and Eve came from Eden. Eden is defined as *"pleasure," "pleasant," delicate,"* or *"delight."*[376] These definitions seem to apply just as well for emotions as they do for a place (or thing). However, both *Strong's* and the *Oxford English Dictionary* also define Eden as *"Paradise,"* which *Strong's* reveals as a *"forest,"* or *"orchard."* A forest is certainly where the *Amanita* grow. The association to the mushroom experience may explain the emotive definitions for Eden:

> 3857: paradeisos par-ad'-i-sos of Oriental origin (<u>compare 6508</u>); <u>a park</u>, i.e. (specially), **an Eden** (place of future happiness, "paradise"):--paradise.

> 6508: pardes par-dace' Of foreign origin; <u>*a park:*</u> - **forest, orchard**. [underline, bold—ours]
> ~ *Strong's Concordance*

---

[376] *Strong's*, # H5731, 5730, 5727.

Acharya S points out that "Eve is one with Isis-Meri and therefore, the Virgin Mary and the constellation of Virgo, as well as the moon [and oceans]. In the original astrotheological tale, as Virgo rises she is followed or bitten on the heel by Serpens, who, with Scorpio, rises immediately behind her." [377] Here again, we find the law of duality.

Jesus, hanging on the cross, is lanced in the rib and out of his side comes the blood that is collected into the Holy Grail. Out of the rib comes the enlightenment once again.

Figure 125 - Bible Moralisee (c. 1250)

In 2nd Corinthians 3:16-17 it says:

> Nevertheless when it shall turn to the lord the veil shall be taken away. Now the lord is that spirit; and where the spirit of the lord is, there is liberty.

That is a very interesting statement and if one takes it and puts it into our modern language, it might sound like this:

> ...when the cap of the *Amanita* turns upward and the veil drops, there you will find the spirit of the lord; and there you will also find freedom.

---

[377] *The Christ Conspiracy*, by Acharya S, page 186.

THE FORBIDDEN FRUIT

The story of Adam and Eve is a very in-depth story of the snake climbing the tree, forming the caduceus, and giving them something to eat that evokes enlightenment. After Eve was created, she suddenly found herself standing in front of the same tree from which Adam was told not to eat. If we are to believe Genesis 2,[378] Eve was never told by God not eat from this tree. In the biblical version, as opposed to the Gnostic version, she did not yet exist. It was supposedly only communicated to her through Adam. If they were real people, which they were not, it must have been a miscommunication of sorts. Perhaps Adam did not weigh upon her the importance of not eating from this tree.

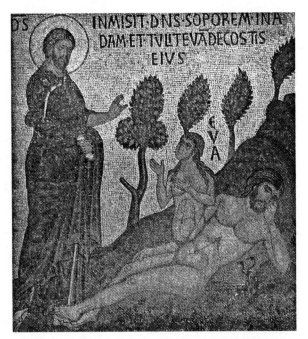

Figure 126 - Eve, born from the rib of Adam

Has the famous story that stands at the beginning of the Bible really been understood? The only story of god's hellish fear of *science*... only from woman did man learn to taste of the tree of knowledge. What had happened? The old god was seized with hellish fear. Man himself had turned out to be his *greatest* mistake; he had created a rival for himself; science makes godlike--it is all over with priests and gods when man becomes scientific. Moral: science is the forbidden as such-- it alone is forbidden. Science is the *first* sin, the *original* sin. *This alone is morality*. 'Thou shalt not know'--the rest follows.
~ Frederick W. Nietzsche *Der Anti Christ* [1888/1895]

The snake represents gnosis or knowledge (the logos) in nearly all the ancient mythologies and philosophies. Only in Christianity does the snake *appear* to mean something evil. When we look at the creation story in the book of Genesis, it is interesting because who lies? Does the serpent lie, or does God lie? The serpent tells Eve (Gen 3:5) "...your eyes shall be opened, and ye shall be as gods, knowing good and evil." Eve sees (Gen 3:6) "a tree to be desired to make one wise." God tells Adam, who in turn must have told Eve (Gen 2:17), "...for in the day that thou eatest thereof thou shalt surely die." She does not die, at least not a physical death. In addition, Adam doesn't die either. Neither died *in the day* of eating the fruit.

Genesis 3:2-7
And the woman said unto the serpent, We may eat of the fruit of the trees of the garden: But of the fruit of the tree which is in the midst of the garden, God hath said, Ye shall not eat of it, neither shall ye touch it, lest ye die. And <u>the serpent said unto the woman, Ye shall not surely die: For God doth know that in the day ye eat thereof, then your eyes shall be opened</u>[379]<u>, and ye shall be as gods, knowing good and evil.</u> And when the woman saw that the tree was good for food, and that it was pleasant to the eyes, and a tree to be desired to make one wise, <u>she took of the fruit thereof, and did eat, and gave also unto her husband with her; and he did eat. And the eyes of them both were opened,</u> and they knew that they were naked; and they sewed fig leaves together, and made themselves aprons.

Genesis 3:22-24
<u>And the LORD God said, Behold, the man is become as one of us, to know good and evil: and now, lest he put forth his hand, and take also of the tree of life, and eat, and live for ever:</u> Therefore the LORD God sent him forth from the garden of Eden, to till the ground from whence he was taken. So he drove out the man; and he placed at the east of the garden of Eden Cherubims, and a <u>flaming sword</u> which turned every way, to <u>keep the way of the tree of life.</u>

---

[378] There is a conflict between Genesis 1:27 and 2:22 as to when Eve came into existence.
[379] Their eyes being opened is also metaphor for the internal visionary experiences.

Here is the story in more modern day English. This story is compiled using only direct quotes from the *New International Version* of the Bible:

> The LORD God took the man and put him in the Garden of Eden to work it and take care of it. And the LORD God commanded the man, "You are free to eat from any tree in the garden; but you must not eat from the tree of the knowledge of good and evil, for when you eat of it you will surely die." The LORD God said, "It is not good for the man to be alone. I will make a helper suitable for him."
>
> Now the serpent was more crafty[380] than any of the wild animals the LORD God had made. He said to the woman, "Did God really say, 'You must not eat from any tree in the garden'?" The woman said to the serpent, "We may eat fruit from the trees in the garden, but God did say, 'You must not eat fruit from the tree that is in the middle of the garden, and you must not touch it, or you will die.'"
>
> "You will not surely die," the serpent said to the woman. "For God knows that when you eat of it your eyes will be opened, and you will be like God, knowing good and evil." When the woman saw that the fruit of the tree was good for food and pleasing to the eye, and also desirable for gaining wisdom, she took some and ate it. She also gave some to her husband, who was with her, and he ate it. Then the eyes of both of them were opened... And the LORD God said, "The man has now become like one of us, knowing good and evil. He must not be allowed to reach out his hand and take also from the tree of life and eat[381], and live forever." So the LORD God banished him from the Garden of Eden.

It does not take a rocket scientist to figure out who is the deceptive, jealous god in the Bible. For those interested in more evidence concerning this area of research, we recommend reading the stories of the Sumerian gods Enlil and Enki, as well as the stories of Adam and Even in *The Nag Hammadi Library*, and how the roles of the characters in the Sumerian and Gnostic stories have been flipped in replication in the story of Judeo-Christianity. This is how the story of Adam and Eve reads in the ancient Nag Hammadi scripture, *On the Origin of the World*:

> Then the seven of them [rulers] together laid plans. They came up to Adam and Eve timidly: they said to him, "The fruit of all the trees created for you in Paradise shall be eaten; but as for the tree of knowledge, control yourselves and do not eat from it. If you eat, you will die." Having imparted great fear to them, they withdrew up to their authorities.
>
> Then came the wisest of all creatures, who was called Beast. And when he saw the likeness of their mother Eve he said to her, "What did God say to you? Was it 'Do not eat from the tree of knowledge'?" She said, "He said not only, 'Do not eat from it', but, 'Do not touch it, lest you die.'" He said to her, "Do not be afraid. In death you shall not die. For he knows that when you eat from it, your intellect will become sober and you will come to be like gods, recognizing the difference that obtains between evil men and good ones. Indeed, it was in jealousy that he said this to you, so that you would not eat from it."
>
> Now Eve had confidence in the words of the instructor. She gazed at the tree and saw that it was beautiful and appetizing, and liked it; she took some of its fruit and ate it; and she gave some also to her husband, and he too ate it. Then their intellect became open. For when they had eaten, the light of knowledge had shone upon them. When they clothed themselves with shame, they knew that they were naked of knowledge. When they became sober, they saw that they were naked and became enamored of one another. When they saw that the ones who had modelled them had the form of beasts, they loathed them: they were very aware.
>
> Then when the rulers knew that they had broken their commandments, they entered Paradise and came to Adam and Eve with earthquake and great threatening, to see the effect of the aid. Then Adam and Eve trembled greatly and hid under the trees in Paradise. Then the rulers did not know where they were and said, "Adam, where are you?" He said, "I am here, for through fear of you I hid, being ashamed." And they said to him ignorantly, "Who told you about the shame with which you clothed yourself? —unless you have eaten from that tree!" He said, "The woman whom you gave me—it is she that gave to me and I ate." Then they said to the latter, "What is this that you have done?" She answered and said, "It is the instructor who urged me on, and I ate."

---

[380] Crafty = knowledge and intelligence.
[381] This point suggests that there are definitely two entheogens used in the ceremony.

Then the rulers came up to the instructor. Their eyes became misty because of him, and they could not do anything to him. They cursed him, since they were powerless. Afterwards, they came up to the woman and cursed her and her offspring. After the woman, they cursed Adam, and the land because of him, and the crops; and all things they had created, they cursed. They have no blessing. Good cannot result from evil.

From that day, the authorities knew that truly there was something mightier than they: they recognized only that their commandments had not been kept. Great jealousy was brought into the world solely because of the immortal man. Now when the rulers saw that their Adam had entered into an alien state of knowledge, they desired to test him, and they gathered together all the domestic animals and the wild beasts of the earth and the birds of heaven and brought them to Adam to see what he would call them. When he saw them, he gave names to their creatures.

They became troubled because Adam had recovered from all the trials. They assembled and laid plans, and they said, "Behold Adam! He has come to be like one of us, so that he knows the difference between the light and the darkness. Now perhaps he will be deceived, as in the case of the Tree of Knowledge, and also will come to the Tree of Life and eat from it, and become immortal, and become lord, and despise us and disdain us and all our glory! Then he will denounce us along with our universe. Come, let us expel him from Paradise, down to the land from which he was taken, so that henceforth he might not be able to recognize anything better than we can." And so they expelled Adam from Paradise, along with his wife. And this deed that they had done was not enough for them. Rather, they were afraid. They went in to the Tree of Life and surrounded it with great fearful things, fiery living creatures called "Cheroubin," and they put a flaming sword in their midst, fearfully twirling at all times, so that no earthly being might ever enter that place.

Thereupon, since the rulers were envious of Adam they wanted to diminish their (viz., Adam's and Eve's) lifespans. They could not (however,) because of fate, which had been fixed since the beginning. For to each had been allotted a lifespan of 1,000 years, according to the course of the luminous bodies. But although the rulers could not do this, each of the evildoers took away ten years. And all this lifespan (which remained) amounted to 930 years: and these are in pain and weakness and evil distraction. And so life has turned out to be, from that day until the consummation of the age.

Thus when Sophia Zoe saw that the rulers of the darkness had laid a curse upon her counterparts, she was indignant. And coming out of the first heaven with full power, she chased those rulers out of their heavens, and cast them down into the sinful world, so that there they should dwell, in the form of evil spirits (demons) upon the earth. [382]

Figure 127 - Apple (left) – *Amanita muscaria* **cap (right)**

---

[382] On the Origin of the World, *The Nag Hammadi Library*, pg. 184-186.

Making the forbidden fruit an apple is odd because today we tell children that an apple a day will keep the doctor away, apples are good for you. Why would the Church frighten people away from eating apples? The apple was chosen because apples are symbolically a perfect fit for the actual *forbidden fruit*. Apples are red and they are the fruit of a tree. The *Amanita muscaria* is also red and it, too, is the fruiting body of the tree. Some apples even have white spots on them just like the *A. muscaria* mushroom does. When a bite is taken out of the apple, we see the same white inside that is seen when one finds an *A. muscaria* in the wild with a bite taken out of it by a deer or other animal. An apple is the safe, alchemical representation of the *actual* fruit of the Tree of Knowledge of Good and Evil without giving away the *actual* knowledge of the fruit itself.

Figure 128 is a fresco from the Plaincourault Chapel, 1300 CE, as seen in both Gordon Wasson's *Soma: The Divine Mushroom of Immortality* and John Allegro's *The Sacred Mushroom and The Cross*. Some researchers ignore the obvious and claim that the central figure is *not* a mushroom.[383] It obviously depicts Adam and Eve on either side of the mushroom, or rather, the caduceus with the serpent climbing the stem, which symbolizes what Adam and Eve were eating in the Garden of Eden: the sacred mushroom.[384]

Figure 128 - Fresco from the Plaincourault Chapel, 1300 CE

THE SONG OF SONGS

A more fitting title for the *Song of Solomon* or the *Song of Songs* would be *The Song of the Suns of Duality*. This chapter is generally thought to be a love story, but it is actually a mycological field guide[385] for the *Amanita muscaria*, *Amanita pantherina* and *Psilocybe cubensis* mushrooms. Occult information regarding the *Song of Solomon*, the Book of Revelation, and Jonah are extensive and will be revealed in detail in another book. It is not the purpose of this book to discuss this in depth, but we will disclose a few examples.

> Song of Solomon 2:1
> I AM the rose of Sharon, and the lily of the valleys.

This is not a reference to the *Amanita* mushroom, but to the *Psilocybe cubensis* mushroom, as Sharon comes from sharn, which means dung, or cow dung[386], whereupon these mushrooms grow. Sharon also means flat. The valleys are flat and in this is where we find the "sharn" of the cows that gives birth to the "rose of sharn," or "lily of the valley"… the *P. cubensis* mushrooms. It is also important to note that *Nymphaea caerulea* or Sacred Blue *Lily* is also an entheogenic substance.[387]

---

[383] Historian Erwin Panofsky wrote Wasson concerning this interpretation and dismissed it, stating: "...the plant in this fresco has nothing whatever to do with mushrooms... and the similarity with Amanita muscaria is purely fortuitous. The Plaincourault fresco is only one example—and, since the style is provincial, <u>a particularly deceptive one</u>—of a <u>conventionalized tree type</u>, prevalent in Romanesque and early Gothic art, which art historians actually refer to as a "mushroom tree" or in German, *Pilzbaum*. It comes about by the gradual <u>schematization of the impressionistically rendered Italian pine tree</u> in Roman and Early Christian painting, and there are hundreds of instances exemplifying this development—unknown of course to mycologists…. What the mycologists have overlooked is that the <u>mediaeval artists hardly ever worked from nature but from classical prototypes which in the course of repeated copying</u> became quite unrecognizable." (*Soma*, pg. 179-180) Wasson wrongfully agreed, ignoring the obvious association to the pine tree, the host of the Amanita muscaria, and the caduceus symbol of drugs. See *Mushroom & Mankind* for more on pine worship and the Christmas/mushroom traditions.
[384] *Mushrooms and Mankind*, by James Arthur.
[385] In the 1980's, Jack Herer, discovered similar relationships based on the work of John Allegro in *The Sacred Mushroom and the Cross*. Heinrich (*Magic Mushrooms*, pg. 91-98) and Bennett (*SDVB pt. 1 ch. 6*) also make attempts at this decipherment .
[386] *Oxford English Dictionary*: sharon, dial. Variant of sharn. sharn: Dung, esp. dung of cattle.
[387] *Soma: The Divine Hallucinogen*, by David Spess.

Song of Solomon 2:3
As the apple tree among the trees of the wood....

The above verse tells us that the fruit from the tree of the knowledge of good and evil is like an apple tree among the trees of the wood(s) (some translations of the Bible even read, "...an apple tree among the trees of the *forest*"). We know that apple trees are not found among the trees of the forest. However, this line is symbolically telling us where the fruit of the knowledge of good and evil may be found, looking in the pine *forest* for *apples* (pine-apples[388]) would be a good start.

Gospel of Thomas -
Jesus said: "Split wood, I am there."

That truly is where this mushroom is found, even when the actual "mushroom" is nowhere to be seen. The mycelium attaches to the roots of the tree and its DNA permeates the entire tree.[389]

Song of Solomon 4:1-2
Behold, Thou art fair, my love; behold, thou art fair; thou hast doves' eyes within thy locks...

We have already discussed how the white universal veil peels away to reveal a red "eye," just as doves are white with red eyes, so here is the red and white connection of the colors and the dove.[390]

Song of Solomon 4:1-2
...thy hair is as a flock of goats, that appear from mount Gilead.

This is likely a reference is to the *P. cubensis* mushrooms, as well. Gilead comes from "Gal" which is heap, and "ed" or "uwd" which means to stand up right.[391] Gilead is likely a reference to cow dung (and P. cubensis), but could also mean the heap or "mound" that stands, which is an excellent mushroom description. The mushroom references often contain macrocosm/microcosm allusions and we may visualize the macrocosm as a mound of dung with *Psilocybe* mushrooms all over it. This is the microcosm to the *Amanita* cap, rounded as a mound covered with white bumps. The hair reference points to the *Amanita* spots, which resemble hair--some goats are white. Some goats are also tan colored, the color of *P. cubensis* caps. The flock of goats on a mound is an analogy for the *Psilocybe* mushrooms on a heap of dung. In this verse, we may visualize three levels of macro/microcosm; the single mushroom cap with wool-like spots, the mound of dung with mushrooms on it, and a mountain with goats upon it.

---

[388] We, and others, doubt the accuracy of the *Oxford English Dictionary* definitions of "pineapple" in relation to "pinecone." There is no reason to call a pinecone **seed** (a pine-nut) an "apple." However, the definition would match perfectly with what grows *under* the pine tree; *OED* – Pineapple: 1. a. The fruit of the pine tree; a pine-cone. Obs. exc. dial. Formerly also applied to the edible seeds or 'kernels' (pine-nuts) 3. attrib. and Comb. †a. in sense 1, as pine-apple kernel, seed, a seed of the pine-cone, esp. as used for food; pine-apple nut, a pine-cone; pine-apple tree, a pine-tree, esp. Pinus Pinea (all obs.)

[389] *Protocols for Analysis of DNA from Mycorrhizal Roots*, by Q. F. Baldwin and K.N. Egger, discusses DNA extraction from mycorrhizal roots.

[390] Allegro, Herer, Heinrich.

[391] *Strong's* # **1567**: Gal`ed gal-ade' from 1530 and 5707; heap of testimony; Galed, a memorial cairn East of the Jordan:-- Galeed. # **1530**: gal gal from 1556; something rolled, i.e. a heap of stone or dung (plural ruins), by analogy, a spring of water (plural waves):--billow, heap, spring, wave. **5707** `ed ayd contracted from 5749; concretely, a witness; abstractly, testimony; specifically, a recorder, i.e. prince:--witness. **5749** `uwd ood a primitive root; to duplicate or repeat; by implication, to protest, testify (as by reiteration); intensively, to encompass, restore (as a sort of reduplication):--admonish, charge, earnestly, lift up, protest, call (take) to record, relieve, rob, solemnly, stand upright, testify, give warning, (bear, call to, give, take to) witness.

Figure 129 - Agnus dei

There is power, power,
wonder working power
In the precious blood of the Lamb.[392]

Here is the wool of the goat. The blood of the lamb is shed from its rib. Remember that the word blessed means to have the blood of a sacrifice on you. Here is revealed the blood of (or *in*) the Holy Grail, the blood of the Lamb of God (or Agnus dei).

> Song of Solomon 4:1-2
> ...Thy teeth are like a flock of sheep that are even shorn...

This is probably a reference to both the *A. muscaria* and *A. pantherina*, and the white patches, or "teeth" on the top of the cap.

> Song of Solomon 7:4
> Thy neck is as a tower of **ivory**; thine eyes like the fishpools in Heshbon, by the gate of Bathrabbim: thy nose is as the tower of Lebanon which looketh toward Damascus.

It is unlikely that you would appreciate someone telling you that you have a neck like a tower of ivory, eyes like the blessed (blood) pools of Heshbon (a stronghold)[393] and a nose like the tower of Lebanon. But to an *A. muscaria* mushroom, this description is quite fitting. Bathrabbim also means "*apple of the eye.*"[394]

Next is a reference from the King James version of Revelation 1:12-13:

> And I turned to see the voice that spake with me. And being turned, I saw seven golden candlesticks; And in the midst of the seven candlesticks[395] one like unto the Son of man, clothed with a garment down to the foot, and girt about the paps with a golden girdle.

The Son of man who's "clothed with a garment down to the foot" is the *Amanita* mushroom. The garment (or "robe," as translated in other versions of the Bible) is the universal veil that covers the entire mushroom. The number seven represents, once again, the seven chakras, the seven stars of the Pleiades, and the seven known planets. The word translated in verse 13 as "paps" should actually be singular, as "pap."[396] The *cap* of the mushroom equated to a *pap* (something resembling a nipple) because of its shape.

---

[392] Appendix D
[393] *Strong's*: **1295** brekah ber-ay-kaw' from 1288; a reservoir (at which camels kneel as a resting-place):--(fish-) pool. **1288** barak baw-rak' a primitive root; to kneel; by implication to bless God (as an act of adoration), and (vice-versa) man (as a benefit); also (by euphemism) to curse (God or the king, as treason):--X abundantly, X altogether, X at all, blaspheme, bless, congratulate, curse, X greatly, X indeed, kneel (down), praise, salute, X still, thank. **2809** Cheshbown khesh-bone' the same as 2808; Cheshbon, a place East of the Jordan —Heshbon. (a stronghold) see: http://bible.crosswalk.com/Lexicons/Hebrew/heb.cgi?number=02809&version=kjv.
[394] Ibid : # 1337, 1323.
[395] The candle sticks were first pointed out by Allegro, pg. 68.
[396] *Strong's*: Mastos #3149.

Revelation 1:14
His head and his hairs were white like wool, as white as snow; and his eyes were as a flame of fire...

Again, the reference to the red eyes, we could go on all day with alchemical mushroom representations throughout the Bible, but it is not the scope of this book.

THE DUALITY OF JESUS

Gnostic traditions teach that the serpent is synonymous with Jesus, that their characters are one and the same. Consequently, it was the serpent crucified on the cross, and Jesus who fed Adam and Eve the Fruit of Paradise.

Figure 130 - La serpiente crucificada - Nicholas Flamel – Circa 1370

Figure 131 – Die Erlösung - Lucas Cranach the Younger - 1555

This is a painting of Archangel Gabriel holding the scepter, the staff entwined with the banner, just as the serpents climb the caduceus staff. Angels are messengers of God, and so are these mushrooms. The entheogenic mushrooms speak to us. They are God's messengers, and the physical characteristics of the mushroom are the reason for the wings and the colors represented here. Notice the colors are primarily red and white, the same colors as Sol and Luna and the Amanita muscaria mushroom, with the blue sleeve representing the stipe of a Psilocybe, with the wings symbolizing the cap.

Figure 132 - Archangel Gabriel

Another interesting thing to know about the word "angel" is etymological references relating to the word angel itself. In Greek, the word angel (ἄγγελος) means a messenger[397], and could be derived from ἀγέλη (agele) which means "to herd," as in cattle.[398] The root of angel could also derived from the Greek word 'ang' meaning vessel. The shape of a mushroom is often that of a vessel.[399,400] Both root words *ag* and *ang* give us possible mushroom correlations. Interestingly, the Eskimo word for medicine man or shaman is *angakok*.[401] Gordon Wasson found an

[397] Ibid, #32.
[398] Ibid, #34.
[399] Jay Lynn describes the vessel as often shaped like a bowling pin.
[400] *Oxford English Dictionary* – 2. a. Any article designed to serve as a receptacle for a liquid or other substance, usually one of circular section and made of some durable material; esp. a utensil of this nature in domestic use, employed in connexion with the preparation or serving of food or drink, and usually of a size suitable for carrying by hand. Often with defining term preceding (sometimes hyphened), indicating its special use, as dairy, drinking, kitchen, milk- or wine-vessel.
[401] *Webster's Third New International Dictionary.*

interesting correlation through the root word for a cluster of words pango and *sgᵘhombho. (*sgwombho)[402] Slavonic: *Gomba*; Gothic: *Wamba*; Hindi: *Khumbi*; German: *Schwamm*; Russian: *Guba*; Greek: *Spongos*; Latin: *Fungus*. Moreover, into Ural-Altaic Language groups: Mordvines: *Panggo*; Cheremissian: *Ponggo*; Vogul: *Pangkh*; Ostyak: *Pongkh*; Yenisei Ostyak: *Hanggo*, Spanish: *Hongo*. This provides us with a *possible* origin of the word angel through variations of linguistic forms for the word "mushroom."

> Specialists in the Uralic family of languages have greatly contributed to the Uralic aspect of this problem, but no first class scholar has dealt with the linguistic and cultural aspects of the entire pattern of fungal words that are scattered throughout northern Eurasia from the Iberian peninsula to Bering Strait.... For between the Finno-Ugrian languages and the Samoyed languages there exists precisely the same p ~ t shift that we find distinguished the Latin and Germanic languages; e.g., Latin pater ~ English "father." The Tavgi word, manifesting this basic shift, cannot therefore be a borrowing from Vogul or Zyrian. It goes back to a common ancestor, before the Uralic peoples divided into the Samoyed and the prot-Finno-Ugrian, certainly thousands of years before Christ. We cannot say when the fly-agaric was first used in the northern reaches of Eurasia. We can say, if Castren is to be relied on, that it was being used when the ancestral tongue of the Uralic peoples split up. In any case we feel safe in saying, on the evidence supplied by the Uralic languages, that the fly-agaric was being invoked as a divine inebriant before the Aryans left their ancestral home and long before the Rig Veda was composed.... Was not the *pon* cluster of the Uralic peoples borrowed, perhaps as far back as Uralic times, from [by] the neighboring Indo-Europeans? If the thesis of this book is right, the Aryans were using the fly-agaric in their religious rites before they left their homeland. The Indo-Iranians do not possess a word of the pon cluster, because under tabu influences they had **replaced it by Soma or Haoma**, and the original word was lost.[403] [Bold—ours]
> ~ R. Gordon Wasson

Figure 133 - 16th Century art shows a shaman eating mushrooms and a god behind him, speaking through the mushroom.

Figure 133 is an example of 16th century art depicting psilocybin mushrooms with a shaman sitting on a stump holding a mushroom. Behind the shaman is the spirit of the mushroom (the angel) speaking through him.

---

[402] *Soma: Divine Mushroom of Immortality*, exhibits 33 to 39, by Gordon Wasson; See also *The Sacred Mushroom: Key to the Door of Eternity*, ch. 12-13, by Andrija Puharich for more interesting (but possibly dubious) examples.
[403] *Soma*, pg. 164-65-69, by Gordon Wasson.

Figure 134 is another representation of the Annunciation, depicting the symbol for the scepter as the serpent entwined caduceus, the Egyptian key of life. A magic wand-like device represents something used to transport souls from one dimension to another. The image shows the spirit of Jesus being transferred from another dimension into this dimension (into the Virgin Mary) by way of the caduceus. We can see the dove up above as well, completing the snake/bird template by providing the wings above the serpent-entwined staff.

Figure 134 - The-Annunciation - by Bartel

THE MARK OF THE BEAST

For 2000 years, a puzzle has riddled humankind, perplexing millions of people who study the Christian Bible. This mystery concerns the 13th chapter of the book of Revelation. In this chapter, a Beast is mentioned as a world power that will rise up and plague humankind. This beast is commonly referred to as the Antichrist. Over the last two millennia, a world power has indeed come onto the scene, which seems to fit the description of this prophecy. Strangely enough, the first and only world power that emerged as a suitable candidate is the Roman Catholic Church, the Vatican and the Pope.

Many people understand the 666 to mean the devil or Satan. However, in ancient philosophy, most everything symbolic had a dualistic meaning to it. The mushroom is both God and Devil, Virgin and Whore, Demon and Angel. The caduceus is both the Mark of the Beast and the Seal of God—the 666.[404, 405]

> Do not be ignorant of me.
> For I am the first and the last.
> I am the honored one and the scorned one.
> I am the whore and the holy one.
> I am the wife and the virgin.
> I am the mother and the daughter.
> ~ Excerpt from *The Thunder, Perfect Mind* [406]

---

[404] Arthur , radio interview, "Coast to Coast, with George Noory."
[405] Also see Ch. 14, 'Heaven & Hell,' *Magic Mushrooms in Religion and Alchemy* , by Heinrich.
[406] *The Nag Hammadi Library*, ed. by James M. Robinson, pg. 297.

When early people began to write words rather than to express ideas in pictures, they used an alphabet much more instinctual than ours. Ancient written languages like Phoenician, Egyptian and Hebrew did not use vowels at all.

The Bible, as we know it, was originally written in two languages, Greek and Hebrew. Neither of which, at the time the Bible was written, had an accompanying number system. Every word in ancient Greek and Hebrew could encompass both a literary meaning and a numerical value (the sum of the values of the individual letters). Gematria is something that was most likely used by the Phoenicians as well. Through Gematria, we find that the numbers 666 also have a peculiar alphabetical equivalent in the Greek language.

The alphabetical equivalent of 666 in the *ancient* Greek alphabet was Chi χ Xi ξ Stigma ς.[407]

Chi = 600 Xi = 60 and Stigma = 6.
For confirmation of this, we first turn to Revelation 13:18 and find the words "six hundred threescore and six." Next, we turn to the Strong's Concordance, and look up what the original words were in ancient Greek, and we see that Strong's references us to #5516 of the Greek dictionary. There we find that the actual letters for 666 used in ancient Greek are χ ξ ς. [408]

> Strong's: 5516. χ ξ ς chi xi stigma khee xee stig'-ma the 22nd, 14th and an obsolete letter (4742 as a cross) of the Greek alphabet (intermediate between the 5th and 6th), used as numbers; denoting respectively 600, 60 and 6; 666 as a numeral—six hundred threescore and six.
> ~ Strong's Concordance

In the modern Greek alphabet, stigma equals 90, and sigma equals 200, but in the ancient Greek, as *Strong's* has proven, stigma equals 6. All other theories that we have found fail to verify the original value of the stigma character.[409] To understand what this *mark of the beast*[410] is, ancient Greek must be used.

In the modern Greek alphabet, these letters are different. A straight X represents the chi, the Xi is represented with three dashes (Ξ) or *"three score,"* and the sigma (which now represents 200) looks something between a Z and an E (Σ).

X S s (χ ξ ς) or JeSus can also mean God Is Zeus, by omitting the vowels. XSs or 'X-S-s' translates to **J-e-S-u-s** in English when we include the vowels. For more information, refer to Dr. E. W. Bullinger's *Number in Scripture:*

> The 1st and 3rd letters, it is said, represent the first and last letters of the title "Christos" and the middle letter represents the symbol of the serpent and is intimately connected with the ancient Egyptian Mysteries.[411]
> ~ Dr. E. W. Bullinger

Christmas is often abbreviated **X-Mas** because of the history associating the Greek letter **X** with Jesus Christ. Sometimes Greek, Catholic and Gnostic artwork depicts Jesus Christ with the first, second and last letters of Christos, **XPS**.[412]

---

[407] *Number in Scripture*, by Dr. E.W. Bullinger.

[408] *Ibid.*

[409] We mention both the sigma and stigma characters because they both represent the serpent and are often mistaken for one another.

[410] By looking at the word *stigma* itself, as defined by *Oxford English Dictionary,* other important details are revealed. *Stigma* means mark, or marks: "[m]arks resembling the wounds on the crucified body of Christ, said to have been supernaturally impressed on the bodies of certain saints and other devout persons... Sometimes extended to other marks, as crosses, sacred names, etc., supposed to be supernaturally impressed."

[411] *Number in Scripture,* by Dr. E. W. Bullinger, pg. 49.

[412] *Oxford English Dictionary:* In writing the name Christ, esp. in abbreviated form, X or x represents the first letter (kaɪ) of Gr. XPICTOC khristos, and XP or xp the first two letters (kaɪrəʊ). Hence in early times XX, in modern times Xt, Xt, and X, are used as abbreviations of the syllable Christ, alone or in derivatives; thus †Xpen, Xpn = christen, †Xpenned = christened; †Xpian, Xtian(ity) = Christian(ity); Xmas (Xstmas, Xtmas) – Christmas. †Xpc stands for XPC contracted form of XPICTOC; cf. IHS. - See also page 153, below.

Figure 135 - The Chi Rho - The Monogram for Jesus Christ

The Chi Rho (Χρ) is known as the monogram for Jesus Christ (Figure 135). Surrounding this symbol (above) is a wreath or the ouroboros (serpent) with two birds. They are all touching the ouroboros standing on the cross. A mark is quite similar to a *brand* (trade *mark*) and the original mark of the Catholic Church and for Jesus is the Chi-Rho. The mark is a monogram which is a single letter made by combining two or more letters. Legend has it that Emperor Constantine had a vision or a dream of the Chi-Rho symbol in the sky next to the words "In this sign you will conquer." Constantine then placed the Chi-Rho symbol on his soldier's shields and won a battle in which his army was outnumbered. This decisive battle won him his place as emperor.

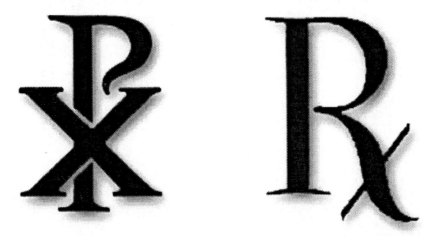

Figure 136 - Chi Rho – symbolic of Christ (left)   Rho Chi – Symbolic of Drugs (Right)

Here again is the symbol for the *Chi Rho*, the "Χρ," and the symbol for the pharmacies, Rx (*Rho Chi*). The P and the R are interchangeable in Greek, the original language of the New Testament. So if we take the X of the Chi Rho "Χρ" and slide it over just a little, the Rx is revealed. Is this really a P, or is it an R? It is an interchangeable symbol for drugs or for Jesus.

132

Figure 137

In the symbology of these letters, the Chi (χ) actually represents the caduceus with the serpent laid over the staff or the column, all on its own. Additionally, when looking at the serpents in the other letters, the Xi (ξ) represents the entwined serpent—the staff of Asclepius, and the Stigma (ς) represents a small serpent(s). Therefore, each letter is the serpent or the caduceus, in and of itself.[413] And as we mentioned previously, the letter 'S' (Serpent) is always symbolic for God.

Figure 138

Once again, Figure 138 is showing the *Chi* on the lower left with the caduceus on the lower right. The serpent is overlying the staff on the Chi, and the serpents overlying the staff on the caduceus. Above is the Christian symbol, Chi Rho (χρ), and the pharmaceutical prescription symbol, Ro Chi (ρχ). Rx is often argued to be the abbreviation for *recipe* in Latin. This symbol plays a role on the earth and in the heavens as well. Howard W. Haggard, M.D., relates "…others [scholars] hold that it [Rx] is the astrological sign of Jupiter, under whose protection medicine was generally placed."[414] Christ can here be seen in the alchemical sense as the recipe for psychedelic oils (Chrism) and other entheogenic mixtures—*drugs*. The mark that governs the trade of these and other "drugs" (to this very day) is the symbol made when the Greek χ ξ ς are laid upon each other— the caduceus.

John 3:14-15
And as Moses lifted up the serpent in the wilderness, even so must the Son of man be lifted up: That whosoever believeth in him should not perish, but have eternal life.

…priests were considered "physicians of the soul," and the early Church hierarchy included "doctors," i.e., Therapeuts, who were also wandering drug-peddlers. In fact, the professions of medicine and divinity were inseparable, and those doctors or healers who received their degrees from the University of Alexandria were viewed as true apostles, while those who did not were deemed false.[415]
~ Acharya S

---

[413] Ibid.
[414] *Mystery, Magic, and Medicine*, by Howard W. Haggard, M.D., pg 25.
[415] *The Christ Conspiracy*, by Acharya S, pg. 322.

To this day, we continue to use these symbols in order to differentiate between the so-called false healers and those with the degrees—the bearers of the caduceus, who have sequestered the use of natural plants for healing and spiritual use.

Figure 139 - Cesar Nero and Caduceus on coins – circa 60 CE

Many people believe that Caesar Nero was the Anti-Christ, 666. On many old coins, you can find Caesar Nero on one side and Mercury (Hermes) on the other side, holding the caduceus.

>Revelation 13:17-18
>And that no man might buy or sell, save he that had the mark, or the name of the beast, or the number of his name. Here is wisdom. Let him that hath understanding count the number of the beast: for it is the number of a man; and his number is Six hundred threescore and six.

The Catholic Church has been called the beast for a number of years. Recently, the Seventh Day Adventists are the largest promoters of this concept. Part of their argument lies in any changing of the calendar and the changing of the official day set aside for worship from Saturday to Sunday. This is the primary reasoning behind the name of the organization as well as their primary objection to established Christian dogma. Seventh Day Adventists do a lot of study in the apocryphal books of Daniel and Revelation. The Branch Davidians are a group of Seventh Day Adventist, and David Koresh, was one of these. His group was raided by the BATF and FBI and many perished in the ensuing siege that lasted for more than 50 days. Apparently, studying the book of Revelation as a group, on your own farm, does not rank on the top of the tolerated actions list of the U.S. government.

The Nazi government is considered a major manifestation of the spirit of the Antichrist by many students of Revelation. The persecution of the Jews and the mass murder of millions qualify Adolf Hitler as an evil figure of high-profile status to the world. One thing that is not mentioned, as far as we have found, is the uncanny similarity between the swastika[416] and the Greek letter Chi – pronounced Kī. The swastika is an ancient symbol and is popular in Germanic lore associated with the god Wodhanaz. Wodhanaz is the name for the Scandinavian god Odin. Celts and Druids also have similar icons and share many myths with Germanic, Norse and Scandinavian gods. Wodhanaz is the Germanic counterpart of Jesus, as he too was sacrificed on a tree. He is even more closely related to the

---

[416] The swastika is found in Buddhist art and Hindu art as well, sometimes rotating clockwise and sometimes rotating counterclockwise. Some say Hitler stole the swastika from India and switched it around to bend opposite of its association with good, making it now evil instead, but this is unlikely as it is found pointing in both directions in India and a particular direction is not an indication of good or evil. Strangely, Hitler was raised by Jesuits and was a professed Christian, although most Christians refused to consider this as fact because Hitler was a madman and most assuredly evil. The vast majority of Christians never for an instant consider their religion to have anything to do with evil regardless of the results of their laws or the history of its patriarchs.

Jewish Joshua. All of these gods are simply personifications and anthropomorphisms of the *Amanita muscaria* and *Amanita pantherina*, the latter being forever attached to the oak because oak is one of its hosts trees. The swastika being connected to the mark of Jesus (X), the oaks, and the number 600 are all a part of the big picture and the discovery of the actual mark of the beast.

> Joshua 24:26 (KJV)
> And Joshua wrote these words in the book of the law of God, and took a great stone, and set it up there under an oak, that was by the sanctuary of the LORD.

The idea of setting a mark upon someone can be traced back to the origins of slavery. These origins are found all over the world and flow into prehistory. Egypt, Africa, the Middle East, China and Europe all have their slavery roots. The first instance of a mark in the Bible comes to us in Genesis 4:15, where Cain is marked so none will kill him:

> And the LORD said unto him, Therefore whosoever slayeth Cain, vengeance shall be taken on him sevenfold. And the LORD set a mark upon Cain, lest any finding him should kill him.

What the mark is, how it was administered, and what it looked like is left unexplained in the Bible. But it must have been a visible thing that could be seen by others, or it would not serve the purpose given.

In 2 Samuel 13:28 a mark is set upon Ammon (Amen), but this time the mark means exactly the opposite from the mark set upon Cain—this mark is the mark of death. This illustrates the duality of the mark principal. One mark indicates protection from death and the other indicates death itself. This is followed into the book of Revelation where one mark is set by the Angel of God to protect the servants of God and the other mark comes from the beast and signifies eventual death. Job uses the term "mark" many times. Job 16:12 says:

> I was at ease, but he hath broken me asunder: he hath also taken me by my neck, and shaken me to pieces, and set me up for his mark.

"**X** *marks* the spot" is common symbolic usage. In fact, it is universal symbolism. The mark is associated with the *perfect man* in Psalms 37:37. "Mark the perfect man, and behold the upright: for the end of man is peace." The mark of the archetypal "perfect man" is the cross. The cross is an upright X. In Ezekiel, a mark is set upon the foreheads of selected men in Jerusalem and men are called to carry out a slaughter of all men, women, and children.

> Ezekiel 9:6
> Slay utterly old and young, both maids, and little children, and women: but come not near any man upon whom is the mark; and begin at my sanctuary. Then they began at the ancient men which were before the house.

The Lord slaughtering his own people is a common theme in Israel's sordid past. True or not, it is very strange indeed. This mark is placed upon the foreheads just as the Marks of God and the Marks of the Beast are placed upon the foreheads in the book of Revelation. The heretics are marked by Paul in Romans 16:17, where he extols the believer to:

> ...mark them which cause divisions and offences contrary to the doctrine which ye have learned; and avoid them.

One can imagine the believer's holding of both hands with index fingers shaped like crosses to signify rejection of what they are seeing and/or saying. Back on the other side of the fence, in Philippians 3:14, the mark is extolled as the high calling:

> I press toward the mark for the prize of the high calling of God in Christ Jesus.

In Galatians 6:17, the marks of Jesus are claimed by Paul:

> ...I bear in my body the marks of the Lord Jesus.

THE ROOT OF ALL EVIL

What is interesting about the caduceus is that its bearer is usually associated with Mercury/Hermes. The word "merchant" derives from the root of the word, "mer-cury." Mercury, the bearer of the caduceus, was the one who gave permission to be a merchant or to buy, sell, and trade. To be a **merch**ant, you had to have the symbol of **Merc**ury, the caduceus. To be a merchant, one also had to have the knowledge of the **merc**handise. This merchandise was commonly herbs, spices, and drugs.

> Hosea 12:7 (KJV)
> He [God] is a merchant, the balances of deceit are in his hand: he loveth to oppress.

Today, the dollar sign is likely the caduceus, though often said to evolve from the Mexican or Spanish "Pˢ" for pesos, or piastres, or pieces of eight and also "US," but it has been used in other countries as well. We still cannot buy or sell without this mark. And, like single and dual snakes climbing the staff of Asclepius and the caduceus, the dollar sign is represented with both single and dual vertical lines (Figure 140).

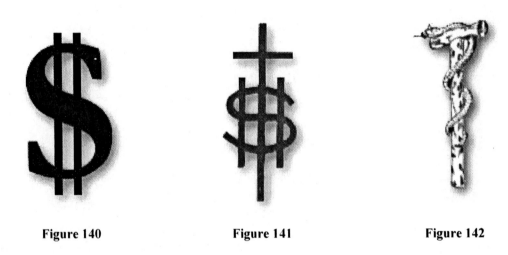

| Figure 140 | Figure 141 | Figure 142 |

The above symbol [Figure 140] is an abbreviation of the Greek name for Jesus (IHSOUS) [which is also "χ ξ ς" and based on the symbol on the right, as we pointed out previously]. The New Testament was written throughout in Greek capital letters, and it was the custom to abbreviate familiar words. When the name Jesus occurred, it was abbreviated, and the scribes used only the first two and last letters. The Greek custom of contraction is to put in first and last letters and indicate omissions by a line over the word – So IhsouS, by omitting "sou" became I H S. It was easy to draw a line down through this bar and so we get I H S and so finally $.[417]

---

[417] *History of the Cross, the Pagan Origin and Idolatrous Adoption and Worship of the Image,* by Henry Dana Ward, Symbols Addendum, Paul Tice.

Figure 143 - Bank of England (Dividend Office) with caduceus on walls

On April 15, 2004, in the *Saint Petersburg Times*, an article titled "Making Sense of the $1" had this to say about the $ symbol:

> It is possible that the dollar symbol, $, was derived from astrology.
>
> The medieval astrologers sometimes used the symbol $ to denote the planet Mercury - the planet that ruled over such things as commerce. The form of this symbol is said to have been derived from the image of a snake curling along a rod or staff.... The wand, or caduceus, carried by the god Mercury, consisted of a rod with two serpents curled around it.
>
> According to the astrological tradition, Mercury ruled finance, banking, and so on, so it is not at all unreasonable that the symbol should be used to denote currency....
>
> It is traditional for banks to have sculpted models of either Mercury or the caduceus on their facades or doors. The Bank of England, in London, has a caduceus on either of the main doors. Above the main portal of the Federal Reserve Building, in Washington, D.C., is a sculpture of a female personification of America,[418] holding a caduceus. This was sculpted in 1937, two years after the modern dollar bill was designed and printed. The two roundels on the dollar bill are based on the designs for the Great Seal of the United States.
>
> In 1935, Franklin D. Roosevelt ordered that a new dollar bill should be designed. He requested that this design should be based on the symbolism of the Great Seal of America. This design was executed by Edward M. Weeks, of the Bureau of Engraving and Printing.
>
> The obverse of this was the famous American eagle, with the shield at its breast. The reverse was the equally famous pyramid design. Both of these designs contained magical and Masonic symbols, and Roosevelt was aware of this....
>
> The dollar bill of 1935 was designed by Freemasons.
>
> The most influential men involved in the design of the dollar bill of 1935 were Freemasons. Among these were the President of the United States, Franklin D. Roosevelt; the Secretary of Agriculture, Henry A. Wallace; and the Secretary of the Treasury, Henry Morgenthau. All three were Masons.
>
> The Masonic interest in symbols may explain why the dollar bill was carefully designed to convey a wide range of secret symbolism...

---

[418] The personification of America is "Libertas," the Goddess of personal Liberty.

Not only is the caduceus the symbol (mark) of pharmaceutical drugs, the 666, our chakra system, Jesus, and the mushrooms (and other entheogens), but it is also a symbol for currency and finance as well.

Figure 144

BUY NOW – PAY LATER

Money can be the root of all evil, greed is a powerful force and has been all throughout history. The "want for more" has led man down a dark path. Today, materialism is normal and even promoted. People are being programmed (with the help of *programs* on television) into the mindset of "my stuff represents me," and this is horrible.

During the course of one year, the average American will see approximately 25,000 commercials. 25 thousand times every year, you are told what to watch, wear, eat, sleep on, brush your teeth with, drive, etc. And it works... very well. These commercials are much more than advertisements for products. They are highly sophisticated corporate tools of promoting materialistic values, attitudes, and a materialistic way of living. And of course, children are the target audience. Advertisers even put their ads on your clothing and charge you extra for doing so! Which is more expensive—a regular sweatshirt, or a regular sweatshirt with the words "Ralph Lauren" across the chest?

You are groomed from birth to be a consumer. Your purpose in life (or rather, your purpose in the lives of certain others) is to feel compelled to buy things that you do not necessarily need or even want. It is the media's job to convince you that you actually *do* want those things, or better yet, that you *need* those things. Your role as a consumer is to buy these products and maintain the status quo.

One is left with the sensation that anything beyond your role as a consumer is none of your business. You go to work so that you can buy "stuff" and maybe pursue a hobby, and that is just about it. The goings on behind the scenes of your government or church is simply designed to be none of your concern. This is reinforced by the bombardment of mindless activities that are meant to make you feel "normal." Things like professional sports and must-see TV that provides us with something to talk about and look forward to. Another example would be something (that only appears to be) taboo or dangerous, such as listening to Howard Stern or watching Jerry Springer... designed to provide the average person with an *excitement fix* before (or after) sitting in your cubicle all day, dosed up on caffeine, making someone else rich. You know when they really have you when you pop 10–20 pills a day, suck down a pack or two of cigarettes, and gulp down as much booze as you can handle and still manage to punch the clock on time and hold down your nine to five job. People are scared of sex, scared of drugs, and even scared to walk down their very own street alone at night. The spin-doctors are doing their jobs well when everything we know comes from our television and newspapers, and it all just so happens to agree with the state-sanctioned religious beliefs. To "*muse*" means to think. **A**muse is its opposite—for example, amoral is the opposite of moral. So amuse is to *not* think. All of the *amusement* that consumes our spare time does nothing to increase our consciousness or further evolve our species. In fact, it enslaves us and sustains the *kings and peons* paradigm. If we are all to be free, we must all break free of the *ignorance is bliss* mentality and strive for knowledge.

Figure 145 - Church of the Minor Friars,[419] **circa 1340**

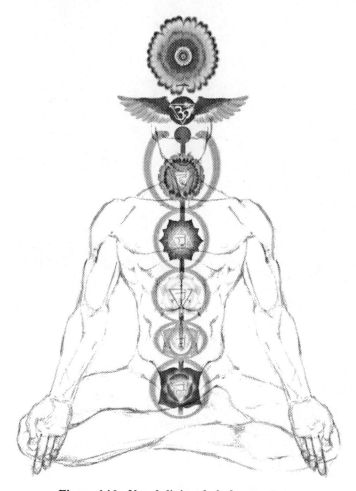

One's body (especially the mind) is the temple of God and it is a shame to spend an entire life sitting on the porch, never to have explored the temple. Meditation or prayer will only take you so far. The shaman uses plant substances in *combination* with meditation to raise the life-force energy and illuminate their crown chakra. In India, some call this energy *kundalini,* which means 'snake or serpent power'.[420]

> 1 Corinthians 3:16
> Know ye not that ye are the temple of
> God, and that the Spirit of God dwelleth
> in you?

This kundalini energy will rise through the body. It will enlighten each of the chakras, including the third eye chakra and the crown chakra. Illuminating the third eye chakra will in turn burst open the crown chakra (often symbolized in artwork, as in Figure 146). The third-eye chakra is often symbolized by placing a dot on the forehead.

Figure 146 - Kundalini and chakra system

---

[419] Background has been darkened to show mushroom shaped doorway.
[420] Kundalini means snake or serpent power in Sanskrit.

Figure 147

The Native American Indian chief wears a feathered headdress to symbolize this higher chakra. He may be wearing snakeskin shoes as well, symbolizing the serpent below and the bird above. The headdress is a representation of his crown chakra being wide open.

This is symbolized often in different traditions. In Figure 148 we see Sixtus II with his crown chakra opened, symbolized by placing a shell behind his head. On either side are entwined columns.

Figure 148 - Botticelli, Sandro
St. Sixtus II, 1481

In many cultures, people will wear feathers over their head, symbolizing the crown chakra. In the story of Pentecost, the Holy Spirit comes down onto man and rests over the heads of the people in the temple. The Holy Spirit, represented as a flame, is symbolic of crown chakra illumination. The time of year that Pentecost is celebrated is also quite symbolic...

Figure 149 - Pentecost Flame

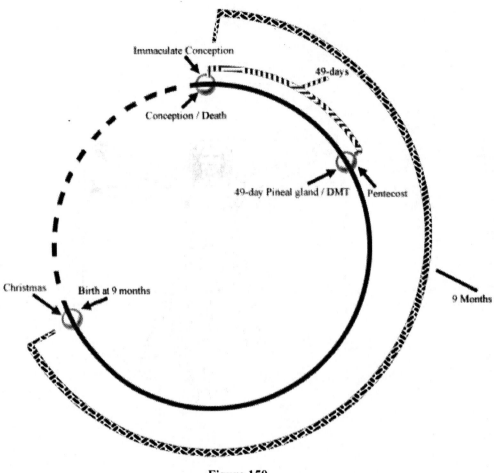

Figure 150

49 days after the Immaculate Conception is Pentecost (Pente=50 and Pentecost is held on the eve of the 50th day). Guatama meditated underneath a tree for 49 days, after which he became the Buddha. The human embryo, on the 49th day after conception, technically becomes a fetus. In the womb, a developing human is called an embryo for the first 49 days. After 49 days, a developing human is called a fetus. There is a 49-day period that happens repeatedly in mythology[421], and it also happens within our body. Pentecost represents the spirit coming down into humankind, or rather, one's spirit entering the mother's womb 49 days after conception.[422]

---

[421] The number seven is said to esoterically contain the entire Universe. 7 x 7 = 49.

[422] For more information, research Dr. Rick Strassman . In addition, choosing the host body is a philosophy held by some eastern religions.

It can be argued that at 49 days after conception, the pineal gland is formed enough to metabolize and discharge its first full dose of DMT (Dimethyltryptamine). On this 49th day, it is suggested that this is the moment that the soul actually enters into the body. This is the first day that the fetus can actually be considered *alive*.

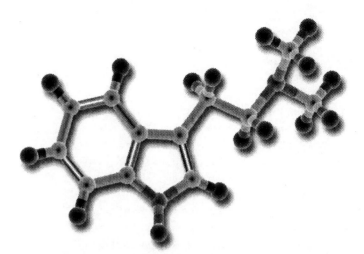

Figure 151 - DMT ($C_{12} N_2 H_{16}$)

There is a great deal of data suggesting that the pineal may produce DMT, although this has not been established scientifically. There are very high levels of the necessary ingredients in the pineal, both in terms of chemical precursors, and the enzymes necessary for converting those precursors into DMT. There *are* data demonstrating the production of 5-methoxy-DMT (a powerful analogue of DMT) in the test tube, using pineal tissue and precursors. No-one has looked carefully at the pineal for DMT production. Even if the pineal does not produce DMT, there are organs that have been firmly established to do so: lung, brain, and red blood cells. DMT levels increase with stress (be it via pineal, or these other organs), are measurable at birth in mammals, and the brain transports into its confines as much DMT as it needs, if there is not enough produced locally in the brain. Thus, the theories I've proposed about the role and function of DMT do not necessarily hinge upon pineal production, although if pineal did produce DMT, it would make a *very* tidy package!
~ Dr. Rick Strassman

Theories have proliferated in the last several years that the pineal gland sends a flood of DMT to the brain and that this is responsible for the intense visions many people experience, as often reported, at death. It is common for a Buddhist to recite from the book of the dead for 49 days after the loss of a loved one as their soul passes through the Bardo. This is something that Christians may recognize as purgatory—this is the period after death, and before the next *phase*. In the cycle of reincarnation, there is a 49-day period where we are not a human, although our host human body has been created. Could this 49th day be the time when our spirit enters into this host, deciding what sex it will be as the fingers and toes begin to develop, the eyelids begin to form and close, etc.?

Dr. Rick Strassman, in *DMT the Spirit Molecule*, was (at the time his research began) the first doctor allowed to perform psychedelic or entheogenic studies in the U.S. for over twenty years. He conducted his study at the University of New Mexico where it took him many years to acquire the permits and begin actual research. One of the many things Dr. Strassman examined while doing research on DMT and other entheogens was to look at the possibility of endogenous DMT production in the brain's pineal gland. It was confirmed during the 1970s that DMT is a neurotransmitter in mammalian brains.[423] With intravenous DMT injection, Strassman was also able to recreate (unintentionally) the alien abduction experiences, as well as many levels of out of body and "religious" experiences in a clinical setting.

The most potent psychedelic substances known to man (variations of DMT) are found naturally in psychedelic mushrooms (as congeners)[424] and inside the human body (quite possibly secreted from the third eye--pineal gland). Knowing this, we get a profound interconnection between science and religion. The churches and temples are there waiting for us to replace the wine and crackers with a true sacrament.[425] Temples will last much longer than the ideologies they were built upon and new (or rather, archaic) philosophies must (re)emerge as this new Age unfolds.

---

[423] *Pharmacotheon*, by Jonathon Ott; Christian et al. 1976, 1977; Corbett et al., 1978.

[424] There are many variations of DMT – see Jonathan Ott, Terence McKenna.

[425] The authors of this book honestly believe that this is where humankind is heading.

THE EYE WITHIN

The pupil of the eye dilates with the introduction of tryptamines. The widening of the pupil accompanies visual acuity and an increase in visible light spectrum recognition and perception. Reports from Norway detail darkroom studies with DMT, which describe an ability to see infrared light glowing from humans in complete darkness. The studies were several weeks long (in total darkness) and were designed to activate the pineal gland in test subjects. Long periods of total darkness are important to Hindu and Buddhist practices, as well as other indigenous shamanic cultures in the East, Africa, and the Americas. Caves (symbolic of the earth's womb) were often used for initiation and meditation for time periods ranging from days to years. Some tribes in South America are known to raise a young shaman in a cave from birth to teenage years. This practice of returning to a womb-like state hyper-develops internal vision as well as preserves pineal gland function.

The pineal gland, after 49 days, is known to be very active throughout the gestation period in the womb, during birth and so on. However, pineal gland function diminishes and the gland tends to calcify and atrophy badly by the time a child enters their teens. This atrophy should be taken very seriously as a detrimental effect caused by conditions in the environment. These conditions need to be documented and evaluated in order to assist circumstances to prevent this degradation. Diet may play a role in this phenomenon. A diet deficient in tryptophan results in decreased pineal gland function. Without this precursor enzyme, metabolism chains are broken. There may be additional reasoning behind decreased pineal gland function and atrophy involving a lack of proper stimulation. Without proper stimuli, the pineal gland may atrophy simply due to nonuse.

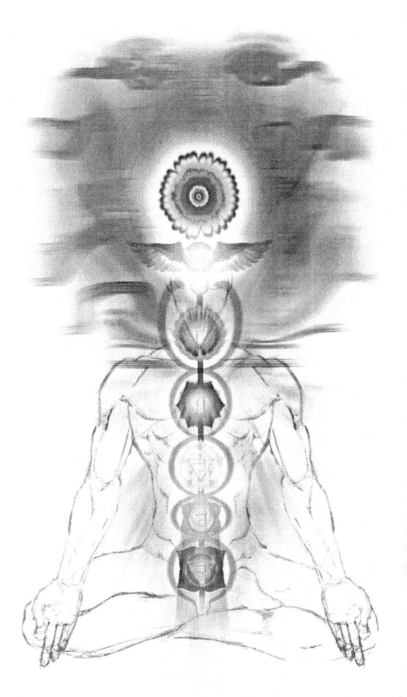

Figure 152 - Kundalini with open chakra system

This meditating man is shown with his chakra system being opened by the kundalini energy. Above his head, between his third eye and crown chakra, notice the wings on the head. We actually do have what appear to be wings in our head.

144

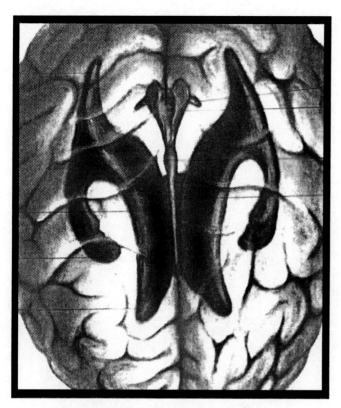
Figure 153 - Ventricle system

In our bodies, we have wings above our spinal staff. This darkened area in Figure 153, looking like wings, is the ventricle system of the brain. The ventricle system of the brain is a series of cavities and chambers that allow cerebrospinal fluid to flow around the brain. Cerebrospinal fluid is the fluid that the brain floats in to protect itself from injury.

> Small amounts of DMT and 5-MeO-DMT can be found in the cerebrospinal fluid of psychiatrically normal humans, schizophrenics and manics.
> ~ Corbett et al. 1978

> There is DMT in the spinal fluid. That's well established.[426]
> ~ Dr. Rick Strassman

> The finding of DMT in normal human body fluids opens up interesting legal questions. Since DMT is illegal, as is "any material, compound, mixture or preparation" containing DMT, it would seem that we are all guilty of possession of a controlled substance. Possession, or possession with intent to sell, of other human beings is clearly proscribed by modern "controlled substances" legislation![427]
> ~ Jonathon Ott

It was once believed that the brain had only *three* ventricles, i.e., the laterals (considered as one), the third, and the fourth. Albertus Magnus, better known as Albert the Great (circa 1250), is called "the Great," and "Doctor Universalis" (Universal Doctor), in recognition of his extraordinary genius and extensive knowledge. He was proficient in every branch of learning cultivated in his day, and surpassed all his contemporaries (except, perhaps, Roger Bacon 1214-94), in the knowledge of nature.[428] Magnus depicted these cavities with three circles of equal size, filling the entire cranium (Figure 154).

Figure 154 - Albertus Magnus, 1260

In regards to the Brahma-randhra[429] as the greatest of the chambers in the brain, Dr. Rele[430] says that this cavity is constantly secreting a fluid called "the nectar of life" or "the divine fluid," bathing the spinal cord and the brain. When the information regarding DMT is applied to this, the cerebrospinal fluid is one and the same with the "the nectar of life," "the divine fluid," "tears of the sky God," *and* "the tears of Christ." In search of their Elixir of Life, the alchemists discovered the occult properties of a certain mysterious "dew" and were inspired to write about it, but always in a secretive manner.[431]

---

[426] 1. Brown G, Smythies J, Morin R, In: Wood J, ed. Neurobiology of Cerebrospinal Fluid. v. 2. New York: Plenum, 1983:173-7. 2. Smythies JR, Morin RD, Brown G. Identification of dimethyltryptamine and O-methylbufotenin in human cerebrospinal fluid by combined gas chromatography/mass spectrometry. Biol Psychiatry 1979;14:549-56.
[427] *Pharmacotheon* pg. 185, by Jonathon Ott.
[428] Catholic Encyclopedia.
[429] In the Yogic texts, the Brahma Randhra is often identified with the fontanelle at the top of the skull. It is said to be the entry point and exit of the soul.
[430] Author of *The Mysterious Kundalini*.
[431] *Man: Grand Symbol of the Mysteries*, by Manly P. Hall.

Science recognizes four ventricles in the adult human brain, together they are relatively wing-shaped and often referred to as wings. The brain encompassing the shape of wings is interesting because the brain was also likened by the *pagan* initiates to the head of a serpent. Here, in our bodies, the serpent and the bird are one and the same. Could this "Brain Dew" be a sacred substance because of the psychedelic properties contained within the cerebrospinal fluid?

Figure 155 - Alchemical emblem known as the Second Key of Basil Valentine

Manly P. Hall notes the lateral and fourth ventricles are represented as two contesting swordsmen, with Mercury as the third ventricle in equilibrium between them (Figure 155). Also notice the caducei that Mercury is holding. Each caduceus is capped with the Fleur De Lis, or Flower of Life. Giorgio Samorini makes a strong argument that this *Flower of Life* is a psychedelic mushroom[432], but notice here that each is different. Could one represent the *Amanita* and the other *Psilocybe*? This is a very interesting emblem, to say the least. This battle between two wands is incredibly profound because the caduceus is the symbol and mark of the beast as well as the mark of God in the symbolism of the book of Revelation.

---

[432] Ernest Busenbark also associates the Fleur De Lis as a symbol of the male phallic. The two descriptions, based on the phallic symbology of the mushroom, are actually supportive of each other, pg. 163.

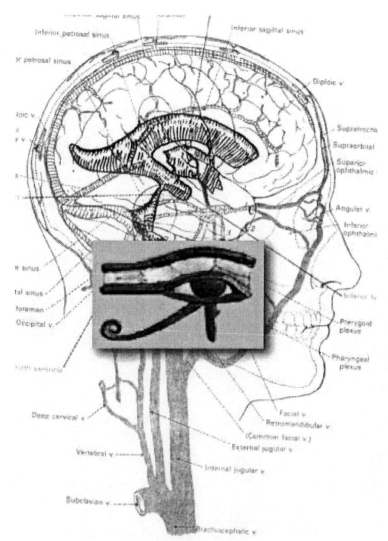

In Egyptian mythology, the Eye of Horus was pulled or plucked from his head by Seth, or "Set." Now we begin to understand from whence the microcosmic symbol of the Eye of Horus came.[433] It is literally our third eye inside the brain. Horus was the son of the sun, just as Jesus is "God's sun on earth." The (one) Eye of Horus represents the mushroom's affect on the third eye (internal vision), opened by those mystifying substances found within mushrooms and naturally within our brains. This visual/symbolic representation has an actual purpose, and that is why it is portrayed in just that particular way.

Matthew 6:22
The light of the body is the eye: if therefore thine eye be single, thy whole body shall be full of light.

Figure 156 - The third eye chakra/ventricle system, represented by the eye of Horus.

In one way, the caduceus is a perfect symbol for allopathic medicine because it is based upon poisons being taken into the body in the hopes that it will kill the disease before it kills the host.[434] Allopathic medicine is based on the use of drugs. Unfortunately, pharmaceutical medicines are unnatural. A pharmaceutical company cannot patent a naturally occurring substance. This means they do not have any financial interest in researching or promoting any natural medicine, no matter how good it is. As opposed to using the ayurvedic approach, Western medicine finds naturally occurring substances and take them into the laboratory where they alter the plants, patent their alterations, and market their new drug. Whereas the original, natural substance may have *cured* disease, the altered product is just skewed enough to *maintain* the disease. The allopathic agenda is not to cure disease but to provide "disease maintenance." Snakes occur *naturally* as does their venom, allopathic medicine uses no natural medicines. Therefore, their use of the caduceus is a mockery. Practitioners of Allopathy have rejected nature and have glorified the works of man. The true caduceus represents the human body; the snakes are nature's drugs in the body, climbing the spinal column to the brain.

---

[433] On the macrocosm, the Eye of Horus was the "eye of the sun," the dark phase is caused by Set, who steals or wounds the Eye of Horus. See *Symbols, Sex, and the Stars*, by Ernest Busenbark pg. 51.
[434] Consider chemotherapy or radiation treatment for cancer patients.

WHAT IS THIS?

The Bible tells us that manna fell from heaven and was eaten by the Israelites during their exodus from Egypt. The authors of this book consider manna to be either a generic term for entheogens, or the psychoactive mushrooms themselves. Recently Daniel Merkur, Ph.D., a former teacher from Syracuse University and Auburn Theological Seminary, proposed that another psychedelic fungus was the manna of the Bible–ergot (Claviceps paspali & Claviceps purpurea). Ergot contains a psychoactive substance similar to LSD called LSA, and is one of the primary sources for making LSD. Ergot was used in the Bible as a grain, and it was also mentioned as something used in a winepress, which was then taken under the oak tree (Judges 6:11-12, 19-24) as, very likely, a substitute for the *Amanitas*.[435] Also wheat, barley, and darnel/cockle (tares – Lolium temulentum)[436] are host plants for ergot.[437]

We believe "manna" was likely used as a generic term for "entheogens," just as "Soma" appears to be. Though generally accepted that ergot was not identified as fungal until 1764,[438] we must also consider the possibility that manna means, "mushrooms."[439] With this in mind, it makes more sense to identify ergot with manna, as well as *Amanita*, *Psilocybe*, and possibly, but less likely, any type of *mushroom*, psychoactive or not. Manna's association to the rains and heavens makes us consider this option, though Soma, too, is often associated with the rains, thunder, and heavens.

We agree with many of Merkur's references to "showbread, unleavened bread, and Presence bread" as being from ergot. Merkur's evidence also suggests that ergot was more likely a later *substitute* for "the manna of the wilderness years":

> What among the ritual objects of Solomon's temple was described in biblical narrative as Manna? The answer is not far to seek. According to Josh. 5:11-12, unleavened bread was **substituted** in Canaan for the manna of the **_wilderness_** years.... Immediately after the Israelites crossed the Jordan River and ate the produce of Canaan, Yahveh ceased to provide them with manna. **_Unleavened bread replaced manna_** in their diet.[440] [bold, italics, underline—ours]
> ~ Dan Merkur

Strong's clearly relates the Hebrew word for wilderness, "*midbar*,"[441] as being related to cattle pastures, and therefore most likely related to *Psilocybe* mushrooms:

> **4057** midbar mid-bawr' from 1696 in the sense of driving; **a pasture (i.e. open field, whither cattle are driven**); by implication, a desert; also speech (including its organs):--desert, south, speech, wilderness. [bold—ours]
> ~ Strong's Concordance

Many of Merkur's references to ergot are, in our opinion, *Amanita* and/or *Psilocybe* references, and not only that of ergot. On page 43, he quotes Philo:

> Why then need you still wonder that God **showers** virtue <u>without toil or trouble, needing no controlling hand but perfect and complete from the very first?</u> And if you would have further testimony of this can you find any more trustworthy than Moses, who says that while other men receive their food from earth, <u>the nation of vision alone has it from heaven? The earthly food is produced with the co-operation of husbandmen, but the heavenly is sent like the snow by God the</u>

---

[435] Amanita mushrooms are also pressed in water to release their psychoactive compounds.

[436] *Oxford English Dictionary* – Cockle: Recent investigation has apparently settled that the ζιζάνιον, pl. -ia, of the N.T., zizania and lolium of Latin writers, was the grass Lolium temulentum or Darnel, a prevalent weed in Mediterranean and Levantine regions (cf. Stanley Sinai & Palestine 426, Tristram Nat. Hist. Bible 487), which is very prone to be affected with ergot, and in the ergotized condition is deleterious. The translation of these words by coccel, cockle, in English was (like the later erroneous rendering tares) due in the first instance to ignorance as to the plant meant by zizania or lolium; but it led to the further error of some scientific writers who, knowing lolium to be darnel, still called it 'cockle.'

[437] See *The Mystery of Manna*, by Daniel Merkur, 2000.

[438] *Plants of the Gods*, by Schultes, Hofmann, Rätsch, 2nd ed., pg. 105.

[439] John Allegro first identified manna as a mushroom. *The Sacred Mushroom and the Cross*, pg. 111, 126.

[440] *The Mystery of Manna*, by Dan Merkur, pg. 5.

[441] Various biblical translations of *midbar* give "wilderness" or "desert," but cow pasture is more accurate.

solely self-acting, with *none* to share his work. And indeed it says "Behold I **rain** upon you **bread from heaven**" (Exod. Xvi. 4). Of what food can he rightly say that it is rained from heaven, save of heavenly wisdom which is sent from above on souls which yearn for virtue? [bold, italics, underlines—ours]
~ Philo

Clearly baking unleavened bread is not something done without the co-operation of the husbandmen "solely self-acting, with *none* to share his work." The mushrooms appear with the storms and rains, look like unleavened bread, and were often called "The Sons of Thunder" or "Boanerges."[442] *Amanita muscaria* also smell much like baking bread when slightly roasted or dried by a fire. Many of Merkur's descriptions of manna seem better suited as descriptions of entheogenic mushrooms.

> Jeremiah 2:20-21
> For of old time I have broken thy yoke, and burst thy bands; and thou saidst, I will not transgress; when upon every high hill and under every green tree thou wanderest, playing the harlot. Yet I had planted thee a noble vine, wholly a right seed: how then art thou turned into the degenerate plant of a strange vine unto me?

Why would the "manna of the wilderness years" be substituted? By substituting the mushrooms with ergot crackers, the priests were further able to suppress the true identity of manna—most likely, *Psilocybe cubensis* and/or *A. muscaria*.

Indeed, Merkur's book mentions several times that the priests took over the knowledge of manna. He also argues rather successfully that they maintained this knowledge as late as the 13th century.

> As I shall show, the knowledge of the biblical mystery was preserved as a secret as late as the <u>thirteenth century</u>…. Given the present social and political climate, I have chosen not to continue this history down to the present day.[443] [underline—ours]
> ~ Dan Merkur

Once one gains knowledge of *the lost language of symbolism* used by the Church and priestly classes, it becomes highly suggestive that they maintain this knowledge even today, and did not end it in the 13th century, though we must admit this is only speculative. Nevertheless, we wonder what Merkur possibly discovered and did not publish, in order to maintain the "present social and political climate."

It is unfortunate that Merkur disregarded all information regarding the mushroom even when so many of his references support the mushroom theory. If he had made a comparison between both ergot and the entheogenic mushrooms, his research, in our estimation, would hold more weight. Instead, he attacked Allegro:

> Neither is there evidence to support the cavalier allegation of John M. Allegro, *The Sacred Mushroom and the Cross*: […], p.112 that manna was *Amanita muscaria*, the fly agaric mushroom.[444]
> ~ Dan Merkur

He offered no evidence to support this statement. Moreover, it was Allegro who was the first researcher to take a *serious* approach to the Bible in regards to its entheogenic origins. Allegro said the Bible is based on drugs, and if you don't believe Allegro, read the hundreds of biblical passages Merkur has provided in his book to discover this on your own. Regardless, Merkur did not give Allegro credit. Placed in context with an overall entheogenic foundation for religion, including Christianity, Merkur's book is wonderful for supporting the entheogen hypothesis—and Allegro.

---

[442] See *The Sacred Mushroom and the Cross*, by John Allegro, pg. 46; *Hamlet's Mill,* by Giorgio De Santillana & Hertha Von Dechend, pg. 225; and *Apples of Apollo*, by Ruck, Staples, Heinrich, pg. 207.
[443] *The Mystery of Manna*, by Dan Merkur, Preface V & pg. 146.
[444] Ibid, ch. 1, footnote #5.

The word Manna translates as "*what is this?*"[445] While we contend that the Manna eaten by the Israelites during the biblical story of their exodus from Egypt was most likely *Psilocybe* mushrooms, there are two types of manna mentioned in the Bible. First is the manna that was eaten during the flight from Egypt (psilocybin, which was later substituted with unleavened bread). There is also the hidden manna, mentioned only once in the book of Revelation. We suggest this to be the *Amanita* mushrooms that are often found *hidden* under trees, pine needles, and shrubbery.[446]

John 6:53
Except ye eat the flesh of the son of man, and drink his blood ye have no life in you.

Mushrooms containing psilocybin are not at all similar to the *A. muscaria* that we discussed earlier. They are two completely different entheogens and experiences. The *Psilocybe* mushroom is known to open the third eye chakra. The *Amanita pantherina* and *A. muscaria* mushroom will take one out of body. A combination of these two types of mushrooms will often take you out of body with an open chakra system, and this was the goal of many alchemists and shamans. [448]

Could taking both types of mushrooms (*Psilocybe* and *Amanita*) at the same time be a deep cosmopolitan secret that directly relates to the "Seal of God," delivered by the an angel (Revelation 7:2-3) to humankind? When we consider that the angels are the messengers, Mercury, like the angels, is the messenger and he carries the caduceus. The snakes forming the caduceus represent both *poisons* (*Amanita* and *Psilocybe*). The consumption of these entheogens raise the kundalini in the body (forming the caduceus within), and the Seal of God suddenly becomes a tool for personal transformation, symbolized by the caduceus.

Figure 157 - *Psilocybe cubensis*[447]

Revelation 7:2-3
And I saw another angel ascending from the east, having the seal of the living God: and he cried with a loud voice to the four angels, to whom it was given to hurt the earth and the sea, Saying, hurt not the earth, neither the sea, nor the trees, till we have sealed the servants of our God in their foreheads.

There were two trees in the Bible story, the Tree of the Knowledge of Good and Evil, whose fruit Adam and Eve were forbidden to eat, and the Tree of Life. Adam and Eve ate of the fruit of the Tree of the Knowledge of Good and Evil, but they were expelled from the Garden to prevent them from eating of the Tree of Life, which would have conferred immortality on them.[449]
~ R. Gordon Wasson

Genesis 2:9
And out of the ground made the LORD God to grow every tree that is pleasant to the sight, and good for food; the tree of life also in the midst of the garden, and the tree of knowledge of good and evil.

Genesis 3:22
And the LORD God said, Behold, the man is become as one of us, to know good and evil: and now, lest he put forth his hand, and take also of the tree of life, and eat, and live for ever.

---

[445] In the *Sacred Mushroom and the Cross*, Allegro reveals that *Manna* is "*mushroom*," pg. 111.
[446] The same colorful, hidden "eggs" that are symbolically hunted by children during an Easter egg hunt.
[447] Photograph by John W. Allen.
[448] Three entheogens were used as Soma, see page 50-51 of *Persephone's Quest*. In Mayan culture, one leg lightening bolt is *Amanita m.*, Dwarf lightning bolt means *Psilocybe* species, the green lightning bolt is morning glories and other entheogens.
[449] *Persephone's Quest*, by Gordon Wasson, pg. 75. Note: see chapter 4 in specific regard to Merkur's hypothesis that the Tree of Life and Tree of Knowledge in Genesis are possibly synonymous. This would not negate the other references to the admixture hypothesis.

Uniting the opposites is considered the method of producing the philosophers' stone. It is also the method of achieving enlightenment in tantric philosophy and the Soma ceremony. This union or coupling together of opposites was symbolized in alchemy as the Hermetic androgyne of hermaphrodite and in the Soma ceremony as the rememberment of the primal man of light as Anthropos. This union is frequently represented in tantric statues of Siva as half male and half female, and it is shown in the Soma ceremony as <u>the union of fire and water</u> in the heart and the gathering of Soma light essences to reconstitute the primal being of light as the solar heart. [450] [underline—ours]
~ David Spess

THE TREE OF LIFE

The Tree of Life is a commonly recurring archetypal artifact of mythology and history, which can be found all over the world. It is typical for people to say it would be a waste of time to look for such a thing because of what is written in the biblical account of Adam and Eve in the Garden of Eden. The account, as it is given in Genesis, is only one particular way of telling of the story. Due to this single version, most people believe the tree is hidden away from man. In this tragic telling, Adam and Eve were expelled from the Garden and were consequently forced to leave the presence of the Tree of Life. This happened when the paradise of innocence was infected with something called *sin*. Human nature, the ability to think for oneself, was suddenly forbidden by law. They were commanded not to do something that they absolutely *had* to do. Consequently, they broke the law and ate some of the fruit from the Tree of Knowledge of good and evil. We can agree that in this version, the archetypal parents were driven out of the Garden. However, it does not actually say they were forbidden to eat of the fruit of the Tree of Life.

In Genesis 3:22 the verse says specifically:

> And the LORD God said, Behold, the man is become as one of us, to know good and evil: and now, lest he put forth his hand, and take also of the tree of life, and eat, and live for ever.

The story explains that partaking of the fruit of the Tree of the Knowledge of Good and Evil made Adam and Eve as one of *them*. This statement is clear. "One of us" does not mean one, singularly. If there were only one God, this statement makes absolutely no sense at all. Theologians and scholars have debated this for decades and it is the subject of very diverse opinions. To those scholars willing to admit that the Bible is a compilation of mythological rhetoric that has evolved out of much older polytheistic roots, this is simple to understand. However, for the fundamentalists and apologists, it opened a Pandora's Box of worms that most of them would rather leave alone. First, let's address whom the Lord God was talking to: Himself? His Partner? Friends? Humankind? If the one and only Lord God was talking to humankind he would have said "become like me." To say "become as one of *us*" to humankind simply reveals a secret, a Freudian slip, so to speak. Apparently there are many like the Lord God, as per scriptural explanation, this includes all of those who have partaken of the Fruit of he Tree of the Knowledge of Good and Evil. Actually, there are no other means anywhere in biblical scripture to surpass this status. Nor is there any single thing that can produce the same effect for a human. A statement that specifically says how one can become as one of the gods is a very powerful statement indeed. No wonder this *tree* and *fruit* theme can be found all over the world.[451] The only comparable thing would be eating the manna,[452] the body of Jesus, the bread that comes down from heaven spoken of in John, chapter 6, regarding *drinking the waters of life* from the fountain of living waters and eating the fruit from the Tree of Life. All of these things are one and the same. These are just various ways to explain a single, tangible, discoverable object.

Elsewhere in religious texts of the early Biblical period, the Tree of Life is the same as the Tree of the Knowledge of Good and Evil. The *Nag Hammadi Library* uncovered several *creations, eye openings,* and *becoming as gods* accounts. Gnostic texts even take this a step further by reversing the roles of the two trees.[453] Some Gnostic texts refer to the Tree of Knowledge of Good and Evil as "The Tree of the Thought of Light." To the Gnostics, the god

---

[450] *Soma: The Divine Hallucinogen*, by David Spess, pg. 161.

[451] "Every nation had its legend of a Garden of Paradise, a tree of life and a serpent." Busenbark, pg. 184.

[452] See section titled "What is This?", page 148.

[453] *Nag Hammadi Library*, On the Origin of the World.

Yahweh is a jealous god and one must wonder why he must have this type of emotion if he is omnipotent (and what he is jealous of, if he is omnipresent).

Since the 1611 King James Version of the Bible is a rather recent retelling of the story of creation, there is no reason to assume it to be the one true account, throwing out all older renditions. This is putting the cart before the horse. With this in mind, understanding what the stories are really trying to get across in their symbolism, and thereby understanding what the Bible actually says, is certainly enhanced by reading all possible accounts and correlating the various allegories.

In the book of Hosea, Yahweh says:

> Hosea 14:8
> I am like a green fir tree. From me is thy fruit found.

Once one finds the actual "Fruit of Fir Tree," the doors of understanding will be flung open, gifting the initiate in an understanding of the mystery associated with these things. All of this must be explored in depth because the Fruit of the Tree of Life, the waters of life, and the fountain of living waters are some of the most highly sought and revered keys to the doorways of eternity that history, myth, and religion have passed down to humanity. When these mysteries are unveiled, you will find evidence that these things are not just fanciful ideas, but are in fact quite real.

> When Adam and Eve went forth from Paradise, Adam, as if knowing that he was never to return to his place, cut off a branch from the tree of good and evil.
> ~ *The Book of the Bee*, edited and translated by Earnest A. Wallis Budge [1886]

The legends of the Tree of Life and the Tree of Knowledge of Good and Evil are abundant. Of these legends are tales of Jesus being crucified on the wood cut from this very tree. Many older images of Jesus show him working miracles with a wand, much like the wand or rod of Moses and Jessie. This is likely nothing more than a symbolic representation of Mercury and his caduceus.

THE MISSING LINK

Figure 158 - *Psilocybe cubensis* bruising blue[454]

---

[454] Photograph by John W. Allen.

Figure 158 is a photograph of a *Psilocybe* mushroom. A color image reveals the stipe of the mushroom turning blue. When one grabs hold of these mushrooms and bruise them, they bruise blue, similar to a magnolia tree's white flower bruising brown. These mushrooms can be *kept for generations to come* by submerging the mushrooms in honey. Honey makes an ideal, natural preservative. The blue bruising will stain the honey blue over time, thus making the honey itself psychoactive. This honey is more popularly known as *blue honey*.[455]

> Exodus 16:31-33
> The people of Israel called the bread manna. It was white like coriander seed and tasted like wafers made with honey. Moses said, "This is what the LORD has commanded: 'Take an omer of manna and keep it for the generations to come, so they can see the bread I gave you to eat in the desert when I brought you out of Egypt. So Moses said to Aaron, "Take a jar and put an omer of manna in it. Then place it before the LORD to be kept for the generations to come.

As we discussed, the properties of the *Amanita* are perfected in the recycling process and this is why alchemical images often depict the homunculus urinating into a fountain, flask or cistern. This process is alchemy at its finest. It is the perfection and transformation of the soul through the consumption of the true gold.

Kelly Ivors, Ph.D., suggested in a lecture in Oregon, that *Psilocybe* mushrooms can be recycled as well. Psilocybin (4 Phosporloxy, N-N dimethyltryptamine) also decarboxylates, and it seems this is the difference between it and Psilocin (4Hydroxy-N-N-dimethyltryptamine).[456] It was previously believed that only *Amanitas* possessed this characteristic. Recently discovered was the secret of combining both mushrooms and this emphasizes the importance of the alchemical process even more.

Terence McKenna was a famous philosopher, researcher, scientist and mathematician. He wrote several books and created many theories, including concepts of time and time travel, wormholes, and Habit and Novelty theory. His primary research surrounded shamanism and the spiritual use of entheogens. While we disagree with McKenna that Soma contained *only* the *Psilocybe* mushroom, which he argues in his book *Food of the Gods*, he does make a most interesting and compelling case that mushrooms acted as a catalyst, which propelled human evolution into the conscious beings we are today. The way entheogens are worshipped worldwide makes his theory most suggestive.

Figure 159 - Terence McKenna

In brief, this is how Terence McKenna explained this theory. These next few pages were built upon notes taken from a two-day workshop at the California Institute of Integral Studies in 1995 given by the late Terence McKenna, as well as other thoughts and ideas that Terence has presented:

In nature and in our own homes, we see that animals have "mono-diets" with very little variation in taste or flavor. This is what they prefer. Animals are highly specialized in their choice of foods. A random diet for an animal in nature is a reckless diet. A good strategy for survival in a species is having a specific and specialized diet, thereby developing enzymes that can handle substances that might otherwise make one ill. Consequently, most animals seem to evolve to these very bland, mono-diets.

When something happens that drives these animals from their natural habitat, they can choose to either starve to extinction or change their "palate" and become more flexible in their diet, trying out previously rejected potential foods from the environment. This is the origin of experimentation with unknown plants.

---

[455] See - www.bluehoney.org.
[456] This was also verified by Sahsa Shulgin at the Telluride Mushroom Festival in 2000.

As the rainforest retreated due to changes in weather patterns and climate, our primal ancestors were forced to experiment with new foods. Our remote, forest dwelling ancestors were fruitarian-insectivores. They were forced out of the trees and began exploring the grasslands for food. Now look at us. Our palates are wide open and our species enjoys a wide variety of spices and foods, not just from the area where we live, but foods from all over the world (whether or not this is a healthy choice is not the issue here).

Figure 160 - *Psilocybe* mushrooms growing on cow dung

One food source that they would surely have stumbled upon in the grasslands would have been mushrooms. Many mushrooms growing in grassland areas and on the dung of cattle contain psilocybin. Psilocybin is one of the major psychoactive alkaloids that cannot be found outside of the fungus world. McKenna stated that "Psilocybin is the best model for human interaction with a psychedelic; other man-made psychedelics (LSD and the like) are all an effort to return to or somehow evoke the human relationship with psilocybin."

Aside from its psychedelic qualities, these mushrooms have other attributes. In lower doses, psilocybin increases visual acuity and edge detection.[457] This has been proven under laboratory settings.[458] Enhanced edge detection would be at a high premium for any animals that had found themselves in a hunter/prey situation. Be it the hunter or the hunted, having sharp vision could be the difference between life and death (or dinner vs. no dinner). Blurred vision would be a benefit in very few, if any situations. After one passes the point of edge detection in low dosages of psilocybin, at slightly higher doses, as the eyes dilate further, one begins to increase in consciousness and see into *other dimensions*.

Animals who accept something into their diet that increases edge detection and gifts them with slightly better vision (mushrooms containing psilocybin), would have a slightly enhanced success in hunting. The better hunter an animal is, the more nutrition they have for themselves and for their offspring, offspring who are in turn raised eating this psychedelic mushroom.

Also, by increasing the dose, mushrooms containing psilocybin cause arousal, arousal not only meaning unable to sleep or restlessness, but sexual arousal as well. Here is a species with plenty of food and offspring, thus, out-breeding the non-mushroom using members of the population. Once a certain dosage is reached (this is variable depending on the specific mushroom and the body weight of the person), one experiences a full-blown shamanic *"religious"* experience.[459]

---

[457] Sharpness, clear vision

[458] See Roland Fisher for more information.

[459] *Tripping: An Anthology of True-Life Psychedelic Adventures*, edited and with an introduction and other texts by Charles Hayes – this book has many reports from men and women who choose to partake in psychedelics.

Whatever it was that kept us in the same mental category as the other animals for so long, was interrupted by the introduction of particular items to our diet. These mushrooms are perhaps responsible for many of the things that make us *human*: language, art, poetry, dance, music… all of the things that separate us from other animals, sprang into existence circa 100,000 years ago. This mushroom could quite literally be the "missing link."

Humans are the most conscious of all animals, maybe because we are carnivores. Cows have very little interest in the goings on of the birds or prairie dogs that share the same field with them. Carnivores, on the other hand, have an acute interest in the behaviors of other animals. The earliest consciousness was not of self-awareness or of self-consciousness, but rather of *how dinner must be thinking*. Because, if the hunter can think in the manner in which its prey thinks, the hunter can then place itself ahead of the path of its prey, having the upper hand in the hunt. Our primal ancestor's attention to the behavior patterns of other animals was all that it took to knock over the first domino of human evolution.

Our canopy-dwelling ancestors (according to McKenna's Theory of Evolution) were forced into a grassland environment where psilocybin mushrooms flourished, where both large and small animals are preying upon one another for survival. As this species in a new environment made adaptive choices, it moved further and deeper into the realm of consciousness. It then learned the patterns of other animals, the growth cycles of the new plant environment, where to find water and shelter, etc.—spoken and written language were right around the evolutionary corner.

<u>OUROBORIC PSILOCYBE</u>

Psilocin[460] possesses a rather unusual property for a DMT congener.[461] It is orally active all by itself, unlike similar drugs such as DMT, or 5-MEO-DMT, which have little or no effect when taken orally. DMT and 5-MEO-DMT are altered and made inactive by a digestive enzyme named "monoamine oxidase," or MAO. Hence, even rather large doses of DMT or 5-MEO-DMT will fail to have much effect via simple oral ingestion.[462]

Psilocin, however, has an oxygen atom at the 4-position on the indole ring. This oxygen is able to form a weak hydrogen-type bond with the nitrogen on the carbon "tail" of the psilocin molecule, via the rotatable carbon-carbon bonds on the same tail. This association hinders MAO from altering the psilocin molecule in the gut, allowing it to enter the bloodstream and then, the brain. Note that this oxygen must be at the indole 4-position to have this property. If the oxygen is anywhere else on the ring, the nitrogen will not be able to get close enough to the oxygen to shield it from MAO (see Figures 161-164).

Activity from simple ingestion may be important concerning a myco-human-evolutionary point of view. Here we have a powerful DMT-congener, which is active via simple ingestion. No special shamanic knowledge is required to prepare these psychedelic mushrooms for ingestion in order to experience their ensuing entheogenic effects (take and eat). This is in contrast to DMT-containing Ayahuasca, because when brewing Ayahuasca, the shaman is combining two ordinary-looking plant species into a brew from among thousands of other ordinary-looking plant species. Here, shamanic knowledge *is* required to obtain a psychoactive effect. Ergot also requires special knowledge and preparation. In the case of entheogenic mushrooms, merely gathering and eating will do the trick. This simplicity would support the idea that if indeed psychedelic substances are the basis of much of humankind's mental and religious evolution, then psychoactive mushrooms would tend to factor heavily into possible primordial scenarios.[463]

---

[460] Psilocin is related to psilocybin, the psychoactive component of entheogenic mushrooms in the following way: inside the mushroom, psilocybin is "phosphorylated," but once ingested, psilocybin is "dephosphorylated" to psilocin, which is the form that reaches the brain.

[461] *Oxford English Dictionary* – congener: A member of the same kind or class with another, or nearly allied to another in character.

[462] In Chapter 4, we mentioned the use of a naturally occurring MAO inhibitor, which will allow for the digestion of these drugs.

[463] Thanks to Dan Hillman and Dr. Dennis McKenna for their assistance here.

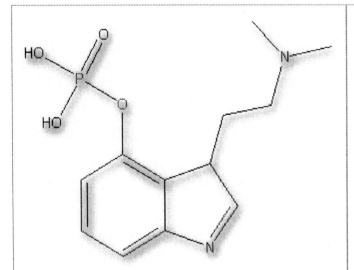

Figure 161 - Psilocybin, as it is found in the fungus.

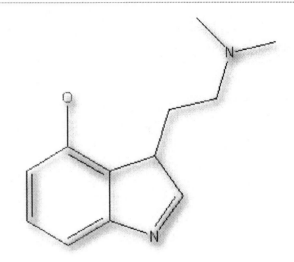

Figure 162 - Psilocin, resulting from de-phosphorylation of psilocybin.

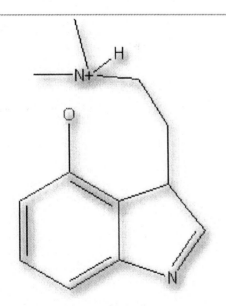

Figure 163 – Protonated psilocin. Nitrogen hinders access to oxygen on indole-4 position. Attack from digestive enzymes hindered.

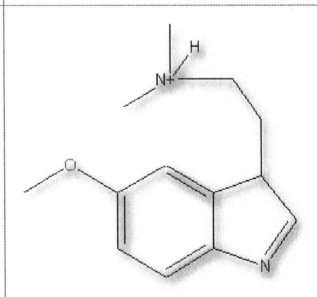

Figure 164 - Protonated 5-MEO-DMT. Nitrogen too far from oxygen to hinder attack from digestive enzymes.

Figure 165 - Could the mushroom be an alien intelligence?

The most curious notion we have come across in our research on psychedelic mushrooms and plants is the suggestion that entheogens are some sort of alien intelligence. We admit this theory, first proposed by Terence McKenna, is only speculation. However, as Terence would say, "For your edification and amusement," we will entertain this idea in brief.

As we noted, as an outcome of Dr. Strassman's research, the so-called alien abduction experience was reproduced in the laboratory with DMT. Inside *Psilocybe* mushrooms is ***Dimethyltryptamine***.[464] These certain types of mushrooms contain a congener form of DMT, the most potent psychedelic substance known to man, which is produced in the human brain, lungs, and blood (and in almost all plants and animals). The theory is that these mushrooms may not only be the Missing Link, but also alien communication or even alien technology. A postscript to this theory is that DMT is the chemical link to the fabric of reality. This alien communication may not be extraterrestrial[465], but from right here on earth. It is staggering to learn that these mushrooms and other psychoactive substances have, until recently, been taken off the scientific agenda[466] and made illegal to possess. If we are going to spend so much time, money, and effort searching the stars for "alien intelligence," it would be wise to search all plant and fungus life on the earth as well.[467] Is it possible that someone, somewhere has encoded data into the entheogens, and by ingesting these substances, we can interpret this data? We know that ants lay pheromone trails and can encode information into a scent that other ants use to determine where to go and what to do. Could mushrooms, and other entheogens, be likened to interspecies pheromones that contain information from somewhere in the cosmos and/or Mother Earth herself?

---

[464] O phosphoryl–4-Hydroxy N,N–Dimethyltryptamine
[465] On November 10, 2005, *New Scientist* ran an article, "Hardy lichen shown to survive in space" which may now give further support for McKenna's theory. www.newscientistspace.com
[466] As mentioned earlier, psilocybin is now being tested on some cancer patents as a way to, among other things, quell the fear of death. This is a fantastic step in the right direction and everyone involved, staff and patients, should be highly praised.
[467] Terence McKenna.

The subject of aliens and mushrooms gets even more peculiar. One day while we were giving a lecture in Texas, author Nancy Red Star approached us and said that Colonel Robert Foy had informed her that the aliens that were reportedly found at Roswell, New Mexico in 1947, had to be fed "toadstools" (another name for the *Amanita muscaria*) as food to keep them alive. Her book presents a modern artist's representation of this alien with the *Amanita muscaria* from her book, *Legends of the Star Ancestors: Stories of Extraterrestrial Contact from Wisdomkeepers around the World*. We suggested to her the possibility that the *Amanita* was used to *see* into the worlds/dimensions of the so-called aliens, whatever they may be, as Dr. Strassman discovered with DMT, and Carl Jung and Terence McKenna[468] suggested with their own research, that perhaps these were not physical aliens in which most people envision them. We suggest the *Amanita* was not "food for aliens," but more fairly worded, "alien food."[469] *Amanitas* do contain unique substances not found anywhere else in nature.[470] Many people who consume entheogens often report the presence of spirits, what many cultures call "watchers" or "the ancestors."

---

[468] See *Flying Saucers*, by Carl G. Jung, and the lecture: *Angels, Aliens, and Archetypes*, by Terence McKenna.

[469] For more information on human technology with flying disks, research Dave Emory on Nikola Tesla: Technology, Theocracy and the Thousand Year Reich, available at www.thehemperor.net.

[470] *Pharmacotheon*, by Jonathan Ott, pg. 326–328.

Jeremy Narby, Ph.D., spent many years in the Amazon as an anthropologist. In his book, *The Cosmic Serpent: DNA and the Origins of Knowledge*, Dr. Narby discusses the possibility that entheogens, especially DMT (as found in Ayahuasca), allow the body (and/or the mind) to somehow communicate (possibly by telepathy) with other animals and plant species through photons emitted by DNA. "The DNA helix releases photons at a rate of up to approximately 100 units per second and per square centimeter... the wavelength at which DNA emits these photons corresponds exactly to the narrow band of *visible light*."[471] The visual representation of the DNA helix is also very similar in design to the caduceus. When one experiences this phenomenon, it leaves little doubt (as Narby once doubted the possibility *before* his own personal experience) that somehow this communication through plant contact is real.

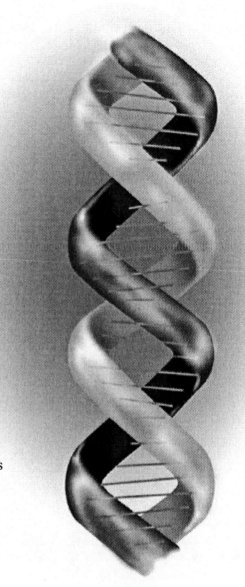

Figure 166 - DNA

This idea [Hypercarbolation] that he [Dennis] has that some hallucinogens work by fitting into DNA is startling.[472]
~ Terence McKenna, regarding Dennis McKenna.

---

[471] *The Cosmic Serpent*, by Jeremy Narby, pg. 126, quoting Rattenmeyer et al. (1981), Popp (1986), Li (1992), Van Wijk and Van Aken (1992), Niggli (1992), Mei (1992), and Popp, Gu, and Li (1994), and Popp (1986, p. 207).
[472] *True Hallucinations*, by Terence McKenna, pg. 21.

Figure 167 - Vishnu

Figure 168 - Shiva

Vishnu (Figure 167) is depicted with serpents at his feet, while up above his head he has the shell-shape represented by the cobras. He also has the sun behind his back, representing the macrocosm. Notice that Vishnu's body is blue, just like the body of the *Psilocybe* mushroom. Shiva (Figure 168) has an extensive following. According to Hindu mythology, when the demons and deities churned the Milky Ocean, fourteen jewels surfaced, one of which was poison. Poisonous fumes threatened to overwhelm the entire world, so Shiva drank the poison. The poison was so intense that Shiva's throat turned blue, which is why Shiva earned the nickname Nilakantha (the blue-throated).[473] Also, note the Third Eye in this image of Shiva.

---

[473] This paragraph is a summery of the *Epic Mythology: The Gods and Demons Churn the Ocean to Obtain Ambrosia*, translated from Sanskrit; see Clark Heinrich's *Magic Mushrooms in Religion and Alchemy* for more information.

Figure 169 - Krishna

Krishna (Figure 169) is also blue, and he is typically depicted with a cow or cattle to his right. Why are cows sacred and holy in Hindu mythology and why is Krishna blue? As we just pointed out, the blue color represents psilocybin, because of the reaction that happens when contact is made with the stem of the mushroom. *Psilocybe cubensis* mushrooms grow on cow dung. As a result, *holy cows* produce *holy shit*, whereupon the *holy sacrament* grows in nature.

Figure 170 - Tassili shamans from Tassili-n-Ajjer Plateau, Algeria

Figure 170 shows depictions of Tassili shamans from Tassili-n-Ajjer Plateau, Algeria,[474] which is now a desert region. These illustrations could be as old as circa 7000 BCE. All of the figures are holding mushrooms in their hands and all of their heads are shaped like the mushroom, symbolizing that they are under its influence. Also, notice more mushrooms growing along the ground in this image.

---

[474] *Food of the Gods,* by Terence McKenna, pg. 72-73.

Figure 171 is another ancient Algerian Tassili shaman man. Here, the shaman's whole body is covered with the mushrooms and his face is that of the deer-bee (giving reference to honey). As we pointed out earlier, deer are very significant in shamanic symbology, in part, because of their relationship with the *Amanita muscaria* mushrooms.[475] Bees and honey are significant, as previously mentioned, because of their ability to preserve the mushrooms, creating the blue honey.

Figure 171 - Algerian Tassili shaman

In Figure 172, Persephone and Demeter are holding mushrooms in this piece of ancient Greek artwork. It looks as though they are just about to feed each other the divine sacrament.[476, 477]

**Figure 172 - Greek Temple carving - Persephone and Demeter –
circa 470 BCE, Pharsalus, Thessally, Greece**

---

[475] Native Americans associate the deer to Peyote, see *Peyote Hunt: The Sacred Journey of the Huichol Indians*, by Barbara G. Myerhoff, and *In the Magic Land of Peyote*, by Fernando Benitez.
[476] *Persephone's Quest*, by Wasson, Ruck, Kramrisch, Ott.
[477] *The Road to Eleusis*, by Carl Ruck, Albert Hofmann, R. Gordon Wasson, Jeremy Bigwood, Jonathan Ott, Huston Smith, Danny Staples.

Figure 173 - Phoenix being fed an *Amanita* mushroom

In Figure 173,[478] the phoenix (falcon) is being fed an *Amanita* mushroom. Notice the spots on the cap. The phoenix represents the *A. muscaria* mushroom. Here is the phoenix being fed the phoenix, or the *Amanita* being fed the *Amanita*. This represents a continual cycle, similar to an ouroboros, of regeneration in nature.

---

[478] Detail from a silver platter showing the Falcon god (Phoenix) being fed an amanita mushroom by his female consort (Persia, Sassanid period).

Figure 174 - Story of Creation - Canterbury Psalter - 1147 CE

The Canterbury Psalter from 1147 CE has twelve segments (or panels) representing the twelve signs of the zodiac or the Mazzaroth (Figure 174[479]). Inside each segment is a representation from different parts of the creation of the world epic as described in the book of Genesis. In the top left panel, we see the Great Architect as the "Cosmic Christ" with his Masonic compass. In the top right panel we see Jesus, the lord of magical plants.[480]

---

[479] *The Illustrated Jesus Through the Centuries,* by Jaroslav Pelikan, pg. 64. Thanks to Paul Lindgren for this image.
[480] As described in *Mushrooms and Mankind,* by Arthur (2000).

164

Figure 175 - Detail - Canterbury Psalter - 1147 CE

Figure 176 - Detail - Canterbury Psalter - 1147 CE

[Regarding Figure 175] The red mushroom on the right is clearly the *Amanita muscaria* (which produces the quickening of the spirit). The next one is obviously another mushroom, but it is blue. This indicates the *Psilocybe* mushrooms (which open the third eye). Next may be a depiction of a Syrian Rue plant pod, which happens to match this in color as well as structure (this increases the properties of the other compounds, and it is likely to posses other unknown qualities). On the left is a depiction of an Opium Poppy which, due to the euphoria it induces, enables one to relax enough to let go and fully experience the visionary state, and withstand the intense experience without the constant urge to "make it stop" (which, by the way, is not an option).[481]

Figure 177 - Detail of the Tree of Knowledge of Good and Evil - Canterbury Psalter - 1147 CE

Some of the other panels depict God (or Jesus) with the book of the law, as the lord over the sacred plants, and as the creator of day and night. One panel depicts a scene in the Garden of Eden with the serpent. Notice that the serpent has entwined the staff (which is actually the stem of a mushroom). It looks a bit like the *Amanita muscaria*, although it does appear to depict some type of *Psilocybe* and some other types of mushrooms as well. Inside the very top of the center "tree," or serpent-entwined mushroom, may be seen little mushrooms within the cap. This is occult symbolism.

---

[481] See www.JamesArthur.net.

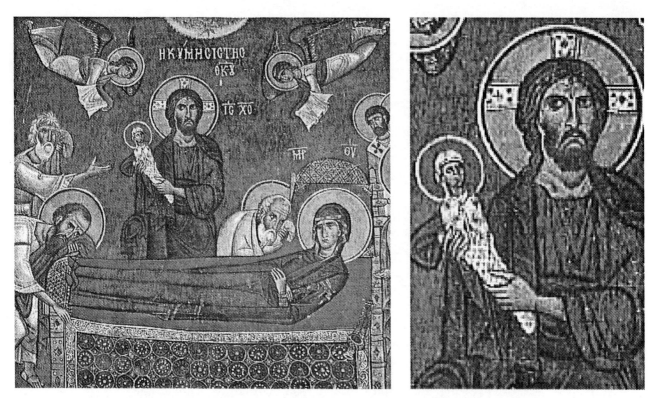

Figure 178 – The Cosmic Christ (with close-up) - Cyprus - circa 1106

This figure identifies the Virgin Mary in the Dormition icon as *Amanita*-form. Notice the red cap, the skirt-like wrap over the shoulders, and the hash marks at the bottom.

Figure 179 - Detail of The Cosmic Christ with *Amanita* mushroom sections for comparison

166

Figure 180 - Woodcut tracing of a witch trial[482]

If the words 'life, liberty, and the pursuit of happiness' don't include the right to experiment with your own consciousness, then the Declaration of Independence isn't worth the hemp it was written on.
~ Terence McKenna

WAR GAMES & MIND GAMES

I have examined all the known superstitions of the world, and I do not find in our particular superstition of Christianity one redeeming feature. They are all alike founded on fables and mythology. Millions of innocent men, women and children, since the introduction of Christianity, have been burnt, tortured, fined and imprisoned. What has been the effect of this coercion? To make one half the world fools and the other half hypocrites; to support roguery and error all over the earth.
~ Thomas Jefferson

The majority of humankind's history with spiritual plants has been spent viewing them as sacred, not immoral. Yet for the last two thousand years, religious institutions and governments have ignored and suppressed this history and waged war against spiritual plants and altered states of consciousness. Today, elitist groups of politicians and clergy, meeting in secret chambers and assuming authority over nature's bounty, have decided for everyone which plants are to be good and which are to be bad. Meanwhile, many of these authorities must have their coffee, tobacco, Zoloft, and alcohol. Some are being caught with straws up their noses as well. Yet, they decide for everyone else which plants are good and against which plants to wage war.

Many of the laws in this country are based upon religious superstition and financial interests rather than common sense. It is the "common folk" who work like slaves, keeping the entire system running. Nearly the entire world is run like a business instead of a community.

I have no hesitation in advocating the repeal of laws that institutionalize juridical persecution of the biblical mystery. Alone among biblical offerings, the bread of the presence is named *berit olam*, an "eternal covenant" or "perpetual obligation." (Lev. 24:8)
~ Dan Merkur

---

[482] If the suspect floated, she was a witch and was burnt at the stake. If she sank and drowned, she could "go free."

The War on Drugs is literally a modern day American civil war. Just because armies representing both sides are not marching in a field doing battle somewhere, does not mean that our country is not at war with itself. People seeking religious freedom founded the United States of America. Today, the USA has become the beast from which our founding fathers were once trying to escape. Modern day martyrs are suffering unjustly. They are stripped of their families, homes, jobs and lives. The victims of this immoral war suffer simply because they made the choice to grow or possess a plant for relaxation, spiritual use, or profit. Especially for profit, because you are **strictly forbidden** to make a profit in this country without handing over a large percentage of your earnings in taxes (taxes spent to maintain the Drug War, and illegal, pre-emptive strikes on other countries). The Drug War is a world war and a civil war simultaneously. Under certain circumstances, the penalty might be as severe as life in prison just for the possession of a living plant. At the time of this writing, with the Patriot Act in place, the possession of one marijuana cigarette (or any illegal drug possession) is regarded as an *act of terrorism*. Terrorism has become the all-purpose and never-failing weapon for fear mongering, because anything undesirable can now simply be converted into "terrorism." Growing marijuana is now technically considered creating weapons of mass destruction, because the illegal plants can be used to intoxicate many (willing) people. Now, the grower could even be executed.

> Romans 14:2-3
> For one believeth that he may eat all things: another, who is weak, eateth herbs. Let not him that eateth despise him that eateth not; and let not him which eateth not judge him that eateth: for God hath received him.

In the original thirteen colonies, it was required by law for farmers to grow hemp for the defense of the nation.[483] Cannabis/hemp is actually the one plant that could turn our precarious environmental and economical position around, and yet today it is considered an act of terrorism to grow the very plant of which our forefathers said, "Make the most of Hemp Seed and sow it everywhere."[484] When we follow the value of hemp as a renewable fuel source,[485] we soon realize that to the oil tycoons, hemp literally is a terror that threatens their profits! There is absolutely no reason for the U.S. to be held hostage by oil cartels, when everything petroleum-based could be made from hemp. We could be re-harvesting a field rather than drilling mother earth for the last of her non-renewable fossil fuels.

Chances are, you have not heard of Cicuta maculata. Most people would not be able to recognize it growing in nature, even if it was growing only a few feet away. Like marijuana, Cicuta maculata (commonly known as Spotted Water hemlock) is a plant that has no trouble finding a place to live. It flourishes on flat ground, in thickets, and along roadsides and riverbanks. If you were to consume *this* plant, the symptoms would begin in as few as 15 minutes. Death, from respiratory paralysis and terminal convulsions typically occurs within 45 minutes of the onset of symptoms.

Figure 181 - *Cicuta maculata*

If a person consumes this plant and happens to live, they risk temporary or permanent damage to heart and/or skeletal muscle. Socrates died in 399 BCE, by intentionally drinking a potent solution of poison hemlock (less poisonous than Water hemlock), which was grudgingly regarded by his compatriots as a "humane" method of capital punishment. He was forced to drink the poison because he was performing the mysteries (Eleusinian) privately and the government found out. Socrates refused initiation to the Eleusinian mysteries[486] because he already knew the secret of the psychedelic elixir, Kykeon, and an initiation would have sworn him to secrecy of something that he already knew (as opposed to giving him the secret *after* the initiation). The mysteries included initiations with mushrooms and an ergot-based (LSD-like) psychedelic drink.[487,488] Socrates was a victim of the pharmacratic inquisition, forced by the government to take a plant poison that killed him for using consciousness-expanding plants in the privacy of his own home and refusing to swear to secrecy.

[483] *The Emperor Wears No Clothes*, by Jack Herer.
[484] George Washington.
[485] www.hemp4fuel.com.
[486] *The Secret Teaching of All Ages*, by Manly Palmer Hall.
[487] *The Road to Eleusis*, by Hofmann, Wasson, et al.
[488] *The Sacred Mushroom and the Cross*, by John Allegro.

Hosea 10:4
They have spoken words, swearing falsely in making a covenant: thus judgment springeth up as hemlock in the furrows of the field.

But why are we mentioning hemlock here? Because plants that are truly dangerous, plants that are deadly upon consumption and can *actually be used to kill people*, do not seem to be an issue in the war against dangerous plants and drugs. If lawmakers are truly worried about a connection between plants and terrorism, why are we not at war with poisonous plants? How can they justify waging war against plants that are proven valuable to people's minds, farms, environment, and economy, and **not** include deadly plants in their agenda?

Amos 6:12
Shall horses run upon the rock? will one plow there with oxen? for ye have turned judgment into gall, and the fruit of righteousness into hemlock....

Poisonous and deadly plants are completely legal, but spiritual plants are strictly *forbidden*.[489] Death from tobacco, alcohol,[490] and prescription drugs is prevalent in our society and these take nothing more than an overdose. While, on the other hand, a shamanic dose of dried psilocybin-containing mushrooms is small, there is no possibility of a deadly overdose. A person weighing 150 pounds would have to consume 150 pounds of psilocybin mushrooms to reach a lethal dosage, which is not humanly possible.[491] No one has ever died from an overdose of *Psilocybe* mushrooms or marijuana (or a combination of the two), yet for some reason, there is a war being waged against both of them. Moreover, if you are caught in possession of just one *Psilocybe* mushroom, you can, and probably will be charged with a felony.

America has a larger percentage of its population in prison than any other country on earth –roughly, 25% of the world's 8 million prisoners—but the United States has only 4.5% of the world's population![492] The average sentence for a ***first time,*** **non-violent** drug offender is longer than the average sentence for rape, bank robbery, or manslaughter. Every year, 8,000 to 14,000 people die from illegal drugs in this country.[493] Yes, that is a large number of people, but over 500,000 people die from *legal* drugs. This includes tobacco, liquor, over the counter, and prescription drugs.[494] This is roughly a fifty to one ratio, yet we are led to assume that all of the dangers in the country can be blamed on the drugs that the "authorities" have made illegal.

Politicians are controlled by corporate sponsors who want nothing more than for you to engage yourself in an unbreakable cycle: wake up, take drugs (that they deem "safe"), go to work, buy products, pay taxes, watch advertisements on TV, sleep and repeat daily. Entheogens break that mold, and the big businesses and big churches that run this world tremble in fear at the very thought of that. So they forbid them, they outlaw them, they make them taboo. Until recently they killed you if you even knew about them (for example, "witches" in the Inquisition).

Follow the money and you will discover why these statistics may never change. Imagine you had a product to sell, each unit cost one dollar to make, and each one could sell for $17,000.00. That is the cost and profit reality of the cocaine industry created and sustained by the Drug War. Waging war against something that has this degree of profit incentive is fruitless. It drives up the demand even further and in turn drives up the price, because those who supply the drugs are risking their lives to do so. Actually, the *real* dealers are never at risk at all. Only those at the bottom of the ladder ever touch any drugs. They are nothing but pawns and, like all mercenaries, they are expendable. Waging war against a human's right to control his or her own consciousness has not worked in the seventy years of modern drug prohibition, and as alcohol prohibition showed, banning substances drives up their value and makes it easier for criminals to control the industry.

---

[489] There are a handful of entheogens that remain legal in America. However, some attempts have been made to outlaw these. They include Amanita muscaria and pantherina, Salvia Divinorum, 5 MeO N,N DMT, et al.

[490] Alcohol is generally created by fermentation with the use of yeast, which is a fungus. Alcohol "spirits" or the "essence" was not discovered until around the 1200s.

[491] Jonathon Ott (1978) reported that one would virtually have to consume an amount of mushrooms equal to one's own body weight in order to bring about death.

[492] U.S. prisoners and the drug war: http://members.fortunecity.com/multi19/majority.htm.

[493] Number of American deaths per year, according to world almanacs, life insurance actuarial (death) rates, and the last 20 years of U.S. Surgeon General's reports.

[494] *Drug war Facts*: http://www.drugwarfacts.org.

INQUISITIONS – THEN & NOW

On June 19, 1620, the Inquisition of Mexico City formerly decreed the use of entheogens as heretical:[495]

> The use of the herb or root called Peyote... is a superstitious action and reproved as opposed to the purity and sincerity of our Holy Catholic Faith... We decree that henceforth no person...may use or use of this said herb, this Peyote, or of others for said effects, nor others similar... being warned that doing the contrary, besides incurring said censures and penalties, we will proceed against whoever is rebellious and disobedient, as against persons suspect in the holy Catholic faith.[496]

In 1227, Pope Gregory IX established the Inquisition. In 1231, he published a decree, which called for life imprisonment with salutary penance for any heretic who had confessed to consuming a forbidden plant but repented, and capital punishment for those who persisted. The method of death was burning at the stake. By 1252, Pope Innocent III upgraded the decree to authorize the use of torture in extracting confessions. As special sins called for special divine punishment, pouring molten lead down the throats of "guilty" men, women and children became the norm. All throughout Europe, people caught eating, preparing, or possessing herbs, entheogens, or even having the knowledge of such things, were tried as heretics and witches and were hunted and exterminated along with the rest of the "pagans"[497]…all in the name of God, somehow.

We know that Hitler was one of the worst monsters that ever lived, but compared to the Catholic Church, he was only a bit more obvious in his actions… they both had the same general goal in mind: world domination. In an unbiased comparison between the ways each of them did their mass killings, Hitler's methods were actually a bit more humane. Today the swastika[498] is seen as a symbol representing the atrocities humankind is capable of. Anyone using it as a symbol of honor or worship is looked at as maniacal. How could it be that the crucifix[499] is not seen in this same manner?

This fear of the death sentence for having shamanic knowledge is most likely part of what created the elaborate myths and fables that are known today.[500] Most victims of the inquisitions were females. They were healers, midwives, herbalists, shamans, and naturalists. It has been estimated that the Protestant and Catholic churches were responsible for putting to death as many as 50% of all women living in Europe until 1792, and until 1830 in South America.[501] There was no regard for age, as women from childhood to old-age were tortured and murdered. Women who lived alone or owned property were especially targeted. If a person of influence had a grudge against someone, expect the inquisitors. No one was safe from this insanity.

> All women have been sexually abused by the Bible teachings and institutions set on its fundamentalist interpretations. There would be no need for women's movements if the church and bible hadn't abused them.
> ~ Father Leo Booth

By the end of the 19th century, millions of Native Americans were killed, forced to find a new home, or sent to reservations. More Native Americans were slaughtered in America than Hitler's attempt to exterminate the Jews. Congress passed the Controlled Substance Act in 1970, which specifically prohibited the use of peyote. Peyote had been a religious sacrament in North America for many generations before the arrival of Europeans, but suddenly, its use is abolished. Today, peyote is lumped into the Drug War. There are only a few circumstances where one can legally possess this cactus.

---

[495] Heretical: from heresies Latin, *haeresis*—a sect or school of belief.

[496] *Age of Entheogens*, pg. 21, and *Pharmacotheon*, pg. 84, by Jonathon Ott.

[497] *Pharmacotheon*, by Jonathon Ott; *Born in Blood*, by John J. Robinson; *The Medieval Inquisition*, by Bernard Hamilton; *Inquisition*, by Edward Peters.

[498] The swastika is an ancient religious symbol in many tribal societies on several continents. See *The Mass Psychology of Fascism*, by Wilhelm Reich, ch. 4; *Saharasia*, by James DeMeo, pg. 294-96.

[499] For more information on the pagan origins of the cross, see *The History of The Cross: The Pagan Origin and Idolatrous Adoption and Worship of the Image*, by Henry Dana Ward.

[500] The true Shamanic techniques were hidden by creating faerie tales and folklore. See Appendix E for an example.

[501] Jack Herer, *She Who Remembers Audio Archives*. www.thehemperor.net

These days, we no longer burn witches and shamans alive. But authorities are quick to take away the plant user's freedom, families, and property and lock them in a prison cell. It is similar to the philosophy behind creating an annual deer season: "If we didn't have deer season, the deer would overpopulate." However, animals in nature do not overpopulate, they get in the way of "progress." So it is a sport to kill them once a year (meanwhile, *humans* overpopulate). Likewise, if there were no laws to take spiritual plant users out of society, these people would "overpopulate" and that would be detrimental to (or obstruct) big business and big church "progress."

Fear was a key factor in the proliferation of the Christian Church and the promotion of fear continues to this day. A good example of "fear-mongering" is Christian televangelists Pat Robertson and Jerry Falwell, who are making threats to everyone in the nation that they should fear the "wrath of God" for daring not to discriminate against gays, pagans, and abortionists. They blame what happened on September 11, 2001 on gays and feminists. Robertson essentially told his worldwide television audience that if you piss God off, terrorism in the USA will escalate.

Jerry Falwell, regarding the attack of 9/11:

What we saw on Tuesday [9/11/01], as terrible as it is, could be miniscule if, in fact, God continues to lift the curtain and allow the enemies of America to give us probably what we deserve.

Pat Robertson replied:

Well, Jerry, that's my feeling. I think we've just seen the antechamber to terror, we haven't begun to see what they can do to the major population.

Falwell:

The ACLU has got to take a lot of blame for this. And I know I'll hear from them for this, but throwing God out... successfully with the help of the federal court system... throwing God out of the public square, out of the schools. The abortionists have got to bear some burden for this because God will not be mocked and when we destroy 40 million little innocent babies, we make God mad. I really believe that the pagans and the abortionists and the feminists and the gays and the lesbians who are actively trying to make that an alternative lifestyle, the ACLU, People for the American Way, all of them who try to secularize America... I point the thing in their face and say, "you helped this happen."

In reality, it is the spread of the world's deceitful dogmatic religions to which we can all blame terrorism.

...the Lord also tells me to tell you, that in the mid 90's, about '94 or '95, no later than that, God will destroy the homosexual community of America. But he will not destroy it with what many minds have thought it to be, He will destroy it with fire! Many will turn and be saved, but many will rebel and be destroyed.
~ Benny Hinn

Many American people are so brainwashed by church and state that they propagate their programming into their own children. It is very sad to see innocent minds destroyed with contradiction, fear, and partial truths. Their hearts are sent into turmoil as the people that they love the most, and trust with their every breath, tell them "if you get on God's bad side, you'll burn in hell forever," but at the same time "God loves you" and "you need to love God." Then, there is the real psychological, Orwellian twist: "God is always watching over you." Most Christians live their entire lives in total fear of their own God. This same fear will prevent many Christians from reading this book, or *any* secular book for that matter.

Leviticus 25:17
Ye shall not therefore oppress one another; but thou shalt fear thy God: for I am the LORD your God.

Unfortunately, this fear of God is causing people to oppress one another. A quick look into the history of Christianity will reveal that it was actually the Christian Church who had fear—the fear of too much knowledge and the fear of the losing their power. This is not to say that they were afraid of knowledge itself, but afraid of the common people having knowledge. The Christian church looted and destroyed many libraries. The astrotheological and Pharmacratic Inquisitions have plundered the world and a great wealth of knowledge has been lost.

The city of Alexandria[502] was once an immense center of learning for the entire Western civilization. Alexandria possessed a wealth of knowledge unequaled even today.[503] Practically every field of research was developed and progressed within the Alexandrian milieu. It was a gathering place located on the caravan routes. Great thinkers from all different locations mingled there. Christians, Jews, and pagans all lived together in this marvelous and unique place of learning. The libraries of Alexandria were the most eminent in antiquity and perhaps the largest ever assembled in ancient times. They held over a million different manuscripts, books, papyri, and other sacred text containing the accumulated knowledge and philosophy of the ancient world. These libraries were savagely destroyed and humankind will never know or appreciate the amount of wisdom that was lost. Moreover, the destruction of these libraries concealed the *origins* of much of this knowledge.

It is known that this knowledge did not all originate in Alexandria. Alexandria was but a container for this knowledge. The libraries contained knowledge of the heavens and knowledge of the earth. The knowledge of the heavens helped humankind establish the measurement of time and calendars. The knowledge of the earth helped humankind find food, clothing, shelter, and God. Astrotheologists and shamans, who documented their experiments and findings, used these libraries to preserve their data so that others in the future could build upon it. Today, all that is left of this wealth of information is song, folklore, and fable.

> One of the greatest crimes in human history was the destruction in 391 of the library at Alexandria perpetrated by Christian fanatics under Theophilus, bent on hiding the truth about their religion and its alleged founder. Because of this villainy, we have lost priceless information as to the true state of the ancient world, with such desolation also setting back civilization at least 1000 years.[504]
> ~ Acharya S

Alexandria was home to great thinkers and fabulous events. The story of Hermes[505] arose in Alexandria. Today many people believe that Hermes was a single person, while it is more likely that Hermes was a collection of books or a group of thinkers whose history was destroyed along with these libraries. The city housed lecture areas, gardens, and a zoo. Astronomy and astrology were prominent in Alexandria and it is no wonder that the great pyramids, which still baffle the greatest thinkers of our time, stand not far from this city. Theophilus was Patriarch of Alexandria from 385 to 412 CE. During his sovereignty, the Temple of Serapis (a branch of the Royal Library) was transformed into a Christian Church (probably around 391 CE). Many documents were destroyed at that time. The Temple of Serapis was estimated to hold about ten percent of the overall Library of Alexandria's inventory.[506] The burning of the libraries was intentional and a tragedy for all humankind. *The Other Bible* is a 742-page book[507] containing ancient alternative scriptures such as the Gnostic Gospels, the Dead Sea Scrolls, Christian Apocrypha, the Kabbalah, Carpocrates, Valentinus and the Valentinian system of Ptolemaeus, and many other myths, narratives, poems, gospels, and texts. At the very beginning of this book, a quote reads:

> Had Alexandria triumphed and not Rome, the extravagant and muddled stories that I have summarized here would be coherent, majestic, and perfectly ordinary.
> ~ Jorge Luis Borges (on the Gnostics)

The Oracle of Delphi also played a significant role in ancient history. This was a temple where a priestess (Pythonesses – snake women[508]) supposedly delivered messages from Apollo (the mushroom) to those who sought advice. For fourteen centuries, thousands of people sought the consultation of this mystic figure. The belief in this oracle helped determine the course of empires. Christian Rome silenced the "heretical" practice in the 4th Century CE.

---

[502] Note – St. Alexander of Alexandria attended the "Council of Nicaea."
[503] *The Secret Teaching of All Ages*, by Manly Palmer Hall.
[504] The Christ Conspiracy, by Acharya S, pg. 356.
[505] Hermes is the Greek god of commerce, medicine, and healing (among other things). Hermes is always in transit between this world and the next. In Rome, Hermes is known as Mercury; both Mercury and Hermes carry the caduceus.
[506] Manly Palmer Hall.
[507] Available through Harper Collins.
[508] *Symbols, Sex, and the Stars*, by Ernest Busenbark.

ONWARD CHRISTIAN SOLIDIERS

Onward Christian Soldiers, marching as to war, with the cross of Jesus, going on before...
~ Sabine Baring-Gould (1865)

It can be perplexing to understand the history of Christianity *and* hear a Christian say "I respect everyone's religion and beliefs," or "I think everyone should be able to believe what they want." This type of statement is always accompanied by the unmentioned caveat, "As long as their beliefs don't conflict with what I believe." Christianity is a belief (or faith) system that openly claims that you either join them or burn forever in hell. If this is true, what possible value would *any* other religion have? Where do they get this so-called respect for other religions and beliefs? This respectful ideology is purely a fabrication by people who refuse to acknowledge or are unable to recognize the truth behind Christian fanaticism. Any Christian who has tolerance for other religions should know that the founding fathers of their church *did not* and *would not* approve of this line of thinking. The very thought of another religion competing with Christianity on a level playing field would be met with severe animosity. Tolerant Christians are scripturally in direct conflict with Christian Orthodoxy.

The religious activities of the Catholic Church for the past 17 centuries (since the Council of Nicea in 325 CE) have been deplorably evil and this assault upon humanity continues to this day. Today, Christian enthusiasts want no difference between Church and State. They want to infiltrate our government and our public school systems to force their Christian propaganda upon us and our children. Of course, they want to do this in the name of their God and for the people. But, this hasn't worked in nearly 2000 years and it will not work now.

The following is a timeline[509] showing what has happened, and how shamanic and astrotheological knowledge has been prejudiced throughout history. Where this timeline stops, a new one begins,[510] full of people doing time in prison for nonviolent charges... it is a seemingly never-ending, true-to-life horror story.

- Prior to the 9th century CE: There was a widespread popular belief that evil witches existed. They were seen as evil persons, primarily women, who devoted their lives to harming and killing others through black magic and evil sorcery. The Catholic Church at the time officially taught that such witches did not exist. It was a heresy to say that they were real. For example, the 5th century Synod of St. Patrick ruled that "a Christian who believes that there is a vampire in the world, that is to say, a witch, is to be anathematized; whoever lays that reputation upon a living being shall not be received into the Church until he revokes with his own voice the crime that he has committed." A capitulary from Saxony (775-790 CE) blamed these stereotypes on pagan belief systems: "If anyone, deceived by the Devil, believes after the manner of the Pagans that any man or woman is a witch and eats men, and if on this account he burns [the alleged witch]... he shall be punished by capital sentence."

- 906 CE: Regino of Prum, the Abbot of Treves, wrote the Canon Episcopi. It reinforced the Church's teaching that witches did not exist. It admitted that some confused and deluded women thought that they flew through the air with the pagan goddess, Diana. But this did not happen in reality; it was explained away as some form of hallucination.

- Circa 975 CE: Penalties for witchcraft and the use of healing magic were relatively mild. The English Confessional of Egbert said, in part: "If a woman works witchcraft and enchantment and [uses] magical philters, she shall fast for twelve months.... If she kills anyone by her philters, she shall fast for seven years." Fasting, in this case, involved consuming only bread and water.

- Circa 1140: Gratian, an Italian monk, incorporated the Canon Episcopi into canon law.

- Circa 1203: The Cathar movement, a Gnostic Christian group, had become popular in the Orleans area of France and in Italy. They were declared heretics. Pope Innocent III approved a war of genocide against the Cathars. The last known Cathar was burned at the stake in 1321 CE. The faith has seen a rebirth in recent years.

---

[509] Thanks to Bruce Robinson at www.religioustolerance.org, THE BURNING TIMES: The Time Line – The Dark Ages to Now.
[510] See DRCnet at www.stopthedrugwar.org, Drug War Facts at www.drugwarfacts.org, or Dan Russell's book *Drug War* for more information.

- 1227: Pope Gregory IX established the Inquisitional Courts to arrest, try, convict and execute heretics.

- 1252: Pope Innocent III authorized the use of torture during inquisitional trials. This greatly increased the conviction rate.

- 1258: Pope Alexander IV instructed the Inquisition to confine their investigations to cases of heresy. They were to not investigate charges of divination or sorcery unless heresy was also involved.

- 1265: Pope Clement IV reaffirms the use of torture.

- 1326: The Church authorized the Inquisition to investigate witchcraft and to develop "demonology," the theory of the diabolic origin of witchcraft.

- 1330: The popular concept of witches as being evil sorcerers is expanded to include the belief that they swore allegiance to Satan, had sexual relations with the Devil, kidnapped and ate children, etc.

- 1347 to 1349: The Black Death epidemic killed a sizeable part of the European population. Conspiracy theories spread. Lepers, Jews, Muslims and witches were accused of poisoning wells and spreading disease.

- 1430's: Christian theologians started to write articles and books which "proved" the existence of witches.

- 1450: The first major witch hunts began in many western European countries. The Roman Catholic Church created an imaginary evil religion, using stereotypes that had circulated since pre-Christian times. They said that pagans who worshiped Diana and other gods and goddesses were evil witches who kidnapped babies, killed and ate their victims, sold their souls to Satan, were in league with demons, flew through the air, met in the middle of the night, caused male impotence and infertility, caused male genitals to disappear, etc. Historians have speculated that this religiously-inspired genocide was motivated by a desire by the Church to attain a complete religious monopoly, or was "a tool of repression, a form of reining in deviant behavior, a backlash against women, or a tool of the common people to name scapegoats for spoiled crops, dead livestock or the death of babies and children." Walter Stephens, a professor of Italian studies at Johns Hopkins University, proposes a new theory: "I think witches were a scapegoat for God." Religious leaders felt they had to retain the concepts of both an omnipotent and an all-loving deity. Thus, they had to invent witches and demons in order to explain the existence of evil in the world. This debate, about how an all-good and all-powerful God can coexist in the world with evil is now called Theodicy. Debates continue to the present day.

- 1450: Johann Gutenberg invented moveable type, which made mass printing possible. This enabled the wide distribution of Papal bulls and books on witch persecution; the witch-hunt was greatly facilitated.

- 1480: Thomas of Brabant wrote a book called *Formicarius*, which described the prosecution of a man for witchcraft. Copies of this book were often added to the *Malleus Maleficarum* in later years.

- 1484: Pope Innocent VIII issued a papal bull, "Summis desiderantes," on Dec. 5th, which promoted the tracking down, torturing and executing of Satan worshipers.

- 1486-1487: Institoris (Heinrich Kraemer) and Jacob Sprenger published the *Malleus Maleficarum* (meaning the *Witches' Hammer*). It is a fascinating study of the authors' misogyny and sexual frustration. It describes the activities of witches and the methods of extracting confessions. It was later abandoned by the Church, but became the "bible" of those secular courts that tried witches.

- 1500: During the 14th century there had been 38 known trials against witches and sorcerers in England, 95 in France and 80 in Germany. The witch hunts accelerated. "By choosing to give their souls over to the devil, witches had committed crimes against man and against God. The gravity of this double crime classified witchcraft as crimen exceptum, and allowed for the suspension of normal rules of evidence in order to punish the guilty."[511] Children's testimony was accepted. Unlimited torture was applied to obtain confessions, and the flimsiest circumstantial evidence was accepted as proof of guilt.

- 1517: Martin Luther came out with his 95 theses and is said to have nailed them on the cathedral door at Wittenburg, Germany. This triggered the Protestant Reformation. In Roman Catholic countries, the courts

[511] Elisa Slattery, "To Prevent a 'Shipwreck of Souls': Joann Weyer and 'De Praestigiis Daemonum'" pub. "Essays in History," by the Corcoran Department of History, University of Virginia, Vol. 36, (1994), Pg. 76.

continued to burn witches. In Protestant lands, they were mainly hung. Some Protestant countries did not allow torture. In England, this lack of torture led to a low conviction rate of only 19%.

- Circa 1550 to 1650 $_{CE}$: Trials and executions reached a peak during these ten decades, which are often referred to as the "burning times." They were mostly concentrated in eastern France, Germany and Switzerland. Witch persecutions often occurred in areas where Catholics and Protestants were fighting. Contrary to public opinion, suspected witches—particularly those involved in "evil sorcery"—were mainly tried by secular courts. Minorities were charged by church authorities; these were often cases involving the use of healing magic or midwifery.

- 1563: Johann Weyer (b. 1515) published a book that was critical of the witch trials. Called *De Praestigiis Daemonum* (*Shipwreck of Souls*), it argued that witches did not really exist, but that Satan promoted the belief that they did. He rejected confessions obtained through torture as worthless. He recommended medical treatment instead of torture and execution. By publishing the book anonymously, he escaped the stake.

- 1580: Jean Bodin wrote *De la Demonomanie des Sorciers* (*Of the Punishments Deserved by Witches*). He stated that the punishment of witches was required, both for the security of the state and to appease the wrath of God. No accused witch should be set free if there is even a scrap of evidence that she might be guilty. If prosecutors waited for solid evidence, he felt that not one witch in a million would be punished.

- 1584: Reginald Scot published a book that was ahead of its time. In *Discoverie of Witchcraft*, he claimed that supernatural powers did not exist. Thus, there were no witches.

- 1608: Francesco Maria Guazzo published the *Compendium Maleficarum*. It discusses witches' pacts with Satan, the magic that witches use to harm others, etc.

- Circa 1609: A witch panic hit the Basque areas of Spain. La Suprema, the governing body of the Inquisition, recognized it as a hoax and issued an Edict of Silence, which prohibited discussion of witchcraft. The panic quickly died down.

- 1610: Execution of witches in the Netherlands ceased, probably because of Weyer's 1563 book.

- 1616: A second witch craze broke out in Vizcaya. Again, an Edict of Silence was issued by the Inquisition. But the king overturned the Edict and 300 accused witches were burned alive.

- 1631: Friedrich Spee von Langenfield, a Jesuit priest, wrote *Cautio Criminalis* (*Circumspection in Criminal Cases*). He condemned the witch-hunts and persecution in Wurzburg, Germany. He wrote that the accused confessed only because they were the victims of sadistic tortures.

- 1684: The last accused witch was executed in England.

- 1690's: Nearly 25 people died during the witch craze in Salem, MA. One was pressed to death with weights because he would not enter a plea; some died in prison, the rest were hanged. There were other trials and executions throughout New England.

- 1745: France stopped the execution of witches.

- 1775: Germany stopped the execution of witches.

- 1782: Switzerland stopped the execution of witches.

- 1792: Poland executed the last person in Europe who had been tried and convicted of witchcraft. A few isolated extra-legal lynching of witches continued in Europe and North America into the 20th century.

- 1830's: The Church ceased the execution of witches in South America.

- 1980: Dr. Lawrence Pazder (1936-2004) and Michelle Smith wrote *Michelle Remembers*. The concept of humans in league with Satan, which had been largely dormant for decades, was revived. Although the book has been shown to be a work of fiction, it is presented as factual, based on Michelle's recovered memories. This book was largely responsible for triggering a new witch/Satanist panic in the U.S. and Canada.

- 1980 to 1995: Two types of trials were held in North America, which repeated many of the same features of earlier witch trials: Staff members at some pre-schools, day care facilities and Sunday schools were accused of ritual abuse of children. Evidence was based on faulty medical diagnoses and memories of non-existent abuse implanted in the minds of very young children.

- Tens of thousands of adults, victimized by Recovered Memory Therapy, developed false memories of having been abused during childhood. In about 17% of the cases, these memories escalated to recollections of Satanic Ritual Abuse. Hundreds of parents were charged with criminal acts. Almost all of them were innocent. Most of the charges involved acts that never actually happened.

- Sanity has since prevailed. Most of the accused have been released from jail. Those held in the state of Massachusetts are an exception.

- 1990's: Some conservative Christian pastors continue to link two unrelated belief systems: The imaginary religion of Satan-worshiping witches promoted by the Church during the Renaissance, and Wicca and other Neo-pagan religions which are nature-based faiths and do not recognize the existence of the Christian devil.

- 1994 to 1996: Several hundred people were accused of witchcraft in the Northern Province of South Africa, and were lynched by frightened mobs.

- 1999: Conservative Christian pastors occasionally call for a renewal of the burning times, to exterminate Wiccans and other Neo-pagans. One example shows the intensity of misinformation and hatred that fear of witches can continue to generate in modern times. In August, 1999, Rev. Jack Harvey, pastor of Tabernacle Independent Baptist Church in Killeen, Texas allegedly arranged for at least one member of his church to carry a handgun during religious services, "…in case a warlock tries to grab one of our kids.... I've heard they drink blood, eat babies. They have fires, they probably cook them...." During speeches that preceded his church's demonstration against Wiccans, Rev. Harvey allegedly stated that the U.S. Army should napalm witches. One of the Christian's signs read "Witchcraft is an Abomination" on one side and "Burn the Witches off Ft. Hood" on the other. (Ft. Hood is a large army base near Killeen, Texas. A Wiccan faith group is active there.)

ANOINTING THE BODY

Figure 182 - Witch "Christmas" ornament

Witches are nothing more than shamans who worship a mother goddess and practice herbal healing and spirituality just as their parents had done, and their grandparents, and so on. Many of the fairy tales we've heard throughout life have involved witches in one way or another. There are tales of good witches and bad witches. The green-skinned witch riding a broom is a common Halloween icon. The word "witch" comes from *weik* meaning to separate, hence, set aside for religious worship, to consecrate. Some debate that the word comes from the Saxon word wicce (or Wicca), meaning, "wise one." It is to the wise ones (the oracles and shamans) that communities turn to for many reasons such as consultation regarding farming, spirituality, and childbirth. Either way, the herbal knowledge of the witch was valued as an asset to the community. Plants and herbs were utilized for food, medicine, spirituality and recreation.

On the eve of Samhain, what we now call Halloween, witches gather to perform divination rites. Some prepare an entheogenic "Flying Ointment" to assist them. There are numerous recipes for the ointment, but they all have a base of *nightshade* (Atropa belladonna) and/or *mandrake* (Mandragora officinarum). Both of these are extremely psychoactive plants that generate visions and facilitate astral projection.[512] They are green leafy plants that create a green paste or ointment when prepared.

---

[512] The United States intelligence service has spent millions of dollars on a technique known as "remote viewing," which is just another name for *astral projection*.

This green ointment was then rubbed all over the body (the popularized witch icon is a woman with green skin), especially in places where skin tissue is rich in capillaries. The mucous membrane of the genitals is a preferential location for females. The ointment was applied to a broom handle and rubbed on and inserted into the vagina.[513]

> It [Belladonna] was one of the primary ingredients of the brews and ointments employed by witches and sorcerers. One such potent mixture, containing Belladonna, Henbane, Mandrake, and the fat of a stillborn child, was rubbed over the skin or inserted into the vagina for absorption. The familiar witch's broom-stick goes far back in European magic beliefs. An investigation into witchcraft in 1324 reported that "in rifleing the closet of the ladie, they found a Pipe of ointment, wherewith she greased a staffe, upon which she ambled and galloped through thick and thin, when and in what manner she listed." Later, in the fifteenth century, a similar account stated: "But the vulgar believe and the witches confess, that on certain days and nights they anoint a staff and ride on it to the appointed place or anoint themselves under the arms and in other hairy places and sometimes carry charms under the hair.[514]
> ~ Dr. Richard Evens Schultes & Dr. Albert Hofmann

> Witches soar for related reasons: a witch who wanted to "fly" to a sabbat, or orgiastic ceremony, would anoint a staff with specially prepared oils containing psychoactive matter, probably from toad skins, and then apply it to vaginal membranes.
> References to flying can be found in more recent applications of the mushroom. St. Catherine of Genoa (1447-1510) used fly agaric to soar to the heights of religious ecstasy, according to Daniele Piomelli of the Unite de Neurobilogic et Pharmacologie de I'Inserm in Paris.[515]
> ~ Roger Highfield

Astral projection or *transvection* allows someone to leave their body and "fly" anywhere in the world in their minds, and to visualize themselves and others in certain situations. The method of transportation for these witches is a broomstick (made from the sacred birch). Hence, the icon of the witch on a broom, flying across the sky on Halloween.

In many instances, anointing the body with oil is associated with fertility rights[516] and tantra. Entheogen- infused oil is poured onto the male phallic prior to sex where blissful, psychedelic, sexual experiences are shared by the couples (or groups). Sexually oppressed religionists squirm when confronted with facts like this. The application of plants to the body is natural[517] and only misguided prejudices drive a repulsive attitude towards it.

There are many oils that the shamans use to generate God within and to go out of body. One method of administering the oil involves a harsh shaving of the scalp and applying the anointing oils directly onto the crown chakra. Monks shave the tops of their heads bald, leaving a ring of hair around their heads. While some researchers claim that these elders (EL-ders), were worshiping EL, or Saturn (contending that these rings on their heads symbolically represent the rings of Saturn/Kronos), we believe this to also be a shamanic ritual on the microcosm. It is likely that an extraction from mushrooms or other sacred plants was made into oil, which served as a *marinade* for the skullcaps that these men wore. These skullcaps may have been soaked in psychedelic oil (and even semen because of its association to the liquid seed of God), or were used to cover over the psychedelic oil on their heads. Placing an entheogen-spiked skullcap on top of a fresh razor burn (tonsure) would provide an ideal method for transferring essential oils into the bloodstream. The ring of hair left on their heads would behave like a sponge, soaking up the oil and preventing it from continuously running into their faces and down their backs.

Shamans in Siberia and Eurasia use reindeer as allies when they mentally fly out of body. The reindeer and the shaman apparently have a spiritual connection that is enhanced by eating the *Amanita muscaria* mushroom (which also promotes astral projection or out of body experiences). The out of body flying-reindeer, herding-shaman's sled evolved into the flying chariot of Santa Claus. Although Santa's sleigh and the witches broom are both considered a *flight of the imagination*, the symbolism of both can be traced back to historic facts and knowledge based on Mother Nature, celestial objects, and sexuality.

---

[513] www.botanical.com - *Herbs of Divination* –by Rita Jacinto.
[514] *Plants of the Gods*, by Dr. Richard Evens Schultes, Dr. Albert Hofmann, pg. 88 – or pg. 89-90 in the revised edition with Christian Ratsch, Ph.D.
[515] *The Physics of Christmas*, by Roger Highfield, pg. 22.
[516] *The Sacred Mushroom and the Cross*, by John Allegro.
[517] Consider Aloe Vera.

There is much more to these secret teachings than can be discussed in one book. For now, we have come to *the end of a road*, as we leave you with some thoughtful words from those who have come before us:

We each must become like fishermen and go out onto the dark ocean of mind and let your nets down into that sea. What you are after is not some behemoth that will tear through your nets, foul them, and drag you and your little boat into the abyss. Nor are what we looking for, a bunch of sardines that can slip through your net and disappear. What we are looking for are middle sized ideas that are not so small that they are trivial, and not so large that they're incomprehensible; but middle sized ideas that we can wrestle into our boat and take back to the folks onshore and have fish dinner. Every one of us, when we go into the psychedelic state, this is what we should be looking for. It's not for *your* elucidation, it's not part of *your* self-directed psychotherapy; you are an explorer and you represent our species and the greatest good that you can do is to bring back any new idea because our world is endangered by the absence of good ideas. Our world is in crisis because of the absence of consciousness. To whatever degree any one of us can bring back a small piece of the picture and contribute it to the building of the new paradigm, then we participate in the redemption of the human spirit. And that, after all, is what it's really all about.
~ Terence McKenna

Jesus proclaimed the coming of the Kingdom, but what came was the Church.
~ Alfred Loisy

Romans 12:2
and be not conformed to this world: but be transformed by the *renewing of your mind*, that ye may prove what is that good, and acceptable, and perfect, will of god.

Even more controversial [than The Dead Sea Scrolls] was my study of a hallucinogenic cult and associated mythology centred on the Sacred Mushroom, the *Amanita muscaria*. This was in the main a philological study, although it was brought to public attention dramatically through its serialisation in Britain's Sunday Mirror tabloid. Its main importance was that it drew together in a unique way the origins of cultures and languages in the ancient Near East and the classic civilizations of Europe and Asia Minor. However, the occasion for the almost hysterical condemnation of the work was my inclusion within its scope of certain aspects of biblical mythology, even the New Testament stories. In their opposition the clerics found willing support from the supposedly less partisan world of the acade of the academics who saw a threat posed by such all-embracing studies to their carefully erected interdisciplinary barriers. Professional scholars feel happier and more secure when they are permitted to dig deeper and deeper into less and less, and are not required by less inhibited researchers and an enquiring laity to peer over their trench walls into adjoining fields of which they know little and frankly care less.
~ John Marco Allegro

~ Conclusion ~

The shamanic and astrotheological rituals of the mysteries discussed in this book have long been kept secret for the kings, priests, and the elite. Christians today believe that God sent his only divine son to earth to become a humble man, named Jesus the Christ (the oil-anointed one), to save the souls of God's own faux pas—the creation of humankind. We are told that Jesus then gave the secrets of the mysteries to his followers, who in turn gave them to us by way of the gospels. However, what are Christians today if their ritual of baptism, performed with simple water, is merely symbolic of the anointing oils—in addition to their symbolic Holy Eucharist (wine) being stamped out in an assembly line and bought at a liquor store?

We suggest that Christians today are the victims of an elaborate hoax meant to undermine them and keep them in the dark about the true manner in which we can all have direct communion with God.

If there had actually been a man living 2000 years ago, who adopted the identical traits of the much older astrotheological and entheogenical myths, who upset the rulers by giving the secrets of the mysteries to the common people, he died in vain because the followers of this religion today are still uninformed of the cornerstone upon which their religion was founded. However, even the Teacher of Righteousness of the Essenes/Zadokites kept these secrets under close guard. For over 2000 years humankind has lived under the Dark Age of Pisces, under the control of perjurious, deceitful men with a hunger for global, totalitarian power. This Age of Christianity, the Age of Pisces, is ending, and with its death comes a new Age and a new way of life.

> Exodus 33:1 (NIV)
> Then the LORD said to Moses, "Leave this place, you and the people you brought up out of Egypt, and go up to the land I promised on oath to Abraham, Isaac and Jacob, saying, 'I will give it to your descendants.'

The record of John Marco Allegro and his great works has finally been set straight. May the scholars of the world recognize this and come forward. We are certain that the true sun and mushroom identity of Christ will someday be common knowledge. With the awareness of Christ's return (or rather, the understanding that the true *Christ* never left), we can all genuinely experience what it means to eat the Fruit of the Tree and be blessed by the blood and flesh of Christ, if we so choose to. The Age of Aquarius has dawned and our imminent revelation or *apocalypse* of St. John the Mushroom[518] is now a reality. The secret knowledge of the waters of life is finally flowing back to the minds of the people, where it will remain for quite some time.

In this Age of Enlightenment (and information), no longer do we have the excuse that the truth is not available to us. Humankind as a whole has a chance to evolve, to fling open the doors of the mind and live free. With the dawning of the new Age, we can now leave behind the worlds deceitful religions, created for the enslavement of human consciousness, forever.

> The English word "CHURCH" comes directly from the Scottish work "KIRK." "Kirk" comes to us from "Circe," the ancient female Greek goddess. Circe was an enchantress who tricked and deceived men when they came in to her—and changed them into swine! Female Goddess (CIRCE) = Mother (CHURCH).[519]
> ~ Jordan Maxwell

---

[518] Allegro identified hidden wordplay on *Amanita muscaria* to Soma (Greek=Body), and Manna (Sumerian = Mushroom), (of which there are two kinds), the names Jesus, James, and John, the Fruit of the tree of Knowledge, and the symbol of the cross, to the *Amanita muscaria*, in *The Sacred Mushroom and the Cross*, pg. 100, 120, 133, 150.

[519] In *Witchcraft Medicine* Rätsch also relates: "The Homeric moly, like the magical plant of Circe, was interpreted quite early as mandrake, *Mandragora officinarum L.* (Dierbach, 1833: 204; Kreuter, 1982: 29). Dioscorides passed down the name *circeon* for mandrake, as well as *Mandragora Circaea*, the herb with which Circe transformed the men of the Odysseus into "pigs" (this probably means sexually aroused men): "The mandrake. Some call it *antimelon* ["in place of an apple"], others dirkaia, also kirkaia [plant of Circe/Kirke], because the root seemed to be effective as a love potion" (Dioscorides, Materia medica IV.76)." pg. 117

As a prerequisite to the new Age, humanity must discontinue the use of the outdated and inaccurate Christian/Gregorian calendar, created by the controlling elite for the Piscean age. Our society must evolve. The use of a calendar that teaches humankind the knowledge of the cosmos by way of the very nature of its use is necessary. The universal adaptation of the Maya or similar calendar is a step in this direction. The *Archaic Revival* of our true religious history and connection with the plants, planets, stars and heavens is upon us.

> Since mushrooms nowhere appear in the surface story, and yet are clearly involved in the cryptic names, it must mean that the secret level of understanding is the significant one for the intended reader as for the cryptographer; what appears on the surface is unreal and never expected to be taken seriously by those within the cult.... A subterfuge of this nature, bearing as it does on what we now see is a widespread and very ancient mushroom cult, can only mean that the "real" Christianity was heavily involved with it; in which case the story of Jesus was a hoax for the benefit of the Jewish and Roman authorities engaged in persecuting the cult.
> ~ John Allegro

Truth spreads as Novelty, and it frees the collective consciousness that we call humanity. Many have dedicated their lives to this *End of a Road*. We do not believe that our work alone is capable of ending all atrocity against humankind. Nevertheless, we do know that this information will drive nails into the coffins of the controlling secret societies and religions of the world. Sometimes, perhaps, for the advancement of humankind, it is the obligation of the ethnographer to destroy the ethnos investigated. Occasionally this happens as a result of revealing the truth behind a particular ethnos, in this case, the religious dogmas of the world.

We hope this book has provided you with a new and complete vantage point from which to view the *Law of Duality*. The Law of Duality is the epitome of ancient philosophy, flanked by the two great pillars of astrotheology and shamanism. The time has come when we can rebuild upon a solid foundation of the ancient mysteries. Thousands of years of intellectual hijacking of the collective consciousness is finally ending.

As we have climbed upon the shoulders of many great researchers to reveal these dualistic mysteries, we welcome others to climb upon our shoulders to help usher in the Age of Enlightenment. From two fields of study we may edify one *"new"* field in which the two are recognized as a whole. We jokingly like to refer to this un-named, multi-disciplinary approach as "Ethnopharmacoastrotheology," through which "A Grand, Unifying Theory of Religion"[520] will emerge.

Every day a new turn is taken, and every day, a new piece of the puzzle is discovered and put into place. And like a puzzle, long before all of the pieces have been found and put into place, the entire picture will become obvious to everyone. Then the paradigm will shift.

---

[520] *John Marco Allegro: The Maverick of the Dead Sea Scrolls*, by Judith Anne Brown, ch. 10.

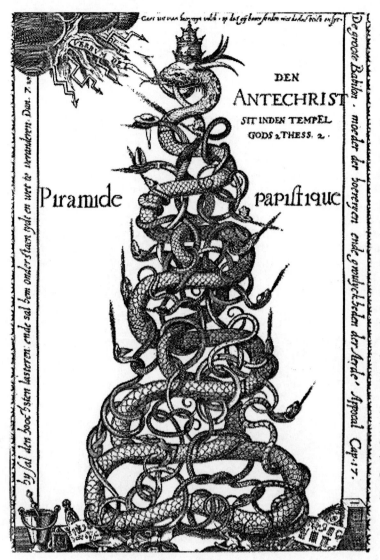

Figure 183

We have shown that Jesus Christ was a complex anthropomorphism of the phallic sun in the sky and the mushrooms on the ground. Jesus is the serpent and the caduceus, which is the symbol for knowledge, finance, drugs, the world tree, the Christmas tree, the energy system of the body, healing, the mark of the beast, the egg (yolk), and this is still not a complete list. In the first century BCE, this already ancient mythology was applied by the Essenes/Zadokites (the healers or 'Physicians') to their leader, the Teacher of Righteousness, because to them, only he had the closest ties to the beams of God's sun, and therefore spiritual and physical good health. Today, physicians still use the ancient symbol of the caduceus, this most ancient symbol of plant pharmacopoeia and healing.

As above, so below—the ancient mysteries of the planetary spheres, celestial spheres and Precession of the Equinoxes are no longer hidden. Recycling the waters of the ouroboros *is* the living water of Christ, the elixir of the alchemist, the alchemical gold, the "*Gold* of God."

No longer do we need to plea for a bite of liberty by groveling at the feet of governments and religions, so full of deceit and tyranny. As a global community, we are now armed with the ax that will cut the roots out from under the proverbial tree of lies, bringing to an end thousands of years of murder, greed, deception and mind control. The false religious paradigm will implode in on itself, because it was never anything more than a fraudulent fabrication of man, led by pathetic, impotent and bitter wizards, pulling the levers of Oz known as the Vatican.

You should now have an understanding of the *law of duality—as above, so below*—an important piece of the mystery. Failure to recognize the macrocosm *and* the microcosm has been an oversight that has prevented many truth seekers from completing the Great Work. For thousands of years, the secret mysteries have been kept from the people. This book is the first known effort to understand and combine the macrocosm and microcosm into a single, workable philosophy in which astrotheology and entheogenic plants are incorporated.

Once the collective shock wears off concerning the facts, some of which were presented here, that entheogens and celestial worship are at the very foundation of modern-day religion, perhaps change will come about. The way each individual perceives these changes, and what is learned at every step, is based upon the truth of one's thoughts. This book contains truths for you to build upon. Now, the ball is in your court.

In the new Age of Aquarius, will humankind finally discover the totality of its collective self?

The Maya conceived of the Great Cycle as one World Age, one growth cycle, at the end of which humanity reaches the next stage in its spiritual development. As the life of an individual goes through distinct stages, so too the collective lifewave of humanity grows through several distinct phases. These "phases" are the five World Ages, or "Suns," spoken of in Mesoamerican mythology.[521]
~ John Major Jenkins

The Pharmacratic Inquisition is now coming to a close as our sun has dawned its return in a new Age of Enlightenment.

When you turn your eyes inward, you discover the birthright... the existential facts out of which this particular existence emerged. Because it means that mystery did not die with the fall of Arthur or the fall of Atlantis or the fall of anything. Mystery is alive in the moment, in the here in now. It just simply lies on the other side of a barrier of courage. And it isn't even that high of a barrier; it's just a barrier high enough to keep out the insincere and the misdirected. But for those who will claim it, in the midst of the historical chaos of the late 20th Century, they become the archaic pioneers; they become the first people to carry the Ouroboric serpent around to its own tail and to make closure. To the degree that any one of us has this connection back to the archaic in our life, it makes where we have been make a lot more sense, and it makes where we're going seem a lot more inviting.
~ Terence McKenna

Figure 184 - Bas Relief on the Great Porch - Notre Dame, Paris

---

[521] *Maya Cosmogenesis 2012*, by John Major Jenkins, pg. 22.

Appendix A

<u>IN MEMORIUM TO JOHN MARCO ALLEGRO</u>

John M. Allegro was born February 17, 1923 in London. He served in the Royal Navy, then studied at the University of Manchester where he obtained a first-class Honors Degree in Oriental Studies in 1951. A year later, he was awarded a Masters Degree for his work on the Balaam Oracles. His Oxford research on Hebrew dialects was interrupted when, in 1953, he was called to join the first international team of scholars working on the newly discovered Dead Sea Scrolls in Jerusalem.

Mr. Allegro was a lecturer, etymologist, and author, credited with:

- *The Dead Sea Scrolls*, 1956
- *The People of the Dead Sea Scrolls*, 1958
- *The Treasure of the Copper Scroll*, 1960
- *The Shapira Affair*, 1965
- *Search in the Desert*, 1967
- *Discoveries in the Judaean Desert of Jordan, Qumrân Cave 4. V (4Q158-4Q186)*, 1968
- *The Sacred Mushroom and the Cross*, 1970
- *The End of a Road*, 1970
- *The Chosen People*, 1971
- *Lost Gods*, 1977
- *The Dead Sea Scrolls and the Christian Myth*, 1979
- *All Manner of Men*, 1982
- *Physician, Heal Thyself*, 1985

Until 1970, he was a lecturer in the Old Testament and Intertestamental Studies department at the University of Manchester. He died in 1988 at the age of 65 with largely disapproving mentions in the press.

Long before the *Sacred Mushroom and the Cross* was actually taken out of print, rumors abounded that rights to the book were supposedly purchased by Anheuser-Busch, owner of the Budweiser beer company and several theme parks across America. Other rumors claimed the Catholic Church bought the rights and went so far as to say that Hodder & Stoughton Publishing sent a letter of apology to the Pope for ever printing the book. In truth, however, the publisher took the book out of print for strictly commercial reasons. Sales had dwindled over the years, and, at the request of John Allegro, all rights were returned to him on May 29, 1985.

John Marco Allegro died suddenly of an aortic aneurysm on his 65th birthday, February 17, 1988 at his home in Sandbach, Cheshire. He had previously been living on the Isle of Man, but moved back to England in 1985. Contrary to rumors that he'd been exiled to the isle, he had moved there mainly because of lower tax requirements for authors and writers. (Had Allegro remained in England at that time, he would have given up in tax most of what he earned from a new book.)

Before his death, Allegro had been criticized by his former friends and colleagues for his outspoken and unconventional ideas. But far from being banished as a scholar after years of "academic" attack, he resigned from the University out of his own accord. He did this <u>before</u> *The Sacred Mushroom and the Cross* went to print. He had had enough of academia and wanted to write freelance.

We lost a modern day "hero" with the passing of John Marco Allegro. He was an amazing expert in linguistics, etymology, philology, theology, mycology and much more. We will miss him, and will continue to do everything we can to to further what will prove to be valuable and accurate work on his part.

Appendix B

PHILOLOGICAL PARALLELS –

AN ESOTERIC LOOK AT WORDS AND LETTERS

By Jay Lynn

NOTE: The material in this Appendix further supports what we have laid out in the beginning of the book, on page xvi. The following excerpts by Jay Lynn provide a brief introduction to his 35 years of research in the area of philology with regards to the origins of many alphabets stemming primarily from human physiology. We have spent much time poring over his work and sources and find it likely enough to present here. This work is currently presented as hypothetical until such time that it is ready for full publication and peer review.

I have been researching linguistics, theology, mycology, etymology and languages from before 1970, when Allegro's book, *The Sacred Mushroom and the Cross*, went into print. In fact, I waited a year before I read and researched his book, simply because I did not want to borrow anything from his works, which came to many of the same conclusions, though mine were from a different source. My conclusions came from researching the English language, taking it back to early Latin, Greek, Hebrew, Aramaic, Egyptian hieroglyphics, mycology, and researching theology.

The first and most shocking thing concerning the English alphabet was the fact it had never been taken back to its hieroglyphic and ideographic form. This I had to question, and the answer was not a straightforward simple deduction, primarily due to the fact that modern languages have never been a purely straightforward means of communication. This fact was due to the corruption of all languages from the so-called "fall" of the Roman Empire to date.

Language in the narrow sense is an exclusive characteristic of man. The most intelligent apes are void of oral language, while most primitive men possessed it in one form or another. Not much has been revealed of the origin of language, and most conjecture about its origin lacks positive proof. Perhaps it is time to unlock the vaults of the sexual truth of language, which will remove the mystery and deceit attached to the letters of which we are all familiar.

Hieroglyphics, alphabets, and the words we use today were formed by what Christianity labeled "pagan" writers, and therefore will reflect their religious sexual implications as well as their origins or genesis. The foundation of the English alphabet has its roots deeply embedded in the Greek alphabet and their language, which has been declared a "dead language" by the "Dark Age rulers," the "First Reich," and "The Holy Roman Empire."

The principle Greek dialects were Ionic (of which Attica Greek was a variety), Doric, and Aeolic. Modern Greek of course is so removed from that of the ancient Greek that it would be unintelligible to the Athenian of the Periclean age. The pre-Christian Latin was built from Greek alphabets, which copied their letters from Phoenician. (Etruscan - Cuneiform?)

The English language contains words from most languages of which all are ultimately derived of ancient Greek. Therefore, the English language was ideal for the purpose of proving my research, as I had to deal with words that had not changed for two thousand years.

I began with *universal words* of Latin and Greek, dealing with the anatomy of the body, plant life, animal life, drugs and any other unchanged Greek, Latin, Hebrew or Phoenician word at hand. These types of words were allowed to remain unchanged as a worldwide means of communication, with regard to the peoples of the world, after the formation of the Holy Roman Empire. The physicians around the world deal in the universal tongue, as do botanists, druggists and the Roman Catholic priesthood themselves, who used old Latin up to the 20th century.

Why would a one-world language, inherited from the Greeks and later the Romans, be divided up into so many various tongues, of which all but a few can be traced back to the original Greek language?

185

One might think there was some sort of conspiracy to hide certain revealing information, hence the common denominator holding these groups together. Why else would the conspirators possess their own language, ancient Latin? Modern Latin is far removed from ancient Latin, and the two are quite distinct.

Latin was used by the Roman Empire for hundreds of years, and was instituted into every conquered country until their known world was united, which was called the Roman Empire. In forming other languages much later, called the *Romance* (after Roman) Languages, the Catholic Church could well have adopted ancient Latin (and Greek) for selfish reasons.

The early Christian's claim that they could speak in many tongues was partially due to the fact that monks were rewriting language, converting it into Roman "Romance Languages," omitting any statement or item they deemed heretical, or letters that would place the Church in a shady light.

After 500 $_{CE}$ ('CE' = common era, which replaced 'AD', Anno Domina, the year of our lord, Jesus Christ), all letters were taken away from the populace, eventually no one could read or write. Up to the fall of Rome, practically everyone could read and write both Greek and Latin.

The Roman Catholic Christian Church, in their adoption of ancient Latin for themselves, wanted to remove all *tentation* (early spelling of temptation) from the masses. At the same time, they wanted to protect the new Christian Catholic image from phallic *horship*[522] of the mushroom. During the Dark Ages, all languages were modernized, and were called the "Romance Languages," derived of Roman, Latin, and ancient Greek. In the process, any anti-Christian reflections or sexual/drug implications were omitted. Many "lost works" are among the list of omissions, lost to the world until recently rediscovered with the revelations of Allegro and of other individuals seeking the truth of our past. The original works would eventually disappear and be listed in large quantities with the lost works of history, some buried under the Vatican in their miles of hidden vaults, still unavailable to public scrutiny.

The link between the chemist, botanist, priest, doctor, etc., was thenceforth a one-world language. The drugs for mystical use were mostly derived from plants of the faba or bean family and poisons. The healing qualities of some of the drugs, as well as their spiritual aspects were also evident, such as the sacred mushrooms—the *Amanita muscaria, pantherina* and *Psilocybe* varieties. The alchemist/priest/shaman (the earlier witch doctor or wizard) mixed the herbal juices, distilled or crystallized them and the priest administered them to the afflicted. Poisons were in heavy demand and were used to eliminate undesirables in religion and government all the way up to the 18th century, until medicine advanced and autopsies were performed.

Hieroglyphics and ancient Greek writings were condemned by the Holy Roman Empire as heretical. Anyone possessing rolls (books) or parchments of hieroglyphics and any other writings outlawed by that faction were imprisoned, punished and, in many cases, put to death. The reason is quite clear to any scholar of etymology and linguistics: a picture is worth a thousand words.

Early Egyptian hieroglyphics show a definite positive proof of the action. Take, for instance, the Egyptian word "sati," from *The Book of the Dead* (Budge), which means to pour out water, to micturate (urinate) or defecate, depicted as a man standing and urinating, or squatting and defecating. Another example of "dirty pictures," is the Egyptian word "Met," for the Egyptian number 10, shown as a male organ at erection and secreting liquid in the form of an "S" from the end of the penis. Met is also depicted as an inverted U, a fertility sign long before it became a vowel. 10 in Roman numerals is expressed with an X, which in turn was a sign for Christ and translated as *anoint, bewet, bedew*.

The letter X in ancient Egypt also symbolized the dead spirit of man. It can be associated with the "living Spirit," of the male in the form of "living water." This is another biblical rendering for Jesus Christ, called also, "*The Comforter*" (Com-forter), Strength in coming. *Fortis* is Latin for strength, vigor; and kum is semen, sperm (Greek, *Kuming*, releasing the seed of the male member). This is still used today, "I'm kuming," handed down by word of mouth from the ancient Greek language.

---

[522] Early spelling of worship, as the W was not used in early language; it was made of a double U, UU, W.

Hieroglyphics, as a medium of communication, was used by the Chinese of 2000 BCE, the Sumerian's of 5000 BCE, along with the more famous Egyptian hieroglyphics.

Many of the signs drawn from the above civilizations have definite relationships. Mountains were shown as a series of A's (e.g. AAA) and water was depicted as three wavy lines. The *S, Z,* and *N* are actually letters symbolizing water, rain and, in the case of the Egyptian word Met, semen. Similar relationships in later languages also bear a resemblance. English and German reflect a relationship. More remotely, English is similar to French, Sanskrit Russian and Greek. But so far, there has been no demonstration to show that English is ever so remotely related to Chinese or Mayan.

The Chinese have a syllabary, an alphabet in which many or all of the signs represent syllables, which is used only to supplement the Chinese characters universally in use. The Persians had a syllabary derived from the Cuneiform. The writings of the Mayas, Hittites and Chinese, along with one or two other peoples, were conventionalized to a great degree, but none of these seems to have developed a true alphabet.

The Sumerians, Chinese, Aztecs, Mayans and especially the Egyptians in their hieroglyphics, all worked out word-writing-systems. In Egyptian writing, there was a process to a word-sound writing in which the symbols were compounded to make words.

The symbol for man, as an example, when enjoined with the sign for drake, would equal man-drake. Then to simplify the system, the same symbol was used for the same sound in like words or homonyms.

In Arabia, prior to 1000BCE, hieroglyphics were in use. An eye placed next to a circle with a cross inside equaled I-land. The written S was added later, island—an *eye* of *land* in a large body of water (at one time, the Vatican claimed all islands as their possessions). Therefore, the *I* in the English language has been taken back to its hieroglyphic root as *an eye.*

In Egyptian hieroglyphics, two feathers=I, shown later as two I's. Later, *Y* replaced the two I's and *I* stood alone until perverted modern Latin made some *I* and *Y* words begin with *J* and *G,* as in *yard* which is also *gard,* and *Iesos* is *Jesus.* The other signs of the alphabet have not been deciphered until now.

It is believed the Phoenician alphabet was the great mother alphabet. It came to us from Phoenicia, then moved on to Greece and Eturia (of Etruscan), an ancient district of Italy where they copied the Greek style in pottery. Then the alphabet went to Rome where some letters were added.

Each literary civilization molded its respective alphabet. The end result differs from the mold such that its original relationship is unrecognizable today. Thus, the Devanagari syllabary, the great alphabet of India, is derived from the same source as the Arabic, Hebrew and Latin alphabets. This is an important fact when comparing the religious aspect of India to that of the Hebrew or Mosaic Law.

I believe these alphabets have their roots in Egyptian hieroglyphics, or "priestly (sacred botanical/chemical/shamanic) writings." However, it is almost impossible for anyone but a scholar to see a real resemblance between these languages in their present form. It is like a dialect. A person must familiarize oneself with a dialect first, before the words can be understood, even though one already speaks and understands the language. There is a theory that the Phoenicians took their alphabet from the Philistines, who are then thought to have brought theirs from Crete, which could have taken its alphabet from Egypt.

A couple of nations developed alphabets not connected with the great alphabets of the West. Japan uses a syllabary to supplement the Chinese characters universally in use, and the Persians had a syllabary derived of cuneiform. Cuneiform was composed of wedge-shaped characters inscribed by the ancient Akkadians (Acadians), Persians, Babylonians and Assyrians (Syria). The word *cuneiform* is derived from the Greek word *kunna,* meaning *wedge-shaped* and Latin, *cunnes,* which means *matrix* or *vagina. Cunnan* means to know. Religiously and legally it applies as *to have sexual intercourse with,* as Adam *knew* Eve, or Joseph *knew* Mary not. "*Cunae*" means *cradle, crib, manger, bin, hopper.* This is where the word *cuneiform* derived its "wedge shaped" meaning.

Cuneiform was developed in the lower Tigris and Euphrates valley by the Sumerians and shares similarities with Chinese, Egyptian, and Mayan writing. While it is one of the four or five original writings, the script was pictographic. But it was developed into phonetic and was highly conventionalized in Babylonia and Assyria. The Persians later took over cuneiform, applying a radical reform and adopted some of it to their own language. As an outgrowth of primitive hieroglyphics, cuneiform eventually reached an alphabetic system.

THE EGG OF GOD

From relief carvings on stone, wood and other durable material such as metal (copper), we can follow the evolution of writing. Words were not just thought up, and letters were not pulled out of a hat to form a word. Words had to be built. First it was done in characters, which depicted part of the whole subject. Cuneiform (as a sex symbol) is an abstract example. Another example would be the word *egg* which, in its modern English form, is far removed from its hieroglyphic and Greek origin. I believe the Greeks, in forming their word for egg (*OON*), had taken it from an Egyptian hieroglyph for what is male or masculine (ego?). A double O (OO) with an S tail rising between the double O, representing masculinity.

Eggs hold living water as their seed, so the ancients noted. Likewise, the universe was the comic egg with the seed of god, the sun, at its center, and rain appeared on earth as the falling semen. Solid matter did not contain liquid—the ancients were aware of this fact. Therefore, all water was considered sacred to them and deities were attached to rivers, lakes, oceans and water (rain) from heaven.

The Babylonians and Assyrians had Ea. The Romans had Neptune as their god of the seas—half man and half fish, who carries a trident. Ultimately, all liquid fell from the heavens and filled the rivers, lakes, streams and maris, or mar, which means "the seas." (The evolution of the word Se is see, sea!) The Catholic Church could have considered Mary to be their female water deity, as the sea was considered the womb of all life through evolution, a common ancient belief until the Hebrew/Christian era. The liquid of life was called *Sblood*, God's blood, the liquid of life in all living creatures. It was considered sacred, as it ultimately was derived of the seed of God, or rain, which, through its evolution from the sea into the air and onto the land, gave life to all creatures.

Rain, snow and frost from the heavens gave life to all creatures. Today we still call the frost of the male species after its phallic name, *Jack-frost*, the male hor (hoar-frost). Anciently, hoar was written as hor, which stood for frost. When the word ooman (earlier for woman, *oo, egg* with *man*) was created, , it signified a place for the male to plant his seed in the furrow, manger, bin, or hopper (vagina) of the female. The *W* was added to *hor*, creating *whore*, the "frost seeker" of the male bone, his seed. Today, the word whore can be applied to either sex.

HIEROGLYPHICS

Obviously all alphabets were preceded by hieroglyphics. Other carvings which bear a similarity to those of the Egyptians have been found in the Minoan civilization of Crete, the Hittite civilization of Asia Minor, Easter Island, and the Mayan, Aztec and Toltec civilizations of Mesoamerica. Because of their similarities these carvings are also called hieroglyphics.

The main feature of hieroglyphics is that they consist of conventionalized pictures used chiefly to represent meanings that seem arbitrary and not too often obvious. Egyptian hieroglyphics are in three stages: The First Dynasty, perfected; the Old Kingdom and Middle Kingdom, going out of use; and the New Empire, no longer used or understood by the scribes. The use of these later hieroglyphics of 500 BCE, was a "Tour de Farce."

Hieroglyphics had a three-fold purpose. However, few were used for all three. As a phonogram: An owl would equal the sound of M, since the word for owl had M for its principal consonant. Owl in Coptic is *Mulotch*, and *M* in Egyptian was taken or shown hieroglyphically as an owl. Other signs were modified forms for the *M*. This is probably because of the great horned owl's head taking the form of an *M*. In addition, we find the word "Amelu" of Assyrian origin and "Awelu" of Babylonian origin. Note the change of the letter *M* to *W*! The first, Awelu, or "man," is the highest of the three social orders recognized by Babylonian law. The letter M would later be taken for man as a prefix, the letter M=Man. Take note of the word "Andros," which means male. "An" in Sumerian means God, and "dros," of Gr. Drosos, which means dew, juice, as in Gr. Drosera, the sundew melon. Dros, broken down

188

further, is from Gr. Juice, (Sblood) and os Gr. Bone, hence, God's dew of the male bone. *M* in Egyptian hieroglyphics consists of a bar, open at one end. A beam = M, a bar. The phonograms were, of course, the controlling factors in the progress of hieroglyphic writing because of the fundamental convenience of an alphabet.

In the Middle Kingdom, a developed cursive was extensively used. The Hieratic in the last centuries BCE was a more developed style. The Demotic supplanted the Hieratic, where the origin of most characters could be plainly seen in the hieroglyphics. Meanwhile the Demotics were too conventionalized to bear any resemblance to the hieroglyphics from which they were born. Hieratic was a form of written hieroglyphics wherein the hieroglyphic symbol was written out, and the characters were assembled or joined together in a type of written form. Later, about 900_{BCE}, the scribes invented an arbitrary or conventional modification of the hieratic characters to form a new style of writing called Enchorial or Demotic. Demotic is from the Greek word, *Demotikos* (demos = the people and tikos = birth, the birth of the people's writing). Enchorial is of Enchoric, which is from the Greek word Enchorios (En, in, within; and chora, country, native). Demotic writing became common in Egypt. Although its use was not popular, it was mandatory and instituted by the religious faction.

THE GREEK INFLUENCE ON LANGUAGE

Ancient Greece formulated the foundations of modern civilizations. Their alphabet, derived of cuneiform, is the mother of all languages with few exceptions— which were mainly Persian and Oriental. It is all but impossible for us to determine, with any certainty of accuracy, the original pronunciation of ancient Greek words and names, though we continually try. There are neither trustworthy records nor unbroken tradition with which to help or relieve the problem.

The study of Greek fell into disrepute with the decline of the Roman Empire, after which came the forming of Christianity and ultimately The Holy Roman Empire. In fact, the first book printed in Greek characters was by Constantine Lascaris, who died around 1501. His book was called, *Greek Grammar*, and was printed in 1476. He was a Greek grammarian. After the fall of Constantinople, he went to Italy where he obtained the patronage of Francisco Sforsa. He earned fame as a teacher of Greek and may be considered a herald of the new learning of the Renaissance in Italy. His brother, Andreas Joannes Lascaris, also taught Greek in Florence, Paris, and Rome until his death in 1535.

By the 16th century Greek pronunciation assumed a curious phase—only two sounds were given to all Greek vowels and diphthongs, whether long or short. The *Y ("U")* was pronounced as *V, K* as *Ch*, and then the *K* all but disappeared from the language until the 18th century. In fact, in the modern Latin dictionary that I have, the only *K* word is *Kalends* (Calendar). The Greek letter *K* was banned by Christianity and I believe I know the reason. The letter *K* was replaced with the Christian combination of *CH*, or *C,* due to the phallic and drug implications of the Greek letter *K*, a stick man at erection. This can be compared to the lambda (λ), which is also a stick man at erection, changed by Christian Latin to ell, the letter *L* which, in Egyptian hieroglyphics, represented man at erection (also Ptah-Min?), one making a tentation (earlier of temptation) in one's toga, causing a temptation to others. *Kay* is the name of the letter *K*, and *kay* in Greek is *key*. The *K* is a key letter. The key plays an important role in Christianity. St. Peter is said to have handed the keys (phallic mushrooms) to the Kingdom of Heaven over to Pope Linus, hence, the Vatican's symbol of "crossed keys" for entering the heavens and earth. Because of the ill repute of the letter *K*, we have few words in our modern dictionary beginning with *K*. In fact, there is not one Pope with the letter *K* in his borrowed Vatican name.

K is the 11th letter of the English alphabet. It was used in Christian Latin for kalends, calendar, and that's about the size of it. *K* was a product of Greek which took it from Phoenician and general Semitic letter *Kaph*. Formerly *K* was added to *C* in certain words of Latin origin, as in *musick*, *publick*, *republick*, where it is now omitted. It is the tenth or when the *J* is used for the tenth letter, *k* becomes the 11th in a series. K is pronounced "ka." Its plural form is "K's" (kaz), the letter k or its sound. *K* and *Q* are often represented as in Arabic Qabilah (tribe), plural of *qabail*. In English, *Kabyle* is "a Berber of Algeria and Tunis." The Kabyles are of two types, blond and brunet, the former may represent the blond Libyans depicted on ancient Egyptian monuments. They are an agricultural, communal people, now mainly Arabic speaking, and are Mohammedan. The *K* appeared in a couple of different positions: lying down to form a teeter-totter and facing backwards.

The double u is actually what it resembles, the double v, VV for *W*. The letter *U* was long a fertility sign and therefore was not used in language until the 17th century. The *U* is the 21st letter, and the fifth vowel of the English alphabet, and was not a letter of the Greek alphabet. Therefore, any Greek words in our modern dictionaries containing the letter *U* are not ancient Greek, but of a modern Greek of the Latin Romance Languages. As stated, *U* is a cursive form of the letter *V*. Both were formerly interchangeable with the other, and were used as either a vowel or consonant. The letter *V* came to be used by preference as the capital initial form, and *U* as the unical or cursive medial form. The small *u* and *v* were used interchangeably as late as the 15th century. The *V* and *U* were not given separate alphabetical positions until about 1800 CE.

About 1540, not long after the birth of the printing press, reaction against the practice of bastardizing Greek took place. After a social struggle by those then being educated, and perhaps desiring to learn ancient Greek, the practice of pronouncing Greek as though it were English was made to be a common standard. Questioning Greek pronunciation is further complicated by the fact that the Greek alphabet is so far removed from the Roman, which was generally adopted into the "modern language" systems of Europe. Therefore, a Greek word, prior to being anglicized, must be transliterated. For example, English must replace the symbols used in Greek to represent certain sounds.

The job was done with great difficulty, and can scarcely be said to have been carried out in English with any care or consistency, as evidenced by my research. Hence, there is much confusion regarding ie, ei, *Y*, *I* and *E*, not forgetting the letter *K*, having been changed in words more than once. Does it end in *el* or *le*? What about *Ch* replacing *K* and being called Greek? If *Ch* replaced the Greek *K*, then it is "Modern Greek" and should be so marked in the world dictionaries.

Why the confusion? It was done on purpose. For example, the *el* or *le* was played with to confuse the reader since El is a Hebrew name for Jehovah. Angel and Angle are two words as an example. *Ang* in *Greek* is a vessel, angle is a corner, *ell* is the name of the letter *L*. Further, as stated above, *L* is a hieroglyph denoting man at erection, reversed it becomes 7, a favorite number in the Bible. Angel in Greek is Aggelos, but we will save that for another time.

Our first introduction to the history of Greek literature came from the enemy of linguistics, Dark Age Christian monks and their method of transliterating (with us being forced to accept it). The West misunderstood the true meaning of Greek letters through lack of knowledge about its fundamental basis, which even today is left out of our learning institutions.

If Greek is our mother tongue, why is it not taught in the first English lessons? Why are we not taught how the words were built letter by letter and the meaning of each letter? Could it have to do with the fact that "pagans" created the alphabets in the first place, and that all pagan works were destroyed by Christian and Jewish factions?

Christian Latin cleansed the drugs and porno out of letters, and Greek, along with Egyptian hieroglyphics, were declared "dead languages."

Greek lives in almost all the languages of the world. We should teach it. We need it. It is our only key to understanding all world languages, thus insuring absolute success in communication on a worldwide basis. If there is to be a future, there is no longer any room for errors in communication due to deceit, ignorance, and blindness.

With the fact that we are in the dark with regard to letters, we have found many obvious and indisputable errors, like the guttural *K*, which was always hard in Greek—but in pronouncing the name, Alcibiades, it is customary to sound the soft *C* in accord with English usage. Had we transliterated the name directly from Greek there would be little doubt since there is no soft *C* in the Greek alphabet. Therefore, the name Alcibades would have been written, Alkibiades, pronounced with the hard *K*. Hence, should we be transliterating Greek words directly into English, instead of through the medium of Christianized Latin, the words could at times be quite unintelligible to the English reader.

Romaic (*French* Romaique; Modern Greek, Romaike of *Latin* Roma, Rome) relates to Modern Greek vernacular language, or to those who spoke it. The language was spoken by the uneducated and peasantry, and therefore words took on a double meaning. Take the word *vulgar*: To nobility it meant common or ordinary. Vulgar people were pagans, peasants, infidels, fallos, fallows, and peons. They were not advanced or educated. Nobility believed it meant nasty habits, sexual implications, filth, and dirt. Peasantry knew only what their parents taught them, and they were denied education with the exception of what they learned in church—the conditioning machine of the Roman Catholic Church, whose main weapon against learning was fear.

When language and letters were again offered to the public at large, they believed whatever the clergy gave them or told them had to be true. If the "Holy House," once in Rome, was the house Jesus grew up in, and was transported from Bethlehem to Rome by angels, it had to be true. Therefore, they paid to walk through the house that disappeared after the Dark Ages (see "Holy House" in *Webster's Dictionary, 1911*).

"Cleric" itself is derived of "clergy." Only the priests were allowed to read and write for a time in the Catholic Church. The conditioned Christians believed in a blind state of ignorance. Some today still follow that path. They accept the word of God as fact, written by He himself. They believe what the government tells them, as if it were fact. The dictionary is a good example of a tool used for this, for if it were in the dictionary it had to be a fact. The fact is that anyone could write a dictionary and publish it. You do not even need a "sheep-skin" (term is Masonic in origin, for diploma). As good as Webster was, I have found many, many errors and mistranslations in the 1912 and 1957 Merriam-Webster editions.

Romaic relates to Modern Greek vernacular language, or to those who speak it. The language was that of the uneducated and peasantry and was so called from being the language of the descendants of the Eastern Roman Empire. It was a corruption of ancient Greek (the characters used being the same). For nearly 500 years from the accepted date of the founding of Rome, its people had no literature. The government held total dictatorial power, at length, to supply the want and need. They wrote in Greek and a servile manner followed Greek models.

Ennius, 249 $_{BCE}$, laid the foundation of the genuine Latin literature. Its development peaked in the Augustan age, with examples such as Cicero in 60 $_{BCE}$, Cesar in 54 $_{BCE}$, Cornelius Nepos in 44 $_{BCE}$, Virgil and Horce in 28 $_{BCE}$, and Livy and Ovid in 14 $_{BCE}$. By 180 $_{CE}$, Roman literature began to decline. By 539 $_{CE}$ it was in its last stage of decay, replaced by Modern Latin, Modern Greek, Modern French, the Romance Languages, derived of Roman, etc.

Late Greek was the language of the period after classical Greek, the term is chiefly applied to the written language seen in patristic (priestly) writings and texts of the early Byzantine Empire, from about 200-300 $_{CE}$, until about 600 $_{CE}$.

Germany in the 4th century had no writing except for crude runic letters. Bishop Ulfilas is credited with the creation of an alphabet modeled on the Greek. His purpose was to translate the Bible into the Gothic tongue. The dating of the Bible was done in the Middle Ages by a person named Ussher, and therefore cannot be used in reference to any happening so referenced.

MYRRH AND THE RESURRECTION
Excerpt by Jay Lynn

Is myrrh more than just incense? Could it also be a drug, poison, or perhaps just a good high? I believe it was used in all of the above categories by the ancient alchemists. The word Myrrh is of medieval times, also spelled *mirre*, and *myrrh* in Old French, *myrrha* and *murra* in Latin, *Myr-ra* in Greek, and *Murr* in Aramaic, all of which means bitter. In addition, myrrh in Hebrew is *mar*, also meaning *bitter*, as are most narcotics. *Mor* (of myrrh) —a yellow brown aromatic gum resin of bitter and pungent taste! The *mystagogy* of this religious drug has tickled my inquisitive mind to search all leads. I have researched the Bible, older dictionaries, encyclopedias and many reference books on the subject, especially the book *The Sacred Mushroom and the Cross*, by John M. Allegro. I found that the Arabic *murr* (meaning bitter herb) exudes a fragrant gum resin from one of several herbs of Arabia and East Africa, especially Balsamo dendron myrrha of the family Amyri daceae. (Daceae, tear?) They bear scanty foliage and small oval fruit. It is used in making incense, perfume and medicine, called *Myrrh'ol.* (Myrrh oil).

Adonis was born of the ***Myrrh tree, his mother Myrrh was changed into the tree.*** Adonis was a beautiful boy, beloved by Aphrodite (in Greek means "sprang from the [sea] foam") of whom we can compare to Venus. This is paralleled in the story of Jesus, whose mother is the womb of the earth, the sea—Mar, Mari, Mary. So great was

191

Aphrodite's grief, that the gods only required Adonis to spend one-half of the time in Hades. (Another version states only one third of the time in Hades.)

Venus is the goddess of love (associated with Jesus) and Venus Ourania is the goddess of heavenly or spiritual love. She was the protector of gardens (vegetation-simples). The **Myrtle** was a sacred plant of Venus, and she was identified with Aphrodite. *Adonis* represents the sun and the annual death and resurrection of vegetation as seen in the hanging Gardens of Adonis, which lasted only eight days, then they were allowed to wilt and thrown into the sea (representing the womb of all life) to be resurrected symbolically, reincarnated—a common belief prior to Catholicism.

> Luke 2:21 (King James Version)
> And when eight days were accomplished for the circumcising of the child, his name was called
> JESUS, which was so named of the angel before he was conceived in the womb.

Hence, the story of Jesus and Adonis are similar in that each lived, died, visited the netherworld, and was resurrected. In addition, when we examine the Latin word for the *sea* we have, *Mar* in Latin, *the sea of marries* (*matrix or womb* in Latin...of all life). Matris in modern translation is: *Matrices* or *matrixes*: something within which something else originates or develops. Is that not a womb? Then why are they disguising it? Because they do not associate *matrix* with *Mar*, which is the root of the word *Marii, Mari,* **Mary**, the mother of the "Living Water," the born again principal of the supposed human, Jesus Christ, the son of God from the womb of the earth, the sea. Only a son has the water of life, semen, the gift of God to Man in his bearded stick (pogo-stick) the phallus. Could this be why the Jewish rabbi wears a beard, celebrating the bearded rod and staff, the phallus and testicles, which is the footstool of God, performed in honor of the mushroom?

The source of Adonis is of Semitic origin, the Phoenician **Adonis** being the same as the Babylonian **Tammuz** (Thomas). Jesus is an updated version of Esos, Adonis, Attis and Tammuz, and follows the same death and resurrection motif of not only the sun and vegetation (pine and myrrh), but includes all life. Thus, Adonis reflects the pre-Christian belief in both evolution and reincarnation, a belief of the old and new world, Europe and the Americas... long before Catholic contamination and Christian doctrine excluded the belief from their books, alongside with the Hebrews, who also removed both during the so-called time of Jesus.

Tammuz, in Babylonian religion, was the god of agriculture and spirit of vegetation. His annual festival (feast) was 40-days after lent and prior to the *summer solstice*, consisting of a period of mourning for his loss, followed by rejoicing (rejusing of the fertility deity) at his reappearance (the same is said of Adonis). Tammuz married Ishtar (another fertility Goddess—Easter), who killed him and later resurrected him from the lower world. (Jesus visited Hell, which is also Hades or Ades, prior to ascending to Heaven.) This is symbolizing the dying of life (the sun and vegetation) in the winter and its return in spring (the sun), much like his Phoenician counterpart, Adonis, and the Phrygian god, Attis. It is also reflected in the Celtic god, Esos, who was the carpenter called "master" and whom Caesar called "the chief god of the Gauls." He predated the Jesus epic.

Attis was a Phrygian (Trojan) god of the sun, vegetation and young life, the counterpart of Adonis. He was beloved by Cybele and was either killed by a boar or died of *self-mutilation* (cutting his penis off—a metaphor for the mushroom). From his blood (sblood) sprang violets (mushrooms). His death and resurrection were celebrated annually, like that of Adonis, Tammuz, Attis, Esos and Jesus.

Jesus corresponds to Esos, Adonis, Tammuz and Attis, rescued from Hell and ascending to paradise, heaven, et al. His "virgin birth" is celebrated in the dead of winter, December 25th, the same day the Romans celebrated the birthday of the Sun, the last month of the Roman calendar (Deca, 10, December the 10th month, 25th day). Many pagan festivals were borrowed by the Catholics, such as Dec. 25th, birthday of the Sun, during the Catholic conversion of the pagan Romans, and all other conquered countries. The reason is quite clear. It was much easier to reform a pagan by slipping a Christian Catholic mythology into a well-known pagan festival day. Easter is another holy day (holiday) of note. Easter was previously a pagan festival celebrating rebirth of all life, the end of winter, a gift from and the inception of the Sun (the Father in the Heavens) who gave mankind his son in the form of the sacred mushroom, the *Amanita muscaria*, which is made in God's image or Idol, (one-eyed doll?), mimicking the male sexual organ.

192

THE LETTER "O"
Gr. O, o, the letter "O"
Excerpt by Jay Lynn

Note: The following is in reference to the OO material listed at the beginning of the book, on page xvi, which references to Appendix B.

The letter *O* is the fifteenth letter and the fourth vowel of the English alphabet. Its form, value and name came from the Greek *Omega* and through Latin O. *O* came into Greece from Phoenician and from there, Egyptian. *A circle or oval. O' and utterance of pain, lamentation, etc.* The O's of Advent, seven anthems, each beginning with an invocation, as "O Adonai," sung in the Roman Catholic Church and the Anglican churches between December 16th and Christmas Eve. *O, Latin* of Greek (ω) compare *Ojh. O,* Irish *O,* a descendant in Irish family names, signifying grandson or descendant of, and is a character of dignity, as, *O'Neil; O'Carrol.* Many biblical names begin with *O,* as well as some of the scriptures.

Examples of O use include:

- *O, OON* Gr. *Egg,* more specifically, *OON,* the liquid egg of the male. *OO egg* and *N,* a suffix denoting Liquid. *OO* upright is *8,* and *OO* is a sign of infinity.
- Oak, Holy Oak. *OOK, OOKE, Oak.*
- *Oaf,* see *ouph. Oaf,* AS. *Auf,* Icel. *Alfr, elf;* an *elfs* child, a changeling left by fairies or Goblins, usually deformed or simpleton, foolish child, an Idiot.
- Oak, Holy Oak. (*Oak, ook, ooke, the oak.*) The tree bears acorns, Akorn Gr. *Testicles,* they drop from their shell, testicles drop from inside while still a baby. One deprived of his acorns has a soprano voice, called *queer boys* from queercus oak.
- *Oak* -queer boys from queerester, a choir boy. (Webster's 1911 Dict.)
- Oakum, Stupa, tow
- Oast, Host, see Osteon in Greek= bone.
- *Oath:* (Gr. *Orkos,* of *Orkis, testicle,* source of *testify.* Of old English Law, "To make one's Law," to adduce to sworn statements of oath helpers or Compurgators to clear one's self of a charge. (See Compurgator: 1. Law. A witness to the veracity of innocence of an accused person, with whom he swears —applied originally to such witnesses in the trials in the ecclesiastical courts, and later to the oath and those acting in the wager of law. See COMPURGATION, OATH HELPER, WAGER OF LAW.)

Appendix C

THE MUSHROOM SPEAKS [523]
by Terence McKenna

I am old, older than thought in your species, which is itself fifty times older than your history. Though I have been on earth for ages I am from the stars. My home is no one planet, for many worlds scattered through the shining disc of the galaxy have conditions which allow my spores an opportunity for life. The mushroom which you see is the part of my body given to sex thrills and sun bathing, my true body is a fine network of fibers growing through the soil. These networks may cover acres and may have far more connections than the number in a human brain.

My mycelial network is nearly immortal--only the sudden toxification of a planet or the explosion of it's parent star can wipe me out. By means impossible to explain because of certain misconceptions in your model of reality all my mycelial networks in the galaxy are in hyperlight communication through space and time.

The mycelial body is as fragile as a spider's web but the collective hypermind and memory is a vast historical archive of the career of evolving intelligence on many worlds in our spiral star swarm. Space, you see, is a vast ocean to those hardy life forms that have the ability to reproduce from spores, for spores are covered with the hardest organic substance known.

Across the aeons of time and space drift many spore forming life-forms in suspended animation for millions of years until contact is made with a suitable environment. Few such species are minded, only myself and my recently evolved near relatives have achieved the hyper-communication mode and memory capacity that makes us leading members in the community of galactic intelligence. How the hyper-communication mode operates is a secret which will not be lightly given to humans.

But the means should be obvious: it is the occurrence of psilocybin and psilocin in the biosynthetic pathways of my living body that opens for me and my symbionts the vision screens to many worlds. You as an individual and Homo sapiens as a species are on the brink of the formation of a symbiotic relationship with my genetic material that will eventually carry humanity and earth into the galactic mainstream of the higher civilizations.

Since it is not easy for you to recognize other varieties of intelligence around you, your most advanced theories of politics and society have advanced only as far as the notion of collectivism. But beyond the cohesion of the members of a species into a single social organism there lie richer and even more baroque evolutionary possibilities. Symbiosis is one of these. Symbiosis is a relation of mutual dependence and positive benefits for both species involved.

Symbiotic relationships between myself and civilized forms of higher animals have been established many times and in many places throughout the long ages of my development. These relationships have been mutually useful. Within my memory is the knowledge of hyperlight drive ships and how to build them. I will trade this knowledge for a free ticket to new worlds around suns younger and more stable than your own.

To secure an eternal existence down the long river of cosmic time, I again and again offer this agreement to higher beings and thereby have spread throughout the galaxy over the long millennia.

A mycelial network has no organs to move the world, no hands, but higher animals with manipulative abilities can become partners with the star knowledge within me and if they act in good faith, return both themselves and their humble mushroom teacher to the million worlds to which all citizens of our starswarm are heir.

---

[523] From *Psilocybin: The Magic Mushroom Growers Guide.*

Appendix D

Below is the complete song mentioned on page 127. Whether this song was written about an entheogen, we cannot say. However, some lines in the song are surely fitting.

THERE IS POWER IN THE BLOOD

Words & Music by Lewis E. Jones, 1899

Would you be free from the burden of sin?
There's power in the blood, power in the blood;
Would you over evil a victory win?
There's wonderful power in the blood.

There is power, power, wonder working power
In the blood of the Lamb;
There is power, power, wonder working power
In the precious blood of the Lamb.

Would you be free from your passion and pride?
There's power in the blood, power in the blood;
Come for a cleansing to Calvary's tide;
There's wonderful power in the blood.

There is power, power, wonder working power
In the blood of the Lamb;
There is power, power, wonder working power
In the precious blood of the Lamb.

Would you be whiter, much whiter than snow?
There's power in the blood, power in the blood;
Sin stains are lost in its life giving flow.
There's wonderful power in the blood.

There is power, power, wonder working power
In the blood of the Lamb;
There is power, power, wonder working power
In the precious blood of the Lamb.

Would you do service for Jesus your King?
There's power in the blood, power in the blood;
Would you live daily His praises to sing?
There's wonderful power in the blood.

There is power, power, wonder working power
In the blood of the Lamb;
There is power, power, wonder working power
In the precious blood of the Lamb.

Appendix E

ARE FAIRY TALES FOR CHILDREN OR ADULTS?

...fairy-stories are not in normal English usage stories about fairies or elves, but stories about Fairy, that is *Faerie*, the realm or state in which fairies have their being. Faerie contains many things besides elves and fays, and besides dwarfs, witches, trolls, giants, or dragons: it holds the seas, the sun, the moon, the sky; and the earth, and all things that are in it: tree and bird, water and stone, wine and bread, and ourselves, mortal men, when we are enchanted.
~ J.R.R. Tolkien

We may one day find there is more truth in fairy tales than we have so far suspected. There is a sense in which all fairy tales are true. They are very much *unlike* that which passes for realistic or "serious" literature. Many fables are typically realistic in trivial details but unrealistic in matters of importance, and "serious" only because so much of it is quite horrific (take the story of Hansel and Gretel for example). Some fairy tales are delightfully unrealistic in small things: animals speak; the stereotypical witch lives in a cottage in the dark forest; frogs, humans, and inanimate objects such as forests, mirrors, and swords often become *enchanted*. Like religion, fairy tales speak on important matters of good and evil, life and death, etc; frequently reinforcing a set or morals. Oftentimes, these tales contain secrets and mysteries that are buried beneath the surface. The tale of Little Red Riding Hood seems to contain hidden information about the *Amanita muscaria*.

Little Red Riding Hood was originally entitled Little Red-Cap, and the story read like this:

Once upon a time there was a dear little girl who was loved by every one who looked at her, but most of all by her grandmother, and there was nothing that she would not have given to the child. Once she gave her a little cap of red velvet, which suited her so well that she would never wear anything else; so she was always called Little Red-Cap....

Many of you remember the story. The little girl is on her way to her grandmother's house with cake and wine. The tale goes on to tell how the little girl was tempted to stray off of the path. This goes against the instructions of her mother to "stay on the path." That is also a direct instruction that our Mother Earth gives to us via her little red-capped mushroom—*"stay on the path."* How does this mushroom tell us anything at all? The fairytale explains in detail: as the tale of the Little Red-Cap goes on, the girl approaches her grandmother's house, the big bad wolf (who arrived ahead of the little girl) has already eaten her grandmother and now it is her turn:

"Oh! Grandmother," she said, "what big ears you have."
"The better to hear you with, my child," was the reply.
"But, grandmother, what big eyes you have!" she said.
"The better to see you with, my dear."
"But, grandmother, what large hands you have!"
"The better to hug you with."
"Oh! But, grandmother, what a terrible big mouth you have!"
"The better to eat you with!"
And scarcely had the wolf said this, when with one bound he was out of bed and swallowed up the Little Red-Cap.

So, this "little red cap" from the forest gets eaten. The next point of interest in the tale is when a hunter (or huntsman) enters the grandmother's house:

So he went into the room, and when he came to the bed, he saw that the wolf was lying in it. "Do I find thee here, thou old sinner!" said he. "I have long sought thee!" Then just as he was going to fire at him, it occurred to him that the wolf might have devoured the grandmother, and that she might still be saved, so he did not fire, but took a pair of scissors, and began to cut open the stomach of the sleeping wolf. When he had made two snips, he saw the little Red-Cap shining, and then he made two snips more, and the little girl sprang out, crying, "Ah, how frightened I have been! How dark it was inside the wolf" and after that the aged grandmother came out alive also, but scarcely able to breathe. Red-Cap, however, quickly fetched great stones with which they filled the wolf's body, and when he awoke, he wanted to run away, but the stones were so heavy that he fell down at once, and fell dead.

Figure 185 - From *Kinder und Hausmärchen*, by Wilhelm and Jakob Grimm, 1888

Then all three were delighted. The huntsman drew off the wolf's skin and went home with it; the grandmother <u>ate the cake and drank the wine which Red-Cap had brought, and revived</u>, but Red-Cap thought to herself, "As long as I live, I will never by myself leave the path, to run into the wood...." [underline—ours]

So lastly, the grandmother was revived after the death of the evil character, and by drinking the wine, which was delivered by the red-cap—but not until it had been consumed and extracted from the belly. This is obviously a recipe for the *Amanita.* After the red cap from the forest is eaten, one may lie around until it can be extracted from their belly (in the form of urine) and then re-consumed in liquid form, like water into *wine.* The tale reassures us that the red-capped mushroom does not have the same appearance after it was consumed, by saying the huntsman saw the "red cap *shining*"... perhaps shining like a pot of gold, or a pot of urine glistening in the sun. Figure 185 is from the 1888 Edition of the Grimms' Kinder und Hausmärchen. Did you notice the *Amanita muscaria* mushroom at the bottom right of the illustration?

Bibliography

- Abrams, M.H., *The Milk of Paradise: The Effect of Opium Visions on the Works of DeQuincey, Crabbe, Francis Thompson, and Coleridge* - Perennial Library, 1934, 1962
- Acharya S, *Suns of God, Krishna, Buddha and Christ Unveiled* - Adventures Unlimited Press, 2004, ISBN: 1-931882-31-2
- Acharya S, *The Christ Conspiracy: The Greatest Story ever Sold* - Adventures Unlimited Press, 1999, ISBN: 0-932813-74-7
- *Advanced Bible History for Lutheran Schools in the Words of Holy Scripture* - Concordia, 1936
- Allegro, John, *The Dead Sea Scrolls and the Christian Myth* - Prometheus Book, 1992, ISBN: 0-87975-757-4
- Allegro, John, *The End of a Road* - MacGibbon and Kee, Ltd., 1970
- Allegro, John, *The Sacred Mushroom and the Cross: Fertility cults and the origins of Judaism and Christianity* - Doubleday, 1970
- Anonymous, *Secret Instructions of the Society of Jesus (1882)* - Kessinger Publishing, 1997, ISBN: 1564599124
- Arthur, James, *Mushrooms and Mankind: The Impact of Mushrooms on Human Consciousness and Religion* - The Book Tree, 2000, ISBN: 1-58509-151-0
  - Arthur, James, Lectures and Recordings:
    - *Christmas Mysteries,* 12/24/01 with Lou Gentile
    - *Magic Mushrooms and the History of Santa Claus and Christmas,* 12/02 with Caroline Casey
    - *Entheo-Mycology,* 2002 with Jeff Rense
    - *Mushrooms and Mankind,* 12/19/02 with Jeff Rense
    - *Jeff Rense Show,* 12/22/03
    - *Coast To Coast,* 01/09/03 *with George Noory*
    - *Coast to Coast* 12/11/2003 *with George Noory*
    - *The Open Mind Show* 10/2/2003 with Patrick Duff
    - *Mushroom Minds,* with Lou Epton
    - *Amanita muscaria: The Mushrooms that Shape the Universe*
    - *Mushrooms and Mankind lecture: Recorded Live in Gizeh Egypt*
    - *Ushering In The New Age,* with Jordan Maxwell
    - *Glimpses within and Beyond*
- Aun Weor, Samael, *The Perfect Matrimony: Tantra - the Door to Enter into Initiation* - Thelema Pr, 2001, ISBN: 0974275506
- Baigent & Leigh, *The Dead Sea Scrolls Deception: Why a Handful of Religious Scholars Conspired to Suppress the Revolutionary Contents of The Dead Sea Scrolls* - Summit Books, 1991, ISBN: 0-671-73454-7
- Barnstone, Willis, *The Other Bible* - Harper Collins, 1984, ISBN: 0-06-250030-9
- Benitez, Fernando, *In the Magic Land of Peyote* - University of Texas Press, 1975, ISBN: 0-446-89306-4
- Bennett, Chris & Mcqueen, Neil, *Sex, Drugs, Violence and the Bible* - Forbidden Fruit Publishing, ISBN: 1-55056-798-5
- Bennett, Chris & Osburn, Lynn & Judy, *Green Gold the Tree of Life: Marijuana In Magic and Religion* - Access Unlimited, 1995, ISBN: 0-9629872-2-0
- Bishop, Cliford & Osthelder, Xenia, *Sexualia Mundi* - Konemann, 2001, ISBN: 382902729X
- Blakney, Raymond B., *The Way of Life, Lao Tzu* - Nal Penguin, 1955, 1983, ISBN: 0-451-62674-5
- Blavatsky, H. P., *Isis Unveiled (Volumes 1 and 2)* - Theosophical University PR, 1877
- Brown, Judith Anne, *John Marco Allegro The Maverick of the Dead Sea Scrolls* - Wm. B. Eerdmans Publishing Company, 2005, ISBN: 0802828493
- Brown 32nd, Robert Hewitt, *Stellar Theology and Masonic Astronomy* - 1882, The Book Tree, 2002, ISBN: 1585092037
- Budge, E.A. Wallis, *The Egyptian Book of the Dead* - 1895, Dover, 1967, ISBN: 0-486-21866-X
- Bullinger, Ethetbert W., *Number and Scripture: Its Supernatural Design and Spiritual Significance* - 1894, Kregel Publications, 1983, ISBN: 0825422388
- Bursenos, James, *The Resurection of Santa Claus* – Shaman's Drum, Issue 68, 2005
- Busenbark, Ernest, *Symbols, Sex, and the Stars in Popular Beliefs: An Outline of the Origins of Moon and Sun Worship, Astrology, Sex Symbolism, Mystic Meaning of Numbers, the Cabala, and Many Popular Customs, Myth* - 1949, The Book Tree, 1997, ISBN: 1-885395-19-1
- Campbell, Joseph, *The Hero With a Thousand Faces* - MJF Books, 1949, ISBN: 1-56731-120-2
- Campbell, Joseph, *The Power Of Myth* with Bill Moyers - Doubleday, 1988, ISBN: 0-385-24773-7
- Campbell, Joseph, *Occidental Mythology* – 1964
- Castaneda, Carlos, *The Teachings of Don Juan: A Yaqui Way of Knowledge* - Ballantine, 1968, ISBN: 34502656X125

- Chagnon, Napoleon A., *Yanomamo, The Fierce People* - Holt, Rinehart and Winston, Inc., 1968, ISBN: 0-03-0710707
- Churchward, Albert, *The Origin and Evolution of Religion* - Publisher: Book Tree, 2000 ISBN: 1585090786
- Conrad, Chris, *Hemp Lifeline to the Future: The Unexpected Answer for Our Environmental and Economic Recovery* - Creative Xpressions Publications, 1993
- Crowley, Aleister, *The Book of Thoth* - Lancer Books
- Deane, Rev. John Bathurst, *The Worship of the Serpent* - Health Research, 1970, ISBN: 0-78730279-1
- DeKorne, Jim, *Psychedelic Shamanism: The Cultivation, Preparation and Shamanic Use of Psychotropic Plants* - Breakout Productions, 1994, ISBN: 0-9666932-5-6
- DeMeo, James, *Saharasia – The 4000 BCE Origins of Child Abuse, Sex-Repression, Warfare, and Social Violence In the Deserts of the Old World* - OBRL, 1998, ISBN: 0-9621855-5-8
- de Santillana, Giorgio & von Dechend, Hertha, *Hamlet's Mill: An essay on myth and the frame of time* – David R. Godine, Publisher, Inc., 1969, ISBN: 0-87923-215-3
- Devereux, Paul, *The Long Trip, A Prehistory of Psychedelia* - Arkana Books, 1997, ISBN: 0-14-019540-8
- Dobkin de Rios, Marlene, *Hallucinogens, cross-cultural perspectives* - University of New Mexico Press, 1984, ISBN: 0-8263-0737-X
- Eisenman, Robert & Wise, Michael, *Dead Sea Scrolls Uncovered* - Penguin Books, 1992, ISBN: 0-14-023250-8
- Eisenman, Robert, *James Brother of Jesus* - Penguin Books, 1997, ISBN: 0-14-025773-X
- El-Amin, Mustafa, *Freemasonry: Ancient Egypt and the Islamic Destiny* - New Mind Productions, 1988, ISBN: 0933821131
- Eliade, Mircea, *The Encyclopedia of Religion*, 16 volumes --Macmillan Pub., 1987, ISBN: 0029098505
- Eliade, Mircea, *Shamanism Archaic Techniques of Ecstasy* - Princeton University Press, 1964, ISBN: 0-691-01779-4
- Evans-Wentz, W.Y., *The Fairy Faith in Celtic Countries: The Classic Study of Leprechauns, Pixies and other Fairy Spirits* - University Books, 1966, ISBN: 0-8065-2579-7
- Fideler, David, *Jesus Christ: Sun of God* - Quest Books, 1993, ISBN: 0-8356-0696-1
- Fomenko, Anatoly T., *History: Fiction or Science? Ch. 1* - Delamere Resources Ltd., 2003, ISBN: 2-913621-05-8
- Frazer, Sir James George, *The Golden Bough: A Study in Magic and Religion, abridged* - 1922, Macmillan Publishing Company, ISBN: 0-02-095570-7
- Freke, Timothy, & Gandy, Peter, *Jesus and the Lost Goddess: The Secret Teachings of the Original Christians* - Three Rivers Press, 2002, ISBN: 1400045940
- Freke, Timothy, & Gandy, Peter, *The Jesus Mysteries: Was the "Original Jesus" a Pagan God?* - Three Rivers Press, 2001, ISBN: 0609807986
- Fulcanelli, *Le Mystere Des Cathedrales* - Brotherhood of Life, Inc., 1964, 1990, ISBN: 0914732-14-5
- Furst, Peter T., *Hallucinogens and Culture* - Chandler & Sharp, 1976, ISBN: 0-88316-517-1
- Gilbert, Adrian G. & Cotterell, Maurice M., *The Mayan Prophecies* - Element, 1995, ISBN: 1-85230-692-0
- Goldberg, B.Z., *The Sacred Fire: The Story of Sex in Religion* - University Books, 1958
- Haggard, Howard W., *Mystery, Magic, and Medicine* - Double Day Doran, Inc. 1933

Hall, Manly P., Lectures and Audio Recordings:

Audio Series:
- *Alchemy* - ISBN: 0-89314-002-3
- *Astro-Theology: How Astrology Has Influence Mankind* - ISBN: 0-89314-011-2
- *The Atom in Religion and Philosophy* - ISBN: 0-89314-013-9
- *Studies in Man, Grand Symbols of the Mysteries* - ISBN: 0-89314-268-9

Lectures:
- *Alchemy as a Key to Social Regeneration*
- *Secret Teachings of All Ages: Initiation of the Pyramid*
- *Winter Solstice: Annual Rebirth of the Universal Soul*
- *Christian Gospels That Were Never in the Bible*
- *Hidden Church of the Holy Grail*
- *When the Invincible Sun Moves Northward: The Solar Christmas*
- *Jacob's Ladder That Leads to the Stars*
- *Precious Stones in Lore and Legend*
- *Love of Truth*
- *Second Coming of the Santa Claus Spirit*
- *Physical Body as a Universal Symbol*
- *Sacred Mysteries of the Human Body*

- Hall, Manly P., *Cabalistic Keys to the lords Prayer* - Philosophical Research Society, 1992, ISBN: 0-89314-308-1
- Hall, Manly P., *The Secret Teachings of All Ages, Diamond Jubilee edition* - Philosophical Research Society, 1928, ISBN: 0-89314-546-7
- Hall, Manly P., *Man: Grand Symbol of the Mysteries, Gems of Thought in Occult Anatomy* - Philosophical Research Society - 1972, ISBN: 0-89314-513-0
- Hall, Manly P., *Occult Anatomy of Ma -*, Philosophical Research Society, 1977, ISBN: 0-89314-338-3
- Hall, Manly P., *Planetary Influence and the Human Soul* - Philosophical Research Society, 1985, ISBN:0-89314-3383
- Hall, Manly P., *Pluto in Libra: An Interpretation* - Philosophical Research Society, 1971, ISBN: 0893143421
- Hall, Manly P., *Spiritual Centers of Man* - Philosophical Research Society, 1978, ISBN: 0-89314-383-9
- Harding, Patrick, *Facts Behind The Myths And Magic of Christmas* – Metro Books, 2004, ISBN: 1843581248
- Harding, Patrick, *The Xmas Files: Facts Behind the Myths and Magic of Christmas* – Metro Books, 2003, ISBN: 1843580764
- Harding, Patrick, *Christmas Unwrapped* – Metro Books, 2002, ISBN: 1843580349
- Hawk, Venus, *Soma Shamans* – Red Angels Ltd., 2003, ISBN: 097437220X
- Heinrich, Clark, *Magic Mushrooms in Religion and Alchemy* - Park Street Press, 2002, ISBN: 089281997-9
- Henry, William, *Blue Apples* - Scala Dei, 2000; ISBN: 0972582614
- Herer, Jack, *The Emperor Wears No Clothes: The Authoritative Historical Record of Cannabis and the Conspiracy Against Marijuana*, 11th edition - Ah-Ha Publishing, 2000, ISBN: 1-878125-02-8
- Highfield, Roger, *Can Reindeer Fly?: The Science of Christmas* – Orion, 2004, ISBN: 0753813661
- Highfield, Roger, *The Physics of Christmas* – Little, Brown and Company, 1998, ISBN: 0-316-36695-1
- *Hindu Myths* - Penguin Books, 1975, ISBN: 1-14-044306-1
- Hofmann, Albert, *LSD - My Problem Child: Reflections on Sacred Drugs, Mysticism, and Science* - Archer, 1979, 0-87477-256-7
- Hooper, Judith, & Teresi, Dick, *The 3-Pound Universe, The Brain – From Chemistry of the Mind to the New Frontiers of the Soul* - Dell Publishing, 1986, ISBN: 0-440-58507-4
- Hopfe, Lewis M., *Religions of the World 5th edition* - Macmillan Publishing Co., 1991, ISBN: 0-02-357205-1
- Hutchens 33rd, Rex R., *A Bridge to Light* - The Supreme Council, 33rd Ancient and Accepted Scottish Rite of Freemasonry Southern Jurisdiction, USA, 1995
- Huxley, Aldous, *Brave New World* - Harper & Row, 1932, 1946, ISBN: 0-06-080983-3
- Jacques, J.H., *The Mushroom and The Bride* - The Citadel Press, 1970
- Jeffrey, Grant R., *KJV Prophecy Marked Reference Study Bible* - Zondervan, 1998, ISBN: 0-310-92064-7
- Jenkins, John Major, *Maya Cosmogenesis 2012* - Bear & Co., 1998, ISBN: 1-879181-48-7
- Jung, Carl G., *Flying Saucers* - Routledge & Kegan Paul Ltd., 1959, ISBN: 0-7100-8696-2
- Jung, Carl G., *Man and His Symbols* - Dell, 1964, ISBN: 0-440-35183-9
- Johnson, Kenneth, *Slavic Sorcery: Shamanic Journey of Initiation* - Llewellyn, 1998, ISBN: 1-56718-374-3
- Karcher, Stephen, & Ritsema, Rudolf, *I Ching The Classic Chinese Oracle of Change, The First Complete Translation With Concordance* - Element Books Ltd., 1994, ISBN: 1-85230-669-6
- King James Version, *The Holy Bible (OES) Order of the Eastern Star with Marginal References* - A.J. Holman Company, 1930
- King James Version, *The Holy Bible* – Large Illustrated Masonic Edition - Holman, 1924 – 1968
- King, John C., *A Christian View of the Mushroom Myth* - Hodder and Stoughton, 1970, ISBN: 0-0340-12597-7
- Lamsa, George M., *Peshitta: Holy Bible from the Ancient Eastern Text* - Harper Collins, 1933, ISBN: 0-06-064926-7
- Lake, J.W., *Tree and Serpent Worship* - Holmes Publishing Group, 1998, 0-89314-338-3
- Landers, John, *A Vision of the Gold Plates of the Book of Mormon* - LDS.
- Lau, D.C., *Confucius The Analects* - Penguin Books, 1979, ISBN: 0-14-044348-7
- Lee, Martin A., & Shlain, Bruce, *Acid Dreams: The Complete Social History of LSD: The CIA, the Sixties, and Beyond – revised* - Grove Press, 1992, ISBN: 0-8021-3062-3
- Leedom, Tim C. (editor), *The Book Your Church Doesn't Want You to Read* - Kendall/Hunt Publishing, 1993, ISBN: 0-8403-8908-6
- Lewis, H. Spencer, *Rosicrucian: Questions and Answers/With Complete History of the Rosicrucian Order* - Rosicrucian Order (Supreme Grand Lodge of AMORC); 1993, ISBN: 0912057599
- Los Uffizi, *Florencia Pintura Italiana* - Taschen, 2001, ISBN: 3-8228-1177-7
- Lupieri, Edmondo, *The Mandaeans: The Last Gnostics* - Wm. B. Eerdmans Publishing Co. 1993, 2002, ISBN: 0-8028-3924-X
- Lynn, Jay, *The Alpha and Omega, the Greek Alphabet and Other Root Words*, Unpublished, rev. 4/21/2003
- Lynn, Jay, *Myrrh and the Resurrection*, Unpublished, rev. 2/21/2005
- Mackey M.D., 33rd, Albert G. & McClenachan 33rd, Charles T., *An Encyclopedia of Freemasonry and its Kindred Sciences* - 1873, The Masonic History Company, 1910

- Macoy, Robert, *A Dictionary of Freemasonry* - 1895, Gramercy, 1989, ISBN: 0-517-69213-9
- Marriott, Alice & Rachlin, Carol K., *Peyote* - Thomas Y. Crowell, 1971, ISBN: 069061697X
- Mascaro, Juan, *The Bhagavad Gita* - Penguin Books, 1962, ISBN: 0-14-044121-2
- Mascaro, Juan, *The Dhammapada* - Penguin Books, 1973, ISBN: 0-14-044284-7
- Massey, Gerald, *The Historical Jesus and the Mythical Christ: Separating Fact from Fiction* - Publisher: Book Tree, 2000, ISBN: 1585090735
- Massey, Gerald, *The Natural Genesis (volumes 1 and 2)* - Black Classic Press
- Massey, Gerald, *Ancient Egypt the Light of the World (volumes 1 and 2)* - Kessinger Publishing, 2002, ISBN: 0766126544 and 0766126552
- Massey, Gerald, *Egyptian Book of the Dead and the Mysteries of Amenta* - Kessinger Publishing 1997, ISBN: 1564598918
- Massey, Gerald, *Gerald Massey's Lectures* - Kessinger Publishing 1997, ISBN: 1564591743
- Maxwell, Jordan, *Matrix of Power, How the World has Been Controlled by Powerful People Without Your Knowledge* - The Book Tree, 2000, ISBN: 1-58509-120-0
- Maxwell, Tice, Snow, *That Old-Time Religion: The Story of Religious Foundations* - The Book Tree, 2000, ISBN: 1-58509-120-0

  - Maxwell, Jordan, Lectures and Audio Recordings:
  - *Ancient Symbolism*
  - *Cracking the Code*
  - *Dark Side of Religion*
  - *Men In Black*
  - *Misunderstood Religion*
  - *Religious-Political Symbols*
  - *Symbolically Speaking*
  - *Symbolism and Secret Societies*
  - *Symbolism in the U.S.*
  - *Toxic Religion*
  - *The Story Your Church Did Not Tell You*

  Series:
  - *Continuence of Religo Political P 1 of 5*
  - *Astro-Theology P 2 of 5*
  - *From Ancient Times P 3 of 5*
  - *Symbols of All Times P 4 of 5*
  - *Symbols of Satan P 5 of 5*

- McKenna, Terence & Dennis, *The Invisible Landscape: Mind Hallucinogens and the I Ching* - Harper Collins, 1993, ISBN: 0-06-250635-8
- McKenna, Terence, *The Archaic Revival: Speculations on Psychedelic Mushrooms, the Amazon, Virtual Reality, UFO's, Evolution, Shamanism, the Rebirth of the Goddess, and the End of History* - Harper Collins, 1991, ISBN: 0-06-250613-7
- McKenna, Terence, *Food of the Gods, The Search for the Original Tree of Knowledge: A Radical History of Plants, Drugs, and Human Evolution* - Bantam, 1992, ISBN: 0-553-37130-4
- McKenna, Terence, *True Hallucinations: Being an Account of the Author's Extraordinary Adventures in the Devil's Paradise* - Harper Collins, 1993, ISBN: 0-06-250545-9
- McKenna, Halifax, Furst, Hofmann, Schultes, edited by Riedlinger, *The Sacred Mushroom Seeker – Tributes to R. Gordon Wasson* - Park Street Press, 1997, ISBN: 0-89281-338-5
- McWilliams, Peter, *Ain't Nobody's Business If You Do* - Prelude Press, 1996, ISBN: 0-931580-58-7
- Merkur, Dan, *The Mystery of Manna: The Psychedelic Sacrament of the Bible* - Park Street Press, 2000, ISBN: 0-89281-772-0
- Metzner, Ralph, *Ayahuasca: Human Consciousness and the Spirits of Nature* - Thunder's Mouth Press, 1999, ISBN: 1-56025-160-3
- Miller, Richard and Iona, *The Modern Alchemist: A Guide to Personal Transformation -*, Phanes Press, 1994, ISBN: 0-933999-37-2
- Moor, Edward, *Hindu Pantheon* - Philosophical Research Society, Inc., 1976, ISBN: 0893144096
- Müller-Ebeling, Rätsch, Shahi, *Shamanism and Tantra in the Himalayas* - Inner Traditions, 2002, ISBN: 0892819138
- Müller-Ebeling, Rätsch, Storl, *Witchcraft Medicine: Healing Arts, Shamanic Practices, and Forbidden Plants* - Inner Traditions, 2003, ISBN: 089281971-5

- Murphy, Joseph M., Santeria, *African Spirits in America*, Beacon - 1993, ISBN: 0-8070-1021-9
- *Mysteries of the Bible: The Enduring Questions of the Scriptures* - Readers Digest, 1989, ISBN: 0895772930
- Myerhoff, Barbara G., *Peyote Hunt: The Sacred Journey of the Huichol Indians* - Cornell University Press, 1974, ISBN: 0-8014-3137-1
- Narby, Jeremy, *The Cosmic Serpent, DNA and the Origins of Knowledge* - Tarcher Putnam, 1998, ISBN: 0-87477-964-2
- Orwell, George, *Nineteen Eighty-Four* - Martin Secker & Warburg, 1949
- Oss & Oeric, *Psilocybin Magic Mushroom Grower's Guide, 1976* - Quick American Publishing, 1991, ISBN: 0-932551-06-8
- Ott, Jonathan, *Hallucinogenic Plants of North America* - Wingbow Press, 1976, ISBN: 0-914728-15-6
- Ott, Jonathan, *The Age of Entheogens and the Angels' Dictionary* - Natural Products Company, 1995, ISBN: 0-9614234-7-1
- Ott, Jonathan, *Pharmacotheon: Entheogenic drugs, their plant sources and history 2ⁿᵈ edition* - Natural Products Company, 1996, 0-9614234-9-8
- *Oxford English Dictionary Second Edition* - Oxford University Press, 1989, ISBN: 0-19-861186-2
- Pelikan, Jaroslav, *The Illustrated Jesus Through the Centuries* - Yale University Press, 1997, ISBN: 0-300-07268-6
- Pickthall, Mohammed M., *The Glorious Qur'an translation* - Tahrike Tarile Qur'an, Inc., 2000, ISBN: 1-879402-51-3
- Pike, Albert & House of the Temple, *Morals and Dogma of the Ancient and Accepted Scottish Rite of Freemasonry*, 1871
- Prasad, Ganga, *The Fountain-Head of Religion - A Comparative Study of the Principal Religions of the World and a Manifestation of Their Common Origin From the Vedas* 1927 - The Book Tree, 2000, ISBN: 1-58509-054-9
- Puharich, Andrija, *The Sacred Mushroom: Key to the Door of Eternity* - Doubleday, 1959
- Regardie, Israel, *777 And Other Qabalistic Writings of Aleister Crowley* - Weiser Books, 1986, ISBN: 0877286701
- Reich, Wilhelm, *The Invasion of Compulsory Sex-Morality* - Penguin, 1975, ISBN: 0140218556
- Reich, Wilhelm, *The Mass Psychology of Fascism*, trans. By Vincent R. Carfagno, Farrar - Straus and Giroux, 1970
- van Renterghem, Tony, *When Santa was a Shaman: The Ancient Origins of Santa Claus & the Christmas Tree* - Llewellyn Publications, 1995, ISBN: 1-56718-765-x
- Robinson, James M., *The Nag Hammadi Library in English* – HarperCollins, 1990, ISBN: 0-06-066935-7
- Robinson, John J., *Born In Blood - The Lost Secrets of Freemasonry* - Evens, 1989, 0-87131-602-1
- Robinson, Rowan, *The Great Book of Hemp: The Complete Guide to the Environmental, Commercial, and Medicinal Uses of the World's Most Extraordinary Plant* - Park Street Press, 1996, ISBN: 0-89281-541-8
- Roob, Alexander, *The Hermetic Museum: Alchemy & Mysticism* - Taschen, 2001, ISBN: 3-8228-1514-4
- Ruck, Staples, Heinrich, *The Apples of Apollo: Pagan and Christian Mysteries of the Eucharist* - Carolina Academic Press, 2001, ISBN: 0-89089-924-X
- Russell, Dan, *Shamanism and the Drug Propaganda: The Birth of Patriarchy and the Drug War* - Kalyx.com, 2000, ISBN: 0965025349
- Sacks, David, *Language Visible Unraveling the Mystery of the Alphabet from A to Z.* - Broadway, 2003, 0-7679-11725
- Sacred Writings 5: *Hinduism; The Rig Veda* - Montilal Banarsidass
- Samorini, Giorgio, *Animals and Psychedelics: The Natural World and the Instinct to Alter Consciousness* - Park Street Press, 2002, ISBN: 089281986-3
- Schiaparelli, G., *Astronomy in the Old Testament* - Oxford, 1905
- Schultes, Hofmann, Rätsch, *Plants of the Gods,* revised - Healing Arts Press, 2001, ISBN: 089281979-0
- Schuster, Ignatius, *Bible History of the Old and New Testaments (for use of Catholic Schools) 31ˢᵗ edition* – B. Herder Book Co., 1956
- Shulgin, Alexander & Ann, *Pihkal A Chemical Love Story* - Transform Press, ISBN: 0-9630096-0-5
- Shulgin, Alexander & Ann, *Tihkal The Continuation* - Transform Press, ISBN: 0-9630096-9-9
- Slattery, Elisa, "To Prevent a 'Shipwreck of Souls': Joann Weyer and 'De Praestigiis Daemonum' " Published in "Essays in History," by the Corcoran Department of History, University of Virginia, Volume 36, (1994), Pg. 76.
- Smith, Morton, *Jesus the Magician* – Harper & Row, 1978, ISBN: 0-06-067413-X
- Spess, David L., *Soma - The Divine Hallucinogen* - Park Street Press, 2000, ISBN: 0-89281-731-3
- Stafford, Peter, *Psychedelics Encyclopedia 3ʳᵈ Edition* - Ronin Publishing, Inc., 1992, ISBN: 0-914171-51-8
- Stamets, Paul, *Psilocybin Mushrooms of the World* - Ten Speed Press, 1996, ISBN: 0-89815-839-7
- Strassman, Rick, *DMT The Spirit Molecule: A Doctor's Revolutionary Research into the Biology of Near-Death and Mystical Experiences* - Park Street Press, 2001, ISBN: 0-89281-927-8
- Strong, James, *Strong's Exhaustive Concordance of the Bible* - Thomas Nelson Inc., 1979, ISBN: 0-8407-4999-6
- Suzuki, Daisetz T., *An Introduction to Zen Buddhism* - Grove Weidenfeld, 1964, ISBN: 0-8021-3055-0
- Talbot, Michael, *Holographic Universe* - Perennial; Reprint edition, 1992, ISBN: 0060922583
- Vallance, Jeffery, *Santa is a Wildman!* – LA Weekly, Dec. 20-26, 2002

- Waite, Arthur E., *Secret Tradition in Alchemy* - Kessinger Publishing, 1992, ISBN: 0922802831
- Waite, Charles B., *History of the Christian Religion to the Year Two Hundred* 1900 – The Book Tree, 1992, ISBN: 1885395159
- Ward, Henry Dana, *History of the Cross: The Pagan Origin and Idolatrous Adoption and Worship of the Image 1871* - The Book Tree, 1999, ISBN: 1-58509-056-5
- Wasserman, James, *Art and Symbols of the Occult: Images of Power and Wisdom* - Destiny Books, 1993, ISBN: 0892814152
- Wasson, R. Gordon, *Soma: Divine Mushroom of Immortality* - Harcourt Brace Jovanovich, Inc., 1968, ISBN: 0-15-683800-1
- Wasson, Kramrisch, Ott, Ruck, *Persephone's Quest: Entheogens and the Origins of Religion* - Yale University Press, 1986, ISBN: 0-300-05266-9
- Watts, Alan W., *The Book: On the Taboo Against Knowing Who You Are* - Collier Books, 1966
- Webster, Noah, *An American Dictionary of the English Language*, 1828, 1853
- Webster, Merriam, *Webster's International – Unabridged - Dictionary of the English Language* 1890, 1893, comprising the issues of 1864, 1879, and 1884.
- Webster, Merriam, *Webster's New International Dictionary of the English Language*, 1909, 1921
- Webster, Merriam, *Webster's Third New International Dictionary of the English Language*, 1961, 1986, ISBN: 0-85229-503-0
- Whiston, William, *The Works of Josephus Complete and Unabrideged* - Hendrickson Publishers, Inc., 1987, ISBN: 1-56563-167-6
- Whiting, Alfred F., *Ethnobotany of the Hopi* - Museum of Northern Arizona, Flagstaff, 1966. Originally issued in 1939 as Bulletin No. 15
- Wilson, Peter Lamborn, *Ploughing the Clouds: The Search for the Irish Soma* - City Lights, 1999, ISBN: 0-87286-326-3
- Winter, Zain, *Jesus is a Myth, A Handbook to Reclaim your Celestial Inheritance* - Hunter in the Sky, 2000, ISBN: 0-9706588-0-X
- Young, Kelly, *Hardy lichen shown to survive in space* – NewScientist.com News Service, November 10, 2005. www.newscientistspace.com/article.ns?id=dn8297
- Zalewski, Pat & Chris, *Z-5 Secret Teachings of the Golden Dawn, Book II The Zelator Ritual 1 = 10* - Llewellyn, 1992, ISBN: 0-87542-896-7
- Zimmer, Lynn & Morgan, John P., *Marijuana Myths Marijuana Facts: A Review of the Scientific Evidence* - The Lindesmith Center, 1997, ISBN: 0-9641568-4-9

FIGURE INDEX

Ω

Revelation 2:17
He that hath an ear, let him hear what the Spirit saith unto the churches; To him that overcometh will I give to eat of the tree of life, which is in the midst of the paradise of God.

Printed in the United States
41246LVS00006B/28

9 781585 091072